COOKING for SPECIAL OCCASIONS

Mrs Cozens

Consultant: Pat Cherry
NFWI Home Economics Adviser

Macdonald Educational in association with WI Books Ltd.

Measures: It is essential to follow *either* the metric *or* the imperial measures in any one recipe.
All spoon measures indicate *level* spoonfuls, except where *rounded* spoonfuls are stated.
Yeast: Quantities of yeast referred to are for *fresh* yeast. If dried yeast is to be used, *halve* the given quantity in the recipe.
Tins and moulds: Accurate sizes have been given as far as possible. However, they vary considerably and often one does not have the exact size required. If in doubt, use a larger rather than smaller mould. Where a 1 lb bread tin is called for, this refers to the professional, rather large, tin.

**Designed and created by
Berkeley Publishers Ltd.
9 Warwick Court
London WC1R 5DJ**

Editor Sally Haylor
Design Peter Davies
Photography Chris Ridley
Illustrations Gabrielle Stoddart

The publishers wish to acknowledge the following organizations for their help in providing accessories for the photographs in this book.
Andrews of Hampstead
Robert Dyas Ltd
Grays Mews Antiques
Tempé Davies, London NW1
That New Shop, London NW3
Waterford Wuidart Limited
Josiah Wedgwood & Sons Ltd

First published 1979
Macdonald Educational Ltd.
Holywell House
Worship Street
London EC2A 2EN

Editorial manager
Chester Fisher
Publishing co-ordinator
Gill Rowley
Production managers
Eva Wrennall

Made and printed by
Purnell & Sons Ltd.,
Paulton

ISBN 0 356 063 119

Contents

Informal Buffets and Supper Parties   1

Imaginative ideas for large-scale catering. Interchange
dishes to satisfy individual tastes and appetites

Picnics, Barbecues, Children's Parties   33

Scores of recipes and helpful suggestions for indoor and
outdoor eating

Freezer Cookery   65

Special dishes for the busy hostess to prepare, cook and
freeze for future party occasions

Dinner Parties   97

Fifteen three-course menus specially planned for the
varying seasons of the year

Conversion Tables   129

Glossary   130

Index   132

Introduction

Cooking for special occasions, whether for a dinner party, a large reception or a children's party, does not differ in essentials from ordinary everyday cooking.

The various sections of this book have been planned bearing in mind that most women today are busy trying to do several jobs at once. None of the dishes requires any particular culinary skill outside the range of normal domestic cooking. The ingredients are generally obtainable and many of the dishes can largely be prepared in advance.

The menus and suggestions for buffets and informal suppers have been carefully chosen so that the programme of work is not too time-consuming or involved. The dinner-party menus may be a little more complicated, and are more suitable for smaller numbers. However, many of them can also be adapted for larger parties.

The question of cost is a personal matter that individuals must decide for themselves. A special celebration or party is sometimes an occasion for justifiable extravagance. It is, however, more sensible to choose a reasonably economical recipe in the first place, rather than trying to cut the cost of a more lavish recipe by substituting cheaper ingredients or leaving out wine or liqueurs. A *coq au vin* without sufficient wine would be a sad affair. It is also inadvisable to experiment with any completely new recipe when cooking for a special occasion unless you are very confident of a successful result. In general, any recipe which is really new to you is best tested when you have time to give it your full attention.

There are one or two points to bear in mind when tackling any out-of-the-ordinary catering problem, particularly one that involves cooking in unusually large quantities.

First, detailed planning is essential. The choice of menu is most important. It must, of course, be suitable for the occasion and within your budget. Consider the availability of all the necessary ingredients and also the question of storing the food during preparation—few modern houses are equipped with a large, cool, flyproof larder. Allow time for last-minute decoration and dishing up. You will probably want to spend as much time as possible with your guests before the meal rather than slaving away in the kitchen until the very last second.

When you have decided upon the menu, list what you will need and devise a work programme. Order or buy all the major ingredients in good time. In rural areas and small towns, supplies of quite ordinary items of greengrocery and meat can be unreliable. For this reason it is often wise to plan alternative dishes in any menu.

The freezer can be a great help to the cook-hostess, because it enables her to do a considerable amount of the basic preparation well in advance. The freezer section of this book has been written with entertaining in mind.

Always remember when using any cookery book that recipes are only a guide. As you become more experienced you should be prepared to adapt and alter a recipe to suit your own taste and way of life. Cooking is an art, not a science. To be a good cook you must enjoy food and be interested in it. If the recipes in this book act as a stimulus for you to try something new, it will be all to the good.

Home Economics Adviser
National Federation of Women's Institutes

informal buffets and supper parties

Food with
that informal touch

Informal buffets and suppers can cover a huge variety of meals given under widely differing circumstances and conditions for any number of people. The menus included here are related to seasons or to occasions but dishes can easily be interchanged to suit your needs. Many can be prepared in advance. Salads and vegetable dishes are given in a separate section and can be used with almost all the menus.

Celebration Buffet for Twenty-five

**Russian Smoked
Salmon Roulades
Terrine aux Herbes
Mousse de Fromage
aux Raisins**

**Summer Chicken
Filet de Boeuf Niçoise**

**Gâteau Forêt Noire
Pavlova**

This is a rather more lavish menu than most of those included in this section and has not been planned with a view to economy. It would be superb for an important occasion such as a silver or golden wedding anniversary. It certainly does not have to be a formal 'sit-down' meal, but it would be more enjoyable if seating of some sort could be arranged for all the guests.

Choose the special smoked salmon starter if cost is no problem and serve it with lemon wedges and thinly sliced brown bread and butter. If you feel this is too extravagant, the *terrine aux herbes* and *mousse de fromage aux raisins* are delicious substitutes. The terrine has the advantage that it can be made four to five days beforehand, the mousse one or two days. Keep both in the refrigerator. Do not unmould and decorate the mousse or turn out the terrine until the day of the party. The terrine, incidentally, is particularly good for summer entertaining as it is lighter than most similar recipes.

The summer chicken is sufficient for eight to ten people, so if this is the only main dish to be served, triple the quantities given here. It is essential to cook the birds well in advance and to use well-jellied stock for the sauce. The rice garnish can have other additions, as pre-ferred. As a general guide when making rice salad for more than twenty people, allow 25 g (1 oz) per head and 100–225 g (4–8 oz) extra, according to the likely appetites of your guests: a middle-aged group will not eat as much as a party of hungry teenagers. The standard allowance of 50 g (2 oz) per head is always too much when catering for large numbers, however. If you feel the rice salad makes this too substantial, omit it and just serve a crisp green salad and some new potatoes with this chicken dish.

If serving the fillet of beef recipe as the only main dish, triple the quantities, using 3 x 1-kg (2¼-lb) fillets. If serving the beef dish with the summer chicken, allow 2 x 900-g (2-lb) fillets and 2 x 1·75-kg (4-lb) chickens and double the rest of the ingredients in both instances.

The *gâteau Forêt Noire* is a delicious, fairly rich pudding which makes an impressive table centre-piece and will serve about twelve people. The cake and hazelnut meringue base can be made in advance and frozen. They should both be quite thin and flat in order that the cake looks well-proportioned when filled. Make two pavlovas of the size recommended (they will serve six to eight people each) rather than trying to double the quantity and make a giant one. If possible, serve both puddings; some people might find the gâteau rather rich and the pavlova would be a lighter alternative.

Russian Smoked Salmon Roulades

275 g (10 oz) cream cheese
*4 x 15 ml spoons (4 tablespoons)
  double cream*
lemon juice to taste
salt and pepper
cayenne
*175 g (6 oz) caviar-style lumpfish
  roe*
*25 slices smoked salmon, weighing
  700 g (1½ lb)*

Beat the cream cheese, cream, lemon juice, salt and pepper together until the mixture is smooth. Adjust the seasoning, then gently stir in the caviar. Divide this mixture between the smoked salmon slices. Roll up each one neatly.

Terrine aux Herbes

Pork and Spinach Terrine with Herbs

*450 g (1 lb) fresh spinach or
  1 large packet frozen leaf spinach*
450 g (1 lb) pork fillet
100 g (4 oz) piece cooked ham
100 g (4 oz) piece green fat bacon
1 large onion
2 cloves garlic
2 eggs
*2 x 15 ml spoons (2 tablespoons)
  chopped parsley*
*1 x 15 ml spoon (1 tablespoon) each
  chopped basil and chervil or
  ½ x 5 ml spoon (½ teaspoon) dried
  herbs*
*225 g (8 oz) pork fat or streaky bacon
  rashers*
nutmeg
salt and pepper

Wash the spinach and cook for 5 minutes in boiling salted water. (If using frozen spinach, cook for 2–3 minutes only.) Rinse under the cold tap, drain well and squeeze hard to remove all moisture. Mince the pork with the spinach. Dice the ham and bacon and peel and chop

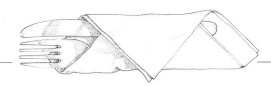

the onion finely. Crush the garlic with a little salt. Mix the garlic, ham, bacon and onion with the chopped herbs. Mix in the pork and spinach. Beat the eggs and gradually add to the mixture, beating well. Season.

Line a terrine or ovenproof dish with the slices of pork fat or rashers of bacon and fill with the meat mixture, pressing it down well. Cover and cook in a baking tin of water for 1½ hours at 180°C, 350°F/Gas 4. Leave to cool under a weight of about 1·5 kg (3 lb).

Mousse de Fromage aux Raisins

Cheese Mousse with Grapes
Serves 8-10
    15 g (½ oz) gelatine
    2 eggs
    300 ml (½ pint) milk
    700 g (1½ lb) cream cheese
    100 g (4 oz) Danish blue cheese
    6-8 spring onions
    black and white grapes
    salt and pepper

Put the gelatine in a bowl with 5 x 15 ml spoon (5 tablespoons) water. Stand this in a pan of hot water until the gelatine has dissolved.

Separate the eggs and mix the yolks with the milk. Cook, without boiling, until the mixture begins to thicken. Add the gelatine and strain into a clean bowl. Put 600 g (1¼ lb) cream cheese in a bowl and crumble in the Danish blue cheese. Trim and chop the onions, add to the cheeses and beat the mixture thoroughly. Beat in the cooled egg mixture gradually and season well. (Alternatively, liquidize all these ingredients.)

When the mixture is cold and on the point of setting, whisk the egg whites stiffly and fold them in gently. Pour into a dampened mould or bread tin and leave to set.

To serve, turn out the mousse on to a flat dish. Beat the remainder of the creamed cheese with a little milk until it is of piping consistency.

Halve the grapes, remove the pips and decorate the mousse with the grapes and the piped cheese.

Aspic Jelly

Aspic jelly is often used in cold buffet dishes. It is added, on the point of setting, to glaze meat or poultry to prevent them drom drying. The dish is then chilled until just before serving.
    1·25 litres (2 pints) well-flavoured
      stock
    brown colouring
    30 g (1 oz, 2 sachets or 10 sheets)
      gelatine
    1 leek
    1 carrot
    1 tomato
    4 egg whites
    parsley stalks
    celery salt
    pepper
    sherry or port to taste

Colour the stock a light golden brown with the colouring and put

Terrine aux Herbes—an unusual combination of pork and spinach with herbs

in a large saucepan (preferably steel). Soak the gelatine in 4 x 15 ml spoons (4 tablespoons) cold water in a small basin and stand in a pan of hot water until the gelatine has dissolved.

Wash the leek and carrot and then chop all the vegetables very finely. Beat the egg whites lightly with half a glass of water and add to the stock with the gelatine, vegetables, parsley stalks, celery salt and pepper. Set over a low heat and stir continuously until the stock begins to cloud. Bring gently to the boil and boil for 3-4 minutes, until there is a thick crust on top and the stock is clear underneath. Strain the stock through a clean damp teacloth or a jelly bag. Remove any grease from the surface with tissue or kitchen paper, and leave to cool. When the jelly is cold, but not set, add the sherry or port to taste.

3

Summer Chicken

1 x 1·75-2-kg (4-4½-lb) chicken
150 ml (¼ pint) dry white wine
1 large carrot
1 large onion
1 stick celery
1 lemon
bouquet garni
salt and pepper

For the garnish

350 g (12 oz) Patna rice
1 green pepper
225 g (8 oz) peas
225 g (8 oz) tomatoes
½ cucumber
2-3 sticks celery
12 black olives
French dressing (see Side Salads)

For the sauce

1 lemon
2 large (or 3 small) egg yolks
300 ml (½ pint) double cream
450 ml (¾ pint) stock from the
   chicken

Truss the chicken and put it in a large pan. Add sufficient cold water to half cover it, then add the wine and some seasoning. Bring slowly to the boil and skim the surface well. Peel the carrot and onion—leave them whole—and wash the celery. Thinly pare the rind from the lemon and squeeze the juice. Add all these to the chicken (break the celery in two if necessary), with the bouquet garni. Simmer for 1-1½ hours, turning the chicken over after 45 minutes. Leave it to cool in the cooking liquor.

Wash the rice well and cook it in boiling salted water for 14-15 minutes. Rinse it under cold water and drain it well. Split the pepper, remove the seeds and dice the flesh. Blanch in boiling salted water for 2 minutes, refresh under cold water and drain. Cook the peas in the same way. Skin and de-seed the tomatoes and dice the flesh roughly. Split the cucumber lengthwise, remove the seeds and dice the flesh. Wash and roughly chop the celery. Stone the olives and cut into quarters. Mix all the vegetables with the rice and put on one side.

When the chicken is cold, strip off all the flesh (discarding the skin) and shred coarsely. Strain the stock and skim it well.

To make the sauce, thinly pare the rind from the lemon and cut it into julienne strips. Blanch these in boiling water for 2 minutes, refresh them under cold water and drain well. Beat the egg yolks with the cream. Bring 450 ml (¾ pint) of the stock from the chicken to the boil and pour it on the egg mixture. Return this to the pan and cook it gently, stirring all the time until the sauce thickens slightly. Remove from the heat. Squeeze the lemon and add the juice to the sauce. Taste for seasoning and let the sauce cool; then pour it over the chicken and mix together well. Chill.

To serve, mix the rice salad with just enough French dressing to moisten. Arrange round a flat serving dish. Pile the chicken in the centre and sprinkle the strips of lemon rind on top.

Filet de Boeuf Niçoise

Beef Fillet Niçoise

1-kg (2½-lb) fillet of beef
butter and oil
salt and pepper

For the salad

2 large aubergines
2 large onions
2 green peppers
450 g (1 lb) tomatoes
garlic to taste
2-3 x 15 ml spoons (2-3 tablespoons)
   olive oil
3 hard-boiled eggs
black olives

Season the fillet and sprinkle with melted butter and oil. Roast for 25-30 minutes at 200°C, 400°F/Gas 7. Remove from the tin and leave to cool.

To prepare the salad, slice the aubergine and sprinkle with salt. Leave for 15-20 minutes, then wipe dry. Peel and thinly slice the onions. De-seed the peppers and shred finely. Skin and de-seed the tomatoes and cut in quarters. Crush the garlic with a little salt. Heat the oil in a strong pan and add the aubergine slices. Fry them briskly for 2-3 minutes, then reduce the heat and add the onion. Cook until soft, but not brown. Add the peppers and garlic. Season well and cook for 2-3 minutes. Add the tomatoes, increase the heat and cook briskly for 3-4 minutes more. Turn into a dish and allow to cool.

To serve, put the salad in the centre of a dish and decorate with quarters or slices of hard-boiled egg and black olives. Carve the meat and arrange in overlapping slices around the salad.

Gâteau Forêt Noire

Black Forest Cake

For the sponge

100 g (4 oz) flour
35 g (1½ oz) cocoa
4 eggs
125 g (4½ oz) sugar

For the hazelnut meringue

2 egg whites
125 g (4½ oz) sugar
50 g (2 oz) ground toasted
   hazelnuts

For the filling and decoration

2 x 400-g (14-oz) cans black
   cherries
juice of half a lemon
50 g (2 oz) sugar
1 x 15 ml spoon (1 tablespoon)
   arrowroot
4 x 15 ml spoons (4 tablespoons)
   brandy
450 ml (¾ pint) double cream

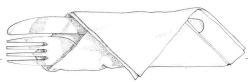

flaked or grated chocolate
flaked browned almonds

To make the sponge, brush out a *moule à manqué* or a 23-cm (9-in) spring-form tin with melted butter and dust with flour. Sift the flour and cocoa together. Put the eggs and sugar in a large bowl and whisk them over a pan of hot water until they are thick and fluffy. Remove from the heat and continue whisking until the mixture is almost cold. Fold in the flour and cocoa and pour the mixture into the prepared tin. Bake for 30 minutes at 190°C, 375°F/Gas 5, until the cake is firm and springy to the touch. Cool on a wire rack.

To make the hazelnut meringue, grease a 23-cm (9-in) sponge tin and line with non-stick paper. Whisk the egg whites stiffly and fold in the sugar and ground hazelnuts. Spread this mixture into the prepared tin and bake for 25–30 minutes at 180°C, 350°F/Gas 4. Cool on a wire rack.

To prepare the filling, drain the cherries and stone them. Put the juice in a pan with the lemon juice and most of the sugar. Bring to the boil. Mix the arrowroot with some water to a smooth paste and use to thicken the syrup until it is the consistency of a thick sauce. Let it cool, then stir in the cherries.

To finish the pudding, split the cake in half and sprinkle each circle with the brandy. Whip the cream stiffly and fold in the rest of the sugar. Put the hazelnut meringue on a serving plate, arrange half the cherries on top and cover with a third of the whipped cream. Put one sponge circle on top, cover it with the rest of the cherries and half of the remaining cream. Top with the other sponge circle. Spread the sides and top of the cake with the remaining cream and decorate it with the flaked nuts and chocolate. Assemble the cake at least 2 hours before serving so the flavours can blend together.

Pavlova

4 egg whites
240 g (8½ oz) castor sugar
3 x 5 ml spoons (3 teaspoons) cornflour
2 x 5 ml spoons (2 teaspoons) vinegar
icing sugar

For the filling

fresh fruit (according to season and taste) or canned white peaches
2 x 15 ml spoons (2 tablespoons) castor sugar
lemon juice
300 ml (½ pint) double cream

Draw a 23-cm (9-in) circle on a piece of non-stick paper. Whisk the egg whites very stiffly. Sift sugar on to a piece of paper, add a quarter to the egg whites and whisk.

Pavlova—a delicate finale to a rich meal, appropriately named after the famous ballerina

---

Add the cornflour and vinegar and whisk again. Fold in the rest of the sugar.

Pile the meringue mixture on to the prepared paper, covering the circle neatly. Hollow out the centre and sprinkle with icing sugar. Bake for 30 minutes at 130°C, 250°F/Gas ½, then reduce the heat as much as you can and bake for a further 1½ hours at least. Leave to cool.

To prepare the filling, sprinkle any fresh white fruit with lemon juice and sprinkle all fresh fruit with 2 x 15 ml spoons (2 tablespoons) sugar. Cover and leave for about 30 minutes so the juice runs. If using canned fruit, drain it well and slice it. Whip the cream, adding the juice from the fresh fruit or a little of the syrup from the can, then fold in the fruit. Pile the fruit and cream into the centre of the pavlova shortly before serving.

Oeufs au Thon
Terrine of Chicken and Walnuts
Roulades au Jambon Dijonnais

Sicilian Steak
Boeuf à la Bourguignonne

Lord John Russell's Pudding
Chocolate and Chestnut Meringue

Roulades au Jambon Dijonnais filled with crunchy walnuts or almonds and Oeufs au Thon in a bed of watercress

The choice of starters and of hot or cold main dishes makes this an ideal menu to serve any time of the year. Serve the *roulades* and *boeuf à la bourguignonne* for an easy stand-up party over the Christmas holiday for example, or the *oeufs au thon* and terrine of chicken and walnuts followed by the Sicilian steak for a summer occasion.

If serving only one of the starters, increase the quantities accordingly. Allow one egg per person for the *oeufs au thon;* make a double quantity of terrine for twenty-five people and make a few extra ham roulades.

Double the quantities of Sicilian steak if serving this as the only main dish. Cook two separate pieces of steak and cool them under a light weight (this makes slicing easier).

Boeuf à la bourguignonne is a perennial favourite and is ideal for a winter buffet. To feed twenty-five people, treble the quantities suggested here. That might sound rather generous, but if any is left

over, it freezes well, and therefore need not be wasted. The meat and the garnish can be cooked in advance and frozen separately (add a little sauce to the mushrooms before freezing), then re-heat them separately after thoroughly thawing. Combine them shortly before serving.

Both puddings should be prepared well in advance. Lord John Russell's Pudding serves eight to ten people and needs, after freezing, at least two hours in the coldest part of the refrigerator to thaw very slightly before serving. Make two quantities of the meringue (so you have six circles altogether) and store them for up to ten days in plastic containers. Omit the cocoa from one set and fill these with coffee- and rum-flavoured cream instead of chocolate. Sandwich the meringues a good three to four hours in advance with the fillings, so they have a chance to soften slightly. The cakes will then cut more easily.

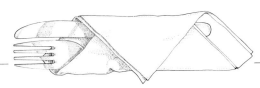

Oeufs au Thon

Eggs with Tuna

> *lettuce or watercress*
> *12 eggs*
> *2 x 15 ml spoons (2 tablespoons)*
>   *mayonnaise*
> *1 x 200-g (7-oz) can tuna*
> *50 g (2 oz) butter*
> *lemon juice* ⎫
> *Tabasco sauce* ⎬ *to taste*
> *cream*
> *chopped parsley*
> *paprika*
> *salt and pepper*

Put the eggs in a pan of cold water. Bring to the boil and simmer for 7-8 minutes (if the eggs are very large, give them a minute or so longer). Run cold water over them immediately, then shell and leave in a bowl of cold water until required.

Prepare the mayonnaise in the usual way (see salad recipes). Cut the eggs in half lengthwise, carefully remove the yolks and sieve these into a bowl or liquidize briefly. Reserve a few spoonfuls for decoration and add the drained, flaked tuna, softened butter and mayonnaise to the remainder. Mash together thoroughly or liquidize all these ingredients. Add the lemon juice, Tabasco sauce and salt and pepper to taste. If the mixture is too stiff to pipe, thin it with a little cream. Put it in a forcing bag with a 1-cm (½-in) plain nozzle. Make sure the egg whites are quite dry, then pipe the mixture into the central cavity neatly. Arrange the eggs on a dish, surround them with shredded lettuce or watercress leaves and decorate with the remaining sieved yolk, chopped parsley and paprika.

Terrine of Chicken and Walnuts

It is not absolutely necessary to make the stock specified in the recipe: instead, the chicken may be boiled with the vegetables. However, the flavour and consistency of the terrine will be much better if the meat stock suggested below is used.

> *1 x 1·75-2-kg (4-4½-lb) chicken*

> *450 g (1 lb) green streaky bacon*
> *350 g (12 oz) lean pork or veal*
> *2-3 bay leaves*
> *75 g (3 oz) walnuts*
> *garlic*
> *2 x 15 ml spoons (2 tablespoons)*
>   *brandy or sherry*
> *salt and pepper*
> **For the stock**
>   *2 pig's trotters*
>   *chicken giblets (except the liver)*
>   *2 large onions*
>   *2 large carrots*
>   *1 stick celery*

To prepare the stock, put the trotters in a pan of cold water, bring to the boil and cook for 5 minutes. Drain and rinse under cold water. Place in a large pan with the chicken giblets, onions, carrots (peeled but left whole) and celery. Add just enough cold water to cover, season well and bring to the boil. Turn down the heat and simmer for 3-4 hours. Leave to cool. Alternatively, cook the stock in a pressure cooker for 40 minutes.

Truss the chicken and put it in a pan with enough stock to come half way up the bird. Cook gently for 1½ hours, turning after 45 minutes. Leave to cool partially in the liquid.

Cook the bacon gently in a pan of water with a few bay leaves until tender (approximately 1 hour). Then leave to cool.

Strip the skin from the chicken and remove all the flesh from the bones. Skin the bacon. Mince the pork or veal and half the bacon. Chop the chicken and the remainder of the bacon fairly finely. Roughly chop the walnuts and add them to the chicken and bacon, then mix in the minced meat, the garlic crushed with a little salt, and the brandy or sherry. Moisten with 4-5 x 15 ml spoons (4-5 tablespoons) of the chicken stock and add lots of seasoning.

Liberally butter 2 x 450-g (1-lb) bread tins (or 1 large terrine dish) and dust out with flour. Fill the tins with the mixture and cover them tightly with foil. Stand in a roasting tin of boiling water and cook for 1½-2 hours at 180°C, 350°F/Gas 4. Cool with a 1-1·5-kg (2-3-lb) weight on top and leave for at least 24 hours before turning out and slicing.

Roulades au Jambon Dijonnais

Dijon Ham Rolls

For a crunchy filling, add 50 g (2 oz) chopped walnuts or almonds to the filling. Grapes make a fresh addition to the salad.

> *25 thin slices of ham*
> *350 g (12 oz) cream cheese*
> *2-3 x 15 ml spoons (2-3 tablespoons)*
>   *cream or top of the milk*
> *4 hard-boiled eggs*
> *1-2 spring onions*
> *2 x 15 ml spoons (2 tablespoons)*
>   *Dijon mustard or similar*
> *chopped parsley or chives*
> *salt and pepper*
> **For the salad**
>   *1 large cucumber*
>   *1 head celery*
>   *450 g (1 lb) tomatoes*
>   *French dressing (see Side Salads)*
>   *watercress*

Beat the cream cheese with the cream or milk until smooth. Chop the hard-boiled eggs coarsely and the spring onions finely. Stir these into the cheese mixture with the mustard, some of the parsley and chives, and seasoning. Spread the ham slices with this mixture and roll them. Cover with cling-wrap and refrigerate until required.

To make the salad, wipe the cucumber, cut it in quarters length-wise and discard the seeds. Dice the flesh. Wash the celery and chop it roughly. Skin and de-seed the toma-toes and cut them in quarters or eighths (depending on their size). Mix all these together and add sufficient French dressing to moisten thoroughly.

Put the roulades in a shallow dish and spoon the salad on top. Sprinkle this with the remainder of the parsley and herbs and put a sprig of watercress at either end.

Sicilian Steak

900 g (2 lb) rump steak in a large
slice
450 g (1 lb) lean chuck steak or
similar
6 eggs
75 g (3 oz) ham
75 g (3 oz) tongue
garlic
3 x 15 ml spoons (3 tablespoons)
fresh breadcrumbs
3 x 15 ml spoons (3 tablespoons)
grated Parmesan cheese
2-3 x 15 ml spoons (2-3 tablespoons)
olive oil
1 onion
1 carrot
1 stick celery
1 wineglass red wine
3 x 5 ml spoons (3 teaspoons)
tomato purée
½ wineglass stock
nutmeg
salt and pepper

Flatten the rump steak and trim off any excess fat. Mince the chuck steak. Hard-boil 4 eggs and plunge into cold water to cool. Cut the ham and tongue into strips and put on one side. Crush the garlic with a little salt; soak the breadcrumbs in cold water and then press out any excess liquid.

Combine the minced beef with the garlic, breadcrumbs, grated cheese and some salt and pepper.

Beat the 2 remaining eggs into the mixture with a little nutmeg. Spread the mixture over the flattened rump steak. Cut the eggs into strips and place on top of the filling with the strips of ham and tongue. Roll up loosely, tucking in the ends if possible to keep the stuffing in place, and tie.

Heat the oil in an oval fireproof casserole and brown the meat on all sides. Peel and chop the onion and carrot. Remove the meat from the pan and brown the onion and carrot in the oil. Replace the meat, wash and chop the celery and add to the casserole. Pour in the wine, tomato purée and stock. Season to taste, then cover and cook for about 1 hour, either by simmering on the top of the cooker or in the oven heated to 160°C, 325°F/Gas 3. Leave to cool in the pan and skim the sauce when it is cold. Serve sliced with the sauce poured on top.

To serve Sicilian steak hot

To serve this dish hot, cook it as described in the recipe, then let the meat cool in the casserole very slightly. Take it out, cut away the string and keep the meat warm. Skim the sauce and add 450 g (1 lb) shelled, blanched peas to the pan. Cook for a further 10-15 minutes, then serve the meat on a dish with the peas and sauce around it.

Boeuf à la Bourguignonne

The meat and the vegetables may be marinated in the wine overnight.

1·5 kg (3½ lb) topside or chuck steak
2 large onions
2 large carrots
50 g (2 oz) dripping
50 g (2 oz) flour
½-1 bottle red wine
stock
bouquet garni
salt and pepper

For the garniture

100-175 g (4-6 oz) piece of
streaky bacon
225 g (8 oz) button mushrooms
50 g (2 oz) butter

20 button onions
4 slices of bread

Cut the meat in 5-cm (2-in) cubes, removing any gristle or fat. Peel the onions and carrots and slice them coarsely. Melt the dripping in a strong pan and brown the meat quickly in batches. Remove the rind from the bacon (used for the garni-ture) and add the rind to the pan with the onions and carrots. Brown them all well. Add the flour and cook for 2-3 minutes. Replace the meat. Add the wine and just enough stock to cover the meat and vege-tables. Season and add the bouquet garni. Cover and simmer very gently for 1½-2 hours.

To prepare the garniture, cut the bacon into thin strips and fry in the melted butter until crisp. Remove from the pan. Wash and dry the mushrooms and cut them into quarters. Fry these in the same pan. Peel the button onions, put them in a pan of cold water and bring to the boil. Fry in rest of fat until golden. Cook gently until almost tender, then mix with the bacon and mush-rooms. Cut the slices of bread into quarters diagonally (to make triangular croûtons) and fry until golden.

Remove the meat from the pan at the end of the cooking time and put it on a warm serving dish. Put the garniture around it. Strain the sauce, skim and boil hard to reduce slightly. Taste for seasoning, then pour over the meat. Cook in the oven at 180°C, 350°F/Gas 4 for 30 minutes, and serve with crisp croûtons arranged around it.

Lord John Russell's Pudding

Serves 8-10

600 ml (1 pint) milk
1 orange
grated rind of 1 lemon
20 g (¾ oz, 1½ sachets) gelatine
6 egg yolks
75 g (3 oz) sugar
50 g (2 oz) crystallized pineapple
50 g (2 oz) raisins

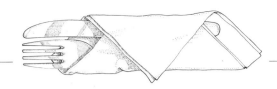

1 sherry glass brandy ·
2 x 15 ml spoons (2 tablespoons)
  Cointreau
300 ml (½ pint) double cream
For decoration
300 ml (½ pint) double cream
glacé cherries
crystallized pineapple

Put the milk in a pan. Grate the rind from the orange and add this with the lemon rind to the milk. Squeeze the juice from the orange and put in a small basin with the gelatine. Stand in a pan of hot water until the gelatine has dissolved.

Bring the milk to the boil. Beat the egg yolks and sugar together and pour the boiling milk on top of them. Return the custard to the pan and cook, without boiling, until it thickens. Cool slightly and strain in the dissolved gelatine. Strain into a clean bowl and chill.

Chop the fruit and soak in the brandy and Cointreau. Whip the cream lightly. When the custard is on the point of setting, fold in the fruit and cream. Pour the mixture into a 1–1·5-litre (2½–3-pint) mould or tin and put in the freezer (or freezing compartment of the refrigerator) for at least 8 hours.

Turn out and decorate with the rest of the cream, stiffly whipped, and the cherries and pineapple.

Chocolate and Chestnut Meringue

5 egg whites
275 g (10 oz) castor sugar
35 g (1½ oz) cocoa
For the filling
73 g (3 oz) plain chocolate
1 x 225-g (8-oz) can sweetened
  chestnut purée
3–4 x 15 ml spoons (3–4 tablespoons)
  brandy or rum
600 ml (1 pint) double cream
For decoration
icing sugar
grated chocolate or chocolate caraque

Line 3 baking sheets with non-stick baking paper and draw 20-cm (8-in) circles on each. Sift the sugar and cocoa together, whisk the egg whites very stiffly and whisk 1 x 15 ml spoon (1 tablespoon) sugar into the mixture. Lightly fold in the rest using a metal spoon. Spoon the meringue into a forcing bag with a 1-cm (½-in) plain nozzle and pipe on to the circles on the paper. Alternatively, divide the meringue into 3 and spread it

Boeuf à la Bourguignonne—a great favourite and ideal when catering for large numbers

over the circles using a palette knife. Bake at 130°C, 250°F/Gas ½ for 30–40 minutes, then reduce the temperature as much as possible and cook for another hour or so (until the meringue has dried out). Cool on a wire rack.

To prepare the filling, break the chocolate and put it in a bowl. Cover with boiling water and leave for 3–4 minutes. Pour off the water, stir in the chestnut purée and the brandy or rum and beat well.

Whip the cream until it begins to thicken and stir in the chocolate and chestnut mixture. Whisk again, until the mixture is stiff. Put one-third aside and sandwich the meringue circles together with the remainder. Dust the top circle with icing sugar and pipe the reserved cream using a forcing bag and star pipe. Decorate with grated chocolate or chocolate caraque.

Ladies' Informal Luncheon for Twelve

Snaffles Mousse

Salade Italienne

**Magda Jelly
Oranges Caramelisées**

There are many occasions that call for an informal luncheon for ladies only—such as a charity or committee lunch. At such times the menu does not need to be quite so substantial as it might be at mixed social functions. The menu given here could easily be adapted to cater for a greater or lesser number and could also be made more substantial by increasing the amount of pasta in the salad.

The Snaffles mousse is a club dish which has a number of variations, such as sherry instead of curry flavouring. The mousse should be made the day before it is required, and the ramekin dishes kept, covered with cling-wrap, in the refrigerator. Decorate just before serving. The gammon could also be cooked and the dressing and mayonnaise made in advance. The pasta and the salad should be prepared in the morning and combined an hour or two in advance of the lunch.

The puddings, which are both light, and excellent to serve at lunch, can be made the day before and finished off in the morning. Brandy snaps filled with whipped cream go well with the oranges and make a delicious dessert.

Snaffles Mousse

1 x 425-g (15-oz) can plain
  consommé
350 g (12 oz) cream cheese
1 x 175-g (6-oz) can condensed
  jellied consommé
curry paste } to taste
garlic salt }
pepper

For the garnish (optional)
  mock caviar
  parsley

Chill the plain consommé and the cheese, but not the condensed consommé. Liquidize the cheese, three-quarters of the plain consommé and all the condensed consommé until smooth. Add the curry paste, garlic salt and pepper, to taste, and liquidize again. Pour into ramekins and chill for at least 4 hours.

Decorate with the remainder of the chilled consommé, chopped, or with mock caviar or parsley.

Canned Consommé
This is very useful for many jellied dishes. Unless a specific variety is mentioned in a recipe, do not use the condensed types. From a flavour point of view, chicken is the best to use.

Always keep any cold dish that contains jellied consommé in the refrigerator until it is needed. It makes a good jelly at refrigerator temperature, but soon turns semi-liquid at room temperature.

Salade Italienne

700 g–1 kg (1½–2¼ lb) middle-cut
  gammon
1 carrot
1 onion
350 g (12 oz) green noodles
  (tagliatelle verdi) or other pasta
225 g (8 oz) mushrooms
100 g (4 oz) black olives
1 green pepper
450 g (1 lb) tomatoes
300 ml (½ pint) mayonnaise
French mustard
boiling water
For the dressing
1 clove garlic
3 x 15 ml spoons (3 tablespoons)
  vinegar
9 x 15 ml spoons (9 tablespoons)
  olive oil

4 x 15 ml spoons (4 tablespoons)
  tomato ketchup or chutney
1 x 15 ml spoon (1 tablespoon)
  Worcestershire sauce
1 x 15 ml spoon (1 tablespoon)
  chopped mixed herbs
salt and pepper

Place the gammon, 24 hours in advance, in a pan of cold water and bring gently to the boil. Peel the carrot and onion, add them to the pan and simmer for 1 hour. Leave the gammon to cool in the cooking liquor.

Cook the pasta in plenty of boiling salted water for about 12 minutes. Wash well under cold water and drain thoroughly. Trim and wash the mushrooms and quarter or slice them, depending on their size. Stone the olives. De-seed the pepper, chop the flesh and blanch in boiling salted water for 2-3 minutes. Refresh under cold water and drain. Put the pasta, mushrooms, olives and green pepper in a large bowl. Cut the cold gammon into strips and add to the bowl.

To make the dressing, crush the garlic with a little salt and mix with the vinegar. Add salt and pepper, then work in the oil, ketchup or chutney, Worcestershire sauce and chopped herbs. Pour this dressing over the gammon and noodle mixture and stir everything together carefully.

Skin and slice the tomatoes. Arrange the noodle mixture in the middle of a serving dish, and put the tomatoes round the edge. Thin the mayonnaise with a little French mustard and boiling water and serve separately.

Magda Jelly

The quantities in this recipe can be doubled to feed 10-12 people, although it is not necessary to double the amount of cream for decoration.

100 g (4 oz) coffee beans or
  2 x 15 ml spoons (2 tablespoons)
  strong instant coffee granules
25 g (1 oz) sugar
700 ml (1¼ pints) boiling water

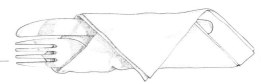

15 g (½ oz, 1 sachet) gelatine
4 x 15 ml spoons (4 tablespoons)
  rum
For decoration
  300 ml (½ pint) double cream
  2–3 large meringues
  25 g (1 oz) plain chocolate

Grind the coffee beans and put them in a warm jug with the sugar. Pour on the boiling water and stand for 30 minutes. Then strain through muslin. Alternatively, make up the strong instant coffee.

Dissolve the gelatine in 2–3 x 15 ml spoons (2–3 tablespoons) of the coffee, then strain it into the remainder. When the coffee is cold, add the rum. Pour into a glass dish and put in the refrigerator to set.

Pour the cream over the jelly and sprinkle with crushed meringue and grated chocolate just before serving.

Oranges Caramelisées
Caramelized Oranges
  12 large seedless oranges
  350 g (12 oz) sugar
  150 ml (¼ pint) cold water
  150 ml (¼ pint) boiling water

Put the sugar in a pan with the cold water and bring gently to the boil. Stir once, then boil briskly until a rich, golden caramel is achieved. Remove from the heat and carefully pour in the boiling water. Return to the heat and boil until the caramel has dissolved. Set aside to cool.

Pare the rind finely from 2 oranges and cut into julienne strips. Blanch in boiling water for 2–3 minutes, then refresh under cold water and drain. Dry on kitchen paper.

Remove the skin and pith from all the oranges and carefully cut each one into 5–6 slices, across the centres of the segments. Hold the oranges together with cocktail sticks so they retain their shape. Pile the oranges in a large glass bowl and sprinkle with the julienne strips. Half an hour before serving, pour the caramel on top.

Salade Italienne—a salad with a difference, including pasta

Summer or Autumn Buffet for Twenty-five

Marinated Smoked Mackerel

Turkey and Ham Salad
Cold Salmon Mayonnaise

Gâteau de Noix des Mesnards
Gâteau Diane
Strawberry Tartlets
Apricot Cheesecake

This menu can easily be adapted to cater for any number of people. The dishes are easy to prepare and should suit all tastes. If you want to keep preparation to a minimum, serve fewer dishes and increase the quantities accordingly.

A simple recipe is included for cold salmon. Salmon is always a great treat, but really only worth serving if fresh salmon is available. The season for this is February to August, with May, June and July being the best months to serve it. For a large party, it is better to use two or three 2–2·5-kg (4½–5-lb) grilse, or young fish, rather than one really large salmon, unless you have a huge fish kettle that will take it. Salmon trout are usually a little smaller than young salmon, but can be cooked and served in the same way. May and June are their peak seasonal months.

This menu includes a wide choice of puddings. The walnut gâteau is unusual, delicious and easy to make. Meringue puddings are always popular and meringues also have the advantage of storing well in plastic containers. *Gâteau Diane* is one of the easiest puddings of all, but will be greeted no less enthusiastically for that: strawberry tartlets are ideal for a stand-up buffet and can be simplified by putting a spoonful of redcurrant or raspberry jelly under the fruit instead of the cream cheese mixture.

Marinated Smoked Mackerel

Use 4 times the quantity of this recipe for 25 people, and serve the fillets with wedges of lemon and thinly sliced brown bread and butter.

> 3 smoked mackerel, weighing approx. 350 g (12 oz) each (or use equivalent weight of smoked mackerel fillets)
> 1 shallot
> 6 x 15 ml spoons (6 tablespoons) oil
> 2 x 15 ml spoons (2 tablespoons) wine vinegar
> 1 x 5 ml spoon (1 teaspoon) dry mustard
> 1 x 15 ml spoon (1 tablespoon) chopped parsley
> salt and pepper

Peel and finely slice the shallot, and mix with all the ingredients except the mackerel and parsley. Season well.

Fillet the fish and put in a dish. Cover with the marinade mixture and then a piece of tinfoil. Chill for at least 3 hours and serve sprinkled with parsley.

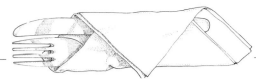

Turkey and Ham Salad

1 x 5·5-6·75 kg (12-15-lb) turkey
600 ml (1 pint) stock
butter
450 ml (¾ pint) mayonnaise
1·75 kg (4 lb) cooked shoulder ham
450 g (1 lb) cooked tongue
salt and pepper

For the sauce

1 litre (1¾ pints) milk
1 small onion
1 bay leaf
60 g (2½ oz) butter
60 g (2½ oz) flour
1 x 5 ml spoon (1 teaspoon)
  French mustard
1 x 5 ml spoon (1 teaspoon)
  paprika
2 x 5 ml spoons (2 teaspoons)
  tomato purée

For the garnish

3 hard-boiled eggs
10-15 black olives
chopped parsley
watercress or lettuce

Truss the turkey, rub with butter and season well. Place breast-side down in a roasting tin and pour the stock over. Cover with tinfoil and roast for 2½-3 hours at 180°-190°C, 350°-375°F/Gas 4-5. Turn the bird over after 1 hour, then turn breast-side uppermost and remove the tinfoil for the last 45 minutes of cooking. Leave to cool.

Marinated Smoked Mackerel—a traditional favourite for cold buffet menus

To prepare the sauce, put the milk in a pan. Peel and thinly slice the onion and add it to the milk with the bay leaf, salt and pepper. Bring slowly to the boil, then remove from the heat and leave, covered, for 10-15 minutes to infuse. Melt the butter in a pan and stir in the flour. Cook for 2-3 minutes, stirring all the time. Remove from the heat and strain in the infused milk. Bring to the boil and cook for 2-3 minutes, stirring all the time to keep the sauce smooth. Add the mustard, paprika and tomato purée and season well. Leave to cool, with wet greaseproof paper on top to prevent a skin forming.

Make the mayonnaise in the usual way (see Side Salads). Mince the ham and chop the tongue. Beat the ham in an electric mixer at a low speed, gradually adding the cold sauce and the mayonnaise. Stir in the chopped tongue. Season very well, adding a little more French mustard if necessary. Cover the bowl tightly with cling-wrap and leave in a cool place.

Remove the flesh from the turkey and cut into neat strips, keeping the dark and white meat separate. Cover with tinfoil or cling-wrap.

When ready to serve, divide the ham mixture between two large dishes and pile neatly in the centre of each. Arrange the turkey on top of the ham with the brown meat underneath and the white meat on top, leaving an oval space in the centre. Separate the yolks from the whites of the hard-boiled eggs. Chop the whites and arrange round the edge of the oval. Sieve the egg yolks and put in the centre. Stone the olives and use to decorate the dish together with chopped parsley. Arrange a little lettuce or watercress round the edge of the dish. Keep tightly covered until ready to serve.

Cold Salmon Mayonnaise

As a general rule, allow about 150-175 g (5-6 oz) fish per serving. This allows for the waste incurred on a whole fish. Traditionally, when a fish was cooked in this way to be served cold, it would be brushed with aspic jelly to prevent it from drying. Wrapping it in cling-wrap achieves the same result.

1 x 2·25-kg (5-lb) salmon
1 onion or shallot
2-3 x 15 ml spoons (2-3 tablespoons)
  white wine
sprig of fennel or tarragon
butter
salt and pepper
450 ml (¾ pint) homemade
  mayonnaise

For decoration

lettuce, cucumber, hard-boiled egg
  and/or prawns

Ask the fishmonger to clean the fish; trim the fins with scissors. Peel and finely chop the onion or shallot. Butter a large piece of tinfoil and sprinkle it with the onion. Put the fish on top. Season well and sprinkle with wine. Put the sprig of fennel or tarragon on top. Cover the fish with buttered greaseproof paper and wrap tightly in the tinfoil. (The join of the foil should be down the back of the fish.) Put the fish parcel on a baking sheet and cook for 1-1¼ hours at 180°C, 350°F/Gas 4, reducing the heat towards the end of the cooking period if necessary. To check whether the fish is cooked, insert a skewer by the back fin and press gently. If the juice runs clear, the fish is cooked. Fish vary in the length of time they take to cook, so test after 1 hour, but leave longer if necessary. Leave to cool in the foil wrapping.

When ready to serve, remove the skin carefully and put the whole fish on a serving dish. Decorate with lettuce, cucumber, hard-boiled egg and/or prawns. Keep the dish tightly covered with cling-wrap until ready to serve. Put the mayonnaise in a jug and serve separately.

13

Pastry

The oven temperature is very important when you are baking pastry or cakes. Opening the door and putting in cold trays of food reduces the temperature by up to 30°C, 50°F/2 gas marks. Therefore, set the oven on at least 15°C, 25°F, or one gas mark higher than you need. For flans and cakes, pre-heat a baking sheet in the oven. This gives more even bottom heat than putting the cake or pastry directly on to an oven rack. Turn the oven down to the required temperature when the pastry or cake has been in the oven for a few minutes.

Gâteau de Noix des Mesnards

Walnut Dessert

275 g (10 oz) shelled walnuts
250g (9 oz) unsalted butter
175 g (6 oz) sugar
3 x 15 ml spoons (3 tablespoons) kirsch
150 ml (¼ pint) double cream

For the crème patissière

3 egg yolks
50 g (2 oz) sugar
15 g (½ oz) flour
15 g (½ oz) potato flour
300 ml (½ pint) milk

For the sauce

225 g (8 oz) plain chocolate
60 ml (2½ fl oz) water
1 x 5 ml spoon (1 teaspoon) instant coffee
25 g (1 oz) castor sugar
1 x 15 ml spoon (1 tablespoon) double cream
50 g (2 oz) unsalted butter

For decoration

double cream
walnut halves

To prepare the *crème pâtissière*, beat the egg yolks and sugar together and gradually work in the flours. Bring the milk to the boil and pour it on to the egg mixture, stirring well. Return to the pan and bring just back to the boil, stirring all the time. When it thickens, cook for 1 minute, then pour into a clean basin, cover and leave to cool.

Chop the shelled walnuts finely (do not grind them). Cream the butter and sugar together until the mixture is soft and white, then beat in the nuts and the cold *crème pâtissière*. Flavour with the kirsch. Lightly whip the cream and fold 2-3 x 15 ml spoons (2-3 tablespoons) into the mixture, reserving some for decoration.

Line the base of a straight-sided 450-g (1-lb) bread tin or charlotte mould with waxed paper and pour in the mixture. Leave in the refrigerator overnight.

To prepare the sauce, break up the chocolate and place in a pan with the water and coffee. Melt over a low heat, stirring frequently. When quite smooth, stir in the sugar and cream. Cool the sauce slightly and add the butter just before serving.

Unmould the pudding and decorate with the remainder of the whipped cream and some walnut halves. Serve the chocolate sauce separately.

Gâteau Diane

Chocolate Meringue

Fill this cake a few hours before serving or, if you prefer, fill it and leave overnight in the refrigerator. Add the final decoration just before serving.

5 egg whites
275 g (10 oz) castor sugar
icing sugar

For the filling

225 g (8 oz) plain chocolate
100 ml (4 fl oz) water
600 ml (1 pint) cream

For decoration

50 g (2 oz) grated or flaked chocolate

Draw 3 circles, 20-cm (8-in) in diameter on non-stick paper and place on baking sheets. Sift the sugar and whisk the egg whites until very stiff. Whisk 3-4 x 15 ml spoons (3-4 tablespoons) sugar into the egg whites. Lightly fold in the rest of the sugar using a metal spoon. Either pipe, using a 1-cm (½-in) plain nozzle, or spread the meringue thinly over the 3 circles. Dust with icing sugar and bake for 1-1½ hours at 130°C, 250°F/Gas ½, reducing the heat after 30 minutes. Make sure the circles are crisp right through before removing from the oven. Cool on the paper on wire racks.

To prepare the filling, break up the chocolate and place in a pan with water. Melt gently, stirring until smooth. Leave to cool. Whip the cream until it begins to thicken, then add the chocolate gradually, beating until the mixture is thick.

Spread each meringue circle with a layer of cream and arrange on top of each other. Cover the sides with cream and put the cake in the refrigerator.

Just before serving, decorate with the grated or flaked chocolate.

Strawberry Tartlets

pâte sucrée using 150 g (5 oz) flour (see Basic Recipes)

For the filling

175 g (6 oz) cream cheese
2-3 x 15 ml spoons (2-3 tablespoons) double cream
1-2 x 15 ml spoons (1-2 tablespoons) castor sugar
225 g (8 oz) small strawberries
225 g (8 oz) redcurrant, raspberry or strawberry jelly

Gâteau Diane is a concoction of chocolate, cream and meringue which looks and tastes delicious

Prepare the pastry in the usual way and leave it to relax for 30 minutes in a cool place. Roll it out and use it to line small tartlet tins. Prick the base of each one and bake for 10-12 minutes at 190°C, 375°F/Gas 5. Cool on a rack.

To prepare the filling, sieve the cheese and beat in the cream and sugar to taste. Pile this into the tartlets shortly before you want to serve them. Put whole small strawberries on top of each tartlet; heat the jelly and boil until smooth. Allow to cool, then brush over the tartlets. Alternatively, just pipe a star of whipped cream on the tops of the strawberries instead of brushing them with jelly.

Apricot Cheesecake

350 g (12 oz) dried apricots
15 g (½ oz, 1 sachet) gelatine
225 g (8 oz) cream cheese
1-2 x 15 ml spoons (1-2 tablespoons) milk (if required)
1 orange
3 eggs
75 g (3 oz) sugar
150 ml (¼ pint) double cream
225 g (8 oz) plain chocolate digestive biscuits
50 g (2 oz) butter

For decoration (optional)
150 ml (¼ pint) double cream

Soak the apricots overnight in just enough water to cover them. Stew them in the soaking liquid until tender and put through a sieve. Leave to cool.

Soak the gelatine in 5 x 15 ml spoons (5 tablespoons) cold water in a small basin. Stand this in a pan of hot water until the gelatine has dissolved.

Sieve the cheese into a bowl and, unless the cheese is very creamy, add the milk. Grate the orange rind and add.

Put the eggs and sugar in an electric mixer and beat until thick and fluffy. Squeeze the juice from the orange and mix with the dis-solved gelatine. Strain this into the egg mixture and beat again. Mix 300 ml (½ pint) of the cold apricot purée into the cheese and fold into the egg mixture.

Lightly whip the cream, and when the apricot mixture is on the point of setting, fold in. Cut a piece of greaseproof paper to fit the base of a 20-23-cm (8-9-in) cake tin or spring mould. Oil the sides of the tin and the paper, pour in the cheesecake mixture and leave in the refrigerator until it begins to set.

Crush the biscuits with a rolling pin. Melt the butter and stir in the biscuit crumbs. Mix together well.

When the cheesecake is beginning to set, spread the surface with the rest of the apricot purée and press the biscuit mixture on top. Leave in the refrigerator overnight.

To serve, run a hot knife around the edge of the tin and turn the cheesecake out on to a large plate. Remove the paper and decorate the top with more whipped cream (optional).

Dishes for Informal Winter Supper and Buffet Parties

**Carrot and Coriander
Soup
Minestra
Smoked Mackerel Pâté**

**Steak Tourte
Carbonnade d'Agneau
Nîmoise
Gougère
English Game Pie**

**Charlotte aux Marrons
Mousse aux Abricots
Salambos Grand
Marnier
Fruits au Vin Rouge
Biscuit au Chocolat
Praliné
Westmorland Raisin
and Nut Flan**

The dishes included here are suitable for informal autumn or winter parties. Unless otherwise stated, quantities are sufficient for eight people, so increase the amounts according to the number of people you are entertaining and the size of their appetites. If the party is for twenty or more, try to give as much choice as possible. There should certainly be at least a couple of different puddings. If possible, also serve alternative main courses, such as a choice of the pies or one pie and perhaps the *carbonnade d'agneau nîmoise*. Casserole dishes are good for winter parties, when cold buffet dishes are generally less appealing.

If the main courses here do not seem to suit the occasion you are planning, you could easily substitute something from one of the other party menus.

Soup is always welcome at a winter gathering. There are two to choose from here—and minestra is almost a meal in itself. The smoked mackerel pâté provides a slightly more sophisticated alternative starter, or could be served in addition to soup.

Most of the puddings are fairly filling and substantial, although there are some lighter ones, such as the *fruits au vin rouge, mousse aux abricots* and *crème caramel*. Include at least one of these for those whose appetites have largely been appeased by the time they get to the pudding.

All these dishes can be prepared in advance and many can be frozen at some stage in their preparation.

Carrot and Coriander Soup

3 large onions
75 g (3 oz) butter
2 cloves garlic
900 g (2 lb) carrots
1 x 15 ml spoon (1 tablespoon)
  coriander seeds
1-2 sherry glasses sherry
600 ml (1 pint) stock
600 ml (1 pint) milk
salt and pepper
For the garnish
cream
chopped parsley

Peel and slice the onions and cook them gently in the butter until they are soft. Crush the garlic with a little salt and add to the onions. Peel and thinly slice the carrots and add to the pan. Season well, add the coriander seeds and the sherry, cover tightly and cook very gently until the vegetables are soft. This will take 10-15 minutes.

Add the stock and cook for a further 15-20 minutes. Then liquidize or sieve the soup and strain it into a clean pan. (Freeze at this stage if desired.)

Add the milk when ready to re-heat. Adjust seasoning. Serve with a spoonful of cream and a sprinkling of chopped parsley in each bowl.

Minestra

1 large carrot
1 large onion
2 sticks celery
1 leek
1 x 15 ml spoon (1 tablespoon) oil
3 rashers bacon
2 litres (3 pints) stock
¼ medium-sized cabbage
1 large potato
1 large tomato
garlic
100 g (4 oz) Cheddar cheese
1 small bay leaf
1 x 15 ml spoon (1 tablespoon)
  chopped parsley
salt and pepper

Peel the carrot and onion, wash the celery and leek and cut them all into strips. Heat the oil and cook the vegetables gently until transparent. Cut the bacon into strips and add to the vegetables. Cook for a further few minutes. Bring the stock to boiling point and pour into the pan with the vegetables and bacon. Slice the cabbage thinly and add it with seasoning and the bay leaf. Simmer for 20-30 minutes.

Peel the potato and cut into strips. Skin and de-seed the tomato. Dice the flesh. Crush the garlic with a little salt. Add all these to the soup and cook for a further 20 minutes. Stir in the chopped parsley.

Grate the cheese and serve it separately. The soup should be thick with chunks of vegetables floating in it. Do not add more stock or water unless absolutely necessary.

Smoked Mackerel Pâté

A little horseradish cream can be added to this pâté if liked. Serve it with hot toast, or thinly sliced brown bread and butter.

2-3 smoked mackerel
225 g (8 oz) cream cheese
1-2 x 15 ml spoons (1-2 tablespoons)
  cream
lemon juice
paprika
salt and pepper

Remove all skin and bones from the mackerel and weigh the flesh – about

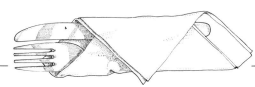

450 g (1 lb) is needed. Place in a liquidizer, ensuring that all the bones have been removed, with the cream cheese, seasoning and lemon juice. Liquidize until smooth. Alternatively, pass the mixture through a sieve or a mouli.

Add the cream and more lemon juice, if the mixture needs to be a little sharper. Adjust the seasoning if necessary.

Steak Tourte

Steak and kidney pie
  rich shortcrust pastry made with
  450 g (1 lb) flour (see Basic Recipes)
  1 egg
For the filling
  1 kg (2¼ lb) chuck steak
  450 g (1 lb) ox kidney
  225 g (8 oz) mushrooms
  seasoned flour
  600 ml (1 pint) stock

Trim the steak and kidney of any fat, gristle and cores. Cut into 2·5-cm (1-in) cubes and roll in seasoned flour. Put in a pie dish and pour the stock on top. Cover tightly with a double layer of foil and bake for 30 minutes at 180°C, 350°F/Gas 5. Reduce the heat to 150°C, 300°F/Gas 2 and cook for a further 2 hours. Cool.

Make the pastry and let it relax in a cool place for 30 minutes. Cut off two-thirds and roll this piece out large enough to line a 20-cm (8 in) springform tin.

Wipe and slice the mushrooms. Put with the cooked meat into the pastry mould, adding a little more stock if the mixture looks very dry. Brush the edge of the pastry with beaten egg. Roll out the remaining third of the pastry, place on top of the meat, trim and seal the edges and decorate the top with pastry trimmings. Leave for 20-30 minutes, then brush with beaten egg and bake for 40-45 minutes at 200°C, 400°F/Gas 6, until the pastry is golden. Leave in the tin until nearly cold.

You can freeze the cooked pie. Thaw for 24 hours and re-heat for 40-50 minutes at 180°C, 350°F/Gas 4.

Carbonnade d'Agneau Nîmoise

Baked Lamb Nîmoise
This serves 6-8 people, depending on their appetites and the amount of vegetables used.
  1 small leg lamb
  100 g (4 oz) lean bacon (preferably
   2 thick gammon rashers)
  garlic
  olive oil
  thyme
  1·5-1·75 kg (3-4 lb) potatoes
  3-4 tomatoes (optional)
  1-2 onions (optional)
  1-2 aubergines (optional)
  chopped parsley
  salt and pepper

Ask the butcher to chop the leg into 3 slices for you. Then lard the meat with slivers of bacon and cloves of garlic. Dice the rest of the bacon. Heat a little oil in a large baking dish and sprinkle in the bacon. Put the lamb on top, season well and add a little crushed thyme. Peel and dice the potatoes and place round the meat. If using any of the other vegetables, skin, de-seed and slice the tomatoes, peel and slice the onions and dice the aubergines. Add to the potatoes. Season everything and cook, uncovered, for 20-30 minutes at 210°C, 425°F/Gas 7. Cover the pan and transfer to a cool oven, 150°C, 300°F/Gas 2, for 3½-4 hours.

Sprinkle with fresh chopped parsley and serve *tel quel*. (This means 'just as it is', but in fact it is easier to serve if the bones are removed and the meat is divided into serving-sized pieces.)

Minestra—a soup which is almost a meal in itself, thick with vegetables and served with cheese

Gougère

Serves 4-6.

This dish can be prepared ready for the oven several hours before it is needed. It will not re-heat, but can be kept hot in a warm oven for at least 20-30 minutes.

90 g (3½ oz) flour
175 ml (6 fl oz) water
75 g (3 oz) butter
3 eggs
75 g (3 oz) Gruyère or Cheddar cheese
salt and pepper

For chicken and mushroom filling

225 g (8 oz) cooked chicken
100 g (4 oz) button mushrooms
2-3 x 15 ml (2-3 tablespoons) water
butter
½ lemon
1 onion
25 g (1 oz) flour
300 ml (½ pint) stock
2-3 x 15 ml spoons (2-3 tablespoons) milk

For alternative prawn and tomato filling

100 g (4 oz) shelled prawns
1 onion
25 g (1 oz) butter
25 g (1 oz) flour
2-3 tomatoes
450 ml (¾ pint) stock
tomato chutney

To prepare the choux pastry, sieve the flour, put the water in a pan with the butter and bring slowly to the boil. When the butter has melted and the mixture is boiling, remove the pan from the heat and fold in the flour. Stir briskly until the mixture forms into a ball which leaves the sides of the pan clean. Add the eggs one at a time, beating each in well. Break the last egg into a bowl and add it gradually: it may not be necessary to add all of it, provided the consistency is firm but pliable. Grate the cheese and stir in most of it. Season well. Butter an oval oven-proof dish and pipe the pastry in a thick border round the edge using a plain 2·5-cm (1-in) nozzle.

To make the chicken and mushroom filling, wipe the mushrooms and put them in a pan with the water, a knob of butter, a squeeze of lemon juice and some pepper and salt. Cover and bring to the boil. Cook for 1-2 minutes, then remove from the heat and leave on one side for 2-3 minutes. Peel and finely chop the onion and fry in 25 g (1 oz) butter until soft. Stir in the flour and cook for 2-3 minutes, stirring all the time. Add the stock and the strained liquor from the mushrooms, stirring continuously to keep the sauce smooth. Bring to the boil, stir in the milk and taste for seasoning. Dice the chicken and add with the mushrooms. Mix everything together well, then leave the mixture to cool.

Pile this mixture into the middle of the choux pastry, sprinkle it with the reserved grated cheese and cook for 35-40 minutes at 200°C, 400°F/ Gas 6.

The prawn and tomato filling is made in a similar way to the chicken and mushroom. Peel and chop the onion and fry in the butter until soft. Add the flour and cook, then make a sauce by adding the stock and bringing this to the boil. Skin and de-seed the tomatoes and dice the flesh. Add with the prawns and tomato chutney to the sauce, mix together well and pour into the centre of the pastry. Top with grated cheese and cook as directed above.

English Game Pie

The long cooking time in this recipe ensures that the game is tender. Any leftovers of cold game or gammon

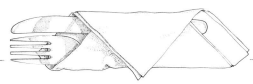

may be added, and the pie can be eaten hot or cold. It is best to use shortcrust pastry if eating the pie cold; puff pastry is best eaten hot on the day it is cooked.

2-4 (depending on the size) casserole game birds, e.g. pheasants, grouse, partridges, or wood pigeon
stock or water
1 onion
1 carrot
1 stick celery
bouquet garni
salt and pepper
rich shortcrust pastry made with 350 g (12 oz) flour or puff pastry made with 225 g (8 oz) flour (see Basic Recipes)

For the stuffing

1 large onion
butter
225 g (8 oz) mushrooms
1 x 15 ml spoon (1 tablespoon) flour
stock
8 rashers lean bacon
4 hard-boiled eggs
chopped parsley

Truss the birds and place in a saucepan. Cover with water or stock and bring gently to the boil. Peel the

Gougère—the delicious filling can be made with chicken or prawns for an interesting alternative

onion and carrot but leave whole. Add to the pan with the celery and bouquet garni. Season well and simmer until the birds are tender. This will take about 2 hours, depending a little on the type, size and age of the birds. Cool slightly, take the birds from the pan and remove the flesh from the carcasses, keeping pieces as large as possible. (Young birds could be cooked in the oven if preferred.)

Make the pastry and put it on one side to relax.

To prepare the stuffing, peel and roughly chop the onion and cook until golden in the butter. Slice the mushrooms and add to the pan. Sauté until golden. Stir in the flour and cook for 2-3 minutes, stirring. Add sufficient stock from the birds to make a thick sauce. Bring to the boil, stirring all the time, taste for seasoning and simmer for 10-15 minutes. Cut the rind off the bacon rashers, stretch them with the back of a knife and make into small rolls. Cook for 5-10 minutes in a hot oven or grill until crisp. Place the game in a 2-litre (4-pint) pie dish. Cut the hard-boiled eggs into quarters and put into the dish with the bacon rolls. Pour the sauce on top, then let the dish cool.

Roll out the pastry and cover the pie dish in the usual way. Decorate with pastry leaves and brush with beaten egg. Leave for 15 minutes in a cool place, then bake for 30-40 minutes at 210°C, 425°F/Gas 7, lowering the heat if the pastry browns too quickly.

Charlotte aux Marrons
Chestnut Charlotte

1 x 450 g (1 lb) can unsweetened chesnut purée plus 50 g (2 oz) castor sugar or
450 g (1 lb) chestnuts, 100 g (4 oz) sugar and a vanilla pod
50 g (2 oz) currants
1 x 15 ml spoon (1 tablespoon) brandy
50 g (2 oz) unsalted butter
100 g (4 oz) plain chocolate

1 x 15 ml spoon (1 tablespoon) strong coffee
300 ml (½ pint) double cream
18 sponge fingers
grated or flaked chocolate

If using fresh chestnuts, slit them and place a few at a time in boiling water. Leave for a few minutes, then remove with a slotted spoon and peel off the skins while still hot. Put them in a pan with 300 ml (½ pint) water, the sugar and vanilla pod. Simmer gently until tender (about 15 minutes), drain and put through a mouli or sieve.

Soak the currants in the brandy for 15 minutes. Cream the butter. Break the chocolate into small pieces, place in a bowl and cover with boiling water. Leave for 5 minutes, then drain off the water and add the coffee to the melted chocolate. Mix well, stir in the butter, the chestnut purée and the currants. Whip half the cream and fold in.

Put a circle of oiled paper on the base of a 1-litre (1¾-pint) charlotte mould. Place the sponge fingers round the sides, then pour in the filling. Tap it down well. Put in the refrigerator and leave for 6-8 hours until firm. Trim the ends of the sponge fingers level with the bottom of the pudding.

Turn out on to a plate. Freeze at this stage if desired. Remove the paper. Whip the rest of the cream stiffly and use it to decorate the pudding, piping it through a star tube. Sprinkle with grated chocolate.

19

Mousse aux Abricots

Apricot Mousse

Crushed meringue makes a good topping for this pudding, particularly if you are serving it to younger children; omit the rum or kirsch in this case. The egg whites should be folded in only a few hours before serving. They will separate out if left too long.

225 g (8 oz) dried apricots
lemon rind
2 large cooking apples
4 x 15 ml spoons (4 tablespoons)
  sugar
2 x 15 ml spoons (2 tablespoons) rum
  or kirsch
3 egg whites
25 g (1 oz) plain chocolate or
  flaked, browned almonds

Soak the apricots and thinly pared lemon rind overnight with just enough water to cover. The next day put them in a pan with the soaking liquor. Thinly slice the apples (there is no need to peel or core them) and add 1 x 15 ml spoon (1 tablespoon) sugar.

Cover and cook gently until the apricots and apples are just soft. Put through a vegetable mill or rub through a sieve. Sweeten to taste and flavour the purée with rum or kirsch when cold.

Whisk the egg whites stiffly and beat in 2 x 15 ml spoons (2 tablespoons) sugar. Fold into the cold purée and pile into a glass dish. Chill and sprinkle with grated chocolate or flaked brown almonds just before serving.

Salambos au Grand Marnier

A 'salambos' is only a rather romantic name for a large oval choux. Serves 6

choux pastry made with 3 eggs
  (see Gougère)
300 ml (½ pint) double cream
1 orange
1-2 x 15 ml spoons (1-2 tablespoons)
  Grand Marnier
1 x 15 ml spoon (1 tablespoon)
  castor sugar

For the icing
225 g (8 oz) castor sugar
3-4 x 15 ml spoons (3-4 tablespoons)
  water
pinch cream of tartar

Make the choux pastry in the usual way. Using a forcing bag and a 1-cm (½-in) plain nozzle, pipe it in small ovals on to a greased baking sheet. Brush with beaten egg and bake for 10 minutes at 210°C, 425°F/Gas 7, then reduce the heat to 180°-190°C, 350°-375°F/Gas 4-5 and cook for another 10-15 minutes, until the buns are well dried. With a small sharp knife, make 2 small holes in the base of each choux. This lets the steam escape and keeps the buns crisp. Cool on a wire rack.

Put the cream in a large bowl. Finely grate the orange rind and add to the cream. Squeeze the juice from the orange. Whisk the cream gently and strain in the orange juice and Grand Marnier gradually as the cream begins to thicken. When it is nearly stiff, whisk in the sugar too. Using a forcing bag and small plain nozzle, fill each bun with the orange-flavoured cream.

To make the icing, put the sugar in a heavy pan with the water and cream of tartar. Bring rapidly to the boil and cook until at *grande casse* (until it is just on the point of caramelizing). Plunge the base of the pan into cold water, then very quickly dip the top of each bun into the syrup. Unless this is done very quickly, the sugar will set before all the buns have been dipped. Cool them on a rack.

Liqueurs and Spirits
Liqueurs and spirits are extremely costly, so either use enough for them to be appreciated or leave them out altogether! There is no point in attempting to economize by reducing the amount used as this merely means there will be no taste of alcohol at all.

Fruits au Vin Rouge

Fruit with Red Wine

The number of people this pudding will serve depends entirely on how much fruit is used. However, the quantity of syrup here is generally enough for 6 servings.

a good variety of fresh fruits in season
  (try to make the colours as varied as
  possible)
300 ml (½ pint) red Bordeaux wine
150 ml (¼ pint) water
4 x 15 ml spoons (4 tablespoons)
  sugar
concentrated vanilla sugar or
  vanilla pod
sprigs of mint for decoration

Put the wine in a pan and boil until reduced by a third. Add the water, sugar and vanilla and bring back to the boil. Remove from the heat, leave to cool, then chill.

Prepare the fruit according to its type: peel pears, apples and peaches and slice them; peel and pith oranges and cut out the segments leaving them free from all skin; stone cherries, grapes and plums; and leave soft fruits whole. Mix all the fruit together, cover and leave in a deep bowl in the refrigerator for 1 hour. Spoon the fruit into individual serving bowls and spoon the wine syrup over each one. Decorate with sprigs of mint.

Biscuit au Chocolat Praliné

Praline Chocolate Biscuit Cake

For the biscuit base
225 g (8 oz) butter
100 g (4 oz) castor sugar
50 g (2 oz) chocolate powder and
  cocoa mixed
225 g (8 oz) flour
1 x 5 ml spoon (1 teaspoon) baking
  powder

For the praline
100 g (4 oz) unblanched almonds
100 g (4 oz) castor sugar

For the cream
100 g (4 oz) plain chocolate
4-5 x 15 ml spoons (4-5 tablespoons)
  water
300 ml (½ pint) double cream

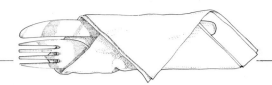

2-3 x 15 ml spoons (2-3 tablespoons) brandy

For decoration
extra cream
grated chocolate

To prepare the biscuit base, cream the butter and sugar together and beat in the chocolate powder and cocoa. Sift the flour and baking powder together and gradually add to the butter mixture to form a paste. Chill, then divide into 4. Pat and roll each one into a rectangle on a greased baking tray (do this directly on to the trays—the paste is otherwise very difficult to handle). Trim each one neatly, to approximately the same size as the top of a 450-g (1-lb) bread tin. Gather up the trimmings and pat out into small biscuits. Bake for 10 minutes at 150°-160°C, 300°-325°F/Gas 2-3. Allow to crisp on baking sheets before cooling completely on a wire rack.

To prepare the praline, put the almonds and sugar together in a strong pan. Cook over a gentle heat until the sugar begins to melt and caramelize. Stir once and continue cooking until a very light smoke comes off the pan. Turn immediately on to an oiled baking sheet and leave to cool. Then grind to powder in a coffee grinder, or put the praline through a nut or cheese mill and reduce to a powder in a liquidizer. (Always check the nuts are golden to the centre before finishing cooking or the mixture will go mouldy.

To prepare the cream, melt the chocolate to a smooth cream with the water. Whip the cream and as it begins to thicken, fold in the praline, brandy and chocolate. Oil a 450-g (1-lb) bread tin and cut a piece of greaseproof paper to fit the bottom. Carefully trim 1 biscuit rectangle to fit the bottom. Cover this with a layer of cream, then another layer of trimmed biscuit and so on, ending with a biscuit. Chill overnight.

When ready to serve, turn out the pudding and decorate it with extra whipped cream and some grated chocolate.

Westmorland Raisin and Nut Flan

An unusual pudding which feeds about 6 sweet-toothed people.

rich shortcrust pastry using 225 g (8 oz) flour (see Basic Recipes)

For the filling
175 g (6 oz) seedless raisins
150 ml ($\frac{1}{4}$ pint) water
1 x 15 ml spoon (1 tablespoon) cornflour
50 g (2 oz) soft brown sugar
1 orange
$\frac{1}{2}$ lemon
50 g (2 oz) walnuts

For decoration
5 x 15 ml spoons (5 tablespoons) double cream
1 x 15 ml spoon (1 tablespoon) rum

Make the pastry in the usual way and leave in a cool place for 30 minutes to relax. Roll out and use to line a 20-23-cm (8-9-in) flan tin. Prick the base and bake blind. Leave to cool on a rack.

Westmorland Raisin and Nut Flan—an unusual dish filled with a rich, sweet mixture of raisins, walnuts and brown sugar

To prepare the filling, put the raisins and water together in a pan and simmer gently for 10 minutes. Mix the cornflour to a paste with 1 x 15 ml spoon (1 tablespoon) water and mix in the sugar. Grate the rind from the orange and half lemon and add. Stir this mixture into the raisins and cook everything together until thick. Remove from the heat. Squeeze the juice from the orange and lemon, add to the mixture, then leave to cool. If it is too thick, add a little more fruit juice.

Chop the walnuts and stir into the mixture. When it is quite cold, pour into the flan case. Whip the cream stiffly adding the rum and, using a forcing bag and star nozzle, pipe cream decoration on top of the filling.

Hot
**Macaroni and Ham
au Gratin
Kidney and Sausage
Casserole
Haricot Beans and
Sausages
Puchero
Crêpes Landaises
Chicken and Leek Pie**

Cold
**Poulet Salade Chantilly
Macédoine Niçoise
Egg Mousse**

Puddings
**Roulade au Chocolat
Almond and
Raspberry Flan
Gâteau Jalousie
Salade des Fruits**

In these dishes, the accent is on economy and substance, bearing in mind that quantity is generally more important than *haute cuisine* quality for hungry teenagers. Nearly all the dishes can be prepared in advance (the hot ones mostly re-heat quite satisfactorily) and they are suitable for various occasions and seasons. Choose according to the numbers and average age of the guests as well as the time of year and type of party, bearing in mind that hot dishes are best for winter parties, while salads get a better reception in the summer.

Unless otherwise stated, quantities in all recipes are generally sufficient for eight people. However it is always hard to judge accurately how younger people will eat. Quantities can therefore be taken only as a rough guide, but the most filling ingredients—the beans, pasta, pastry, rice, potato—in all these recipes can each be increased. Correspondingly they could also be decreased for an older gathering.

The best way to deal with the pudding course on such occasions is to make a huge bowl of fruit salad, rather than trying some of the more substantial pastry or cake puddings. A fruit salad can be made to go further by serving a big plate of individual meringues or palmiers with it (see Basic Recipes). Sandwich small individual meringues together with whipped cream.

Macaroni and Ham au Gratin

450 g (1 lb) macaroni or spaghetti
225-350 g (8-12 oz) ham in one piece
2 x 15 ml spoons (2 tablespoons) chutney
4 x 15 ml spoons (4 tablespoons) tomato ketchup
50 g (2 oz) Cheddar cheese
salt and pepper

For the sauce
50 g (2 oz) butter
35 g (1½ oz) flour
1 litre (1¾ pint) milk and water, mixed
2-3 x 15 ml spoons (2-3 tablespoons) French mustard
2 eggs

To prepare the sauce, melt the butter in a pan and, when it is foaming, add the flour. Cook, stirring all the time, for 2-3 minutes, then add the milk and water gradually. Bring to the boil, stirring continuously to keep the sauce smooth, and cook for another 2-3 minutes. Season well. Remove from the heat and add the mustard to taste. Cool slightly and beat in the eggs.

Cook the macaroni or spaghetti in boiling salted water for 10-12 minutes. Drain and rinse well under cold water. Re-heat and keep warm.

Chop the ham roughly and mix it in a bowl with the chutney and ketchup. Mix the pasta with the mustard sauce (the mixture should be quite wet) and put one quarter in a well-buttered casserole or 2-litre (3-pint) soufflé dish. Spoon half the ham mixture on top and cover with another quarter of the pasta and sauce. Repeat this process in a similar sized dish.

Grate the Cheddar cheese and sprinkle this on top, then bake for 30-60 minutes at 180°-190°C, 350°-375°F/Gas 4-5. (The longer time is necessary if the dish is being re-heated from cold; cover it for the first 30 minutes in this case.)

Kidney and Sausage Casserole

12 lamb's kidneys
450 g (1 lb) chipolata sausages
18 button onions
50 g (2 oz) butter
225 g (8 oz) button mushrooms
1 x 15 ml spoon (1 tablespoon) flour
2 x 15 ml spoons (2 tablespoons) sherry or 150 ml (¼ pint) red wine
300 ml (½ pint) stock
2 x 5 ml spoons (2 teaspoons) tomato purée
4 slices of bread
oil
chopped parsley
salt and pepper

Peel the onions and blanch in boiling

Kidney and Sausage Casserole—a good hot dish and a sound choice when feeding a gathering of young people on a cold day

salted water for 2–3 minutes. Drain and refresh under cold water.

Skin the kidneys, split in 2 lengthwise and remove the cores. Heat the butter in a sauté pan until foaming and brown the kidneys. Remove and brown the chipolatas gently. Remove and add the onions. Wipe the mushrooms, cut into quarters and add to the pan. Cook briskly for 2–3 minutes, then add the flour. Stir well and cook for 1–2 minutes. Add the sherry or wine, the stock, tomato purée and some salt and pepper. Bring everything to the boil and replace the kidneys. Cut the chipolatas into two and put back in the pan. Cover and simmer for about 20–25 minutes.

Cut each bread slice into 4 triangular croûtons and fry in hot oil until golden. Serve the kidneys in a dish surrounded by the croûtons. Sprinkle with chopped parsley.

Haricot Beans with Sausages

> *225–350 g (8–12 oz) haricot beans*
> *450 g (1 lb) pork sausages or chipolatas*
> *1 large onion*
> *25 g (1 oz) butter*
> *2 x 5 ml spoons (2 teaspoons) flour*
> *150 ml ($\frac{1}{4}$ pint) stock*
> *1 x 15 ml spoon (1 tablespoon) tomato purée*
> *salt and pepper*

Soak the beans overnight in plenty of cold water. Drain and put them in a large pan. Cover with warm water and bring slowly to the boil. Simmer until tender—this will take about 1 hour. Drain and rinse well under cold water.

Fry the sausages or chipolatas (there is no need to add any fat) until brown. Add the beans and cook until they have absorbed all the fat from the sausages and are slightly brown. Put beans and sausages into a casserole dish and keep warm.

Peel and finely chop the onion. Fry in the butter until brown. Then stir in the flour and cook for a few minutes. Add the stock, tomato purée and seasoning, bring to the boil, stirring all the time, and cook

for 5 minutes. Pour over the beans and sausages and serve very hot.

Puchero

This dish re-heats very well. Add any pieces of leftover cold poultry you may have at the same time as the sausage.

> *450 g (1 lb) red or brown beans*
> *450 g (1 lb) green gammon or salt pork*
> *1 large onion*
> *1 large carrot*
> *2 red peppers or 1 small can*
> *2 x 15 ml spoons (2 tablespoons) olive oil*
> *2–3 cloves garlic*
> *900 ml (1$\frac{1}{2}$ pints) stock*
> *2 x 5 ml spoons (2 teaspoons) tomato purée*
> *bouquet garni*
> *2 saveloy sausages or 1 Polish boiling sausage*
> *350 g (12 oz) tomatoes or 1 medium can*
> *beurre manié*
> *chopped parsley*
> *salt pepper*

Soak the beans overnight. Drain, rinse and put in a large pan of cold water. Bring to the boil slowly (do not season) and simmer gently for

23

approximately 1 hour. Drain.

Soak the gammon or pork in cold water for about 1 hour. Peel and slice the onion and carrot. De-seed and slice the peppers into strips (if using fresh ones). Heat the oil and cook the onion, carrot and fresh peppers for 5-10 minutes. Crush the garlic with a little salt and add to the pan. Add the drained beans and cook for another 5 minutes. Add sufficient stock to cover, then add the tomato purée and the bouquet garni. Season well and bring to the boil. Add the gammon or pork. Simmer the stew until the beans are tender, which will take 1-1½ hours.

Slice the sausage. Skin and chop the tomatoes and add them to the stew. (If using canned peppers, drain and chop them and add them now too.) Cook for another 30 minutes.

Remove the bouquet garni and the gammon. If the stew is too thin, add a little beurre manié, made with 25 g (1 oz) each of butter and flour, stirring well until the desired consistency is reached. Slice the gammon and put it in a serving dish. Spoon the stew over the top and sprinkle with chopped parsley.

Crêpes Landaises

The quantity of filling is sufficient for about 15 small pancakes.

For the batter
100 g (4 oz) flour
2 egg yolks
1 egg
300 ml (½ pint) milk
2 x 5 ml spoons (2 teaspoons) butter
salt

For the filling
1 onion
2-3 x 15 ml spoons (2-3 tablespoons)
 oil
225 g (8 oz) mushrooms
75 g (3 oz) sausage meat
100 g (4 oz) gammon rasher
garlic
2-3 x 15 ml spoons (2-3 tablespoons)
 fresh breadcrumbs
chopped parsley
salt and pepper

For the sauce
1 onion
25 g (1 oz) butter
1 x 15 ml spoon (1 tablespoon) flour
1 x 400-g (14-oz) can tomatoes
300 ml (½ pint) stock
1 x 5 ml spoon tomato purée
garlic
bouquet garni
salt and pepper

To prepare the batter, put the flour in a bowl with a pinch of salt. Make a well in the centre and add the egg yolks and whole egg. Bring the flour into the centre gradually, adding the milk little by little until a creamy consistency is reached. Beat well to make sure there are no lumps at all in the batter. Then leave to stand for 30 minutes. Stir the melted butter into the mixture just before cooking.

To prepare the filling, peel and finely chop the onion and fry in the oil until soft. Wipe and finely chop the mushrooms and add to the pan. Cook for a few minutes, before stirring in the sausage meat. Cut the rasher into small cubes and add together with the garlic crushed with a little salt. Cook gently, stirring frequently, for about 10 minutes. Season and stir in sufficient breadcrumbs to give a fairly stiff mixture. Stir in 1 x 15 ml spoon (1 tablespoon) chopped parsley. Keep the filling warm.

To prepare the sauce, peel and finely chop the onion and fry in butter until soft. Stir in the flour and cook for 1-2 minutes, then add the tomatoes, stock, tomato purée, garlic crushed with a little salt and the bouquet garni. Season well and bring to the boil. Simmer for 10-15 minutes. Remove the bouquet garni and pass the sauce through a mouli or liquidizer.

Cook the pancakes and pile them on a plate placed over a pan of hot water. Then put a spoonful or so of the filling in each, roll up and arrange in a buttered ovenproof dish. Re-heat the sauce and pour it over the pancakes. Serve sprinkled with more chopped parsley.

Chicken and Leek Pie

This pie may be eaten hot or cold.

1 boiling or roasting chicken
 weighing 1·5 kg (3¼ lb)
1 large onion
1 carrot
2 sticks celery
bouquet garni
100 g (4 oz) cooked tongue
6 medium leeks
2 x 15 ml spoons (2 tablespoons)
 chopped parsley
1 x 15 ml spoon (1 tablespoon) flour
2 x 15 ml spoons (2 tablespoons)
 double cream
salt and pepper
rich shortcrust pastry using 225 g
 (8 oz) flour (see Basic Recipes)
1 egg

Truss the chicken and put in a large pan. Half cover with cold water, bring to the boil and skim well. Peel the onion and carrot, but leave whole. Add to the pan with the celery, bouquet garni and seasoning. Cover and simmer until the bird is tender, turning it over halfway through the cooking. Allow 1 hour cooking time for a roasting bird and at least 3 hours for a boiler. Leave to cool in the liquid.

Take all the chicken flesh off the carcass and cut it into neat pieces, discarding the skin. Arrange it in a 2-litre (3½-pint) pie dish. Cut the tongue into neat pieces and add to the chicken. Wash and trim the leeks and cut into small pieces. Cook briskly in boiling, salted water for 3-4 minutes. Rinse under cold water and drain well. Add to the pie dish. Then stir in the parsley and flour, mixing everything together very thoroughly. Season well. Add just enough cold stock (from the chicken) to cover the mixture and pour in the cream.

Make the pastry in the usual way and leave it to relax for 30 minutes in a cool place. Roll it out so it is larger than the dish. Cut a 1-cm (½-in) strip and put this round the edge of the dish. Brush with beaten egg, then cover with the remaining pastry. Trim off any surplus, press the edges together well and knock

up the edges. Decorate with pastry leaves and brush with beaten egg. Leave in a cool place for 10-15 minutes.

Bake for 10-15 minutes at 210°C, 425°F/Gas 7, then lower the heat to 180°-190°C, 350°-375°F/Gas 4-5 and bake for a further 30 minutes.

Poulet Salade Chantilly

Chicken Salad Chantilly

    1 x 1·5-1·75 kg (3-4 lb) chicken
      (roasted)
    1 large red pepper
    5 x 15 ml spoons (5 tablespoons) oil
    5 x 15 ml spoons (5 tablespoons)
      white wine (optional)
    ½ lemon
    stock
    100 g (4 oz) mushrooms
    10 button onions
    1 large tomato
    1 bay leaf
    50 g (2 oz) butter
    225 g (8 oz) Patna rice
    150 ml (¼ pint) double cream
    300 ml (½ pint) mayonnaise
    salt and pepper

For the garnish

    1 lettuce
    1 hard-boiled egg

De-seed the pepper, slice the flesh finely and blanch in boiling salted water for 2 minutes. Rinse under cold water and drain.

Put the oil and wine in a pan. Squeeze the lemon and add the juice to the pan with 150 ml (¼ pint) stock. Wipe the mushrooms and cut them into quarters. Peel the onions. Skin and slice the tomato. Add all these to the pan with the bay leaf, cover and cook gently for 6-10 minutes. Strain off the liquor and make it up to 600 ml (1 pint) with some extra stock.

Melt the butter in a strong pan, add the rice and cook gently for 3-4 minutes, stirring frequently. Add the stock and the mushroom, onion and tomato mixture and adjust the seasoning. Transfer to an ovenproof dish, cover with grease-proof paper and a lid and cook for 25-30 minutes at 190°C, 375°F/Gas 5. *Do not stir*. When the rice is cooked, remove the dish from the oven and spread the mixture on a large plate to cool. Add the red pepper.

Carve the chicken and cut the flesh into shreds, discarding the skin. Whip the cream lightly and fold into the mayonnaise. Season well and fold in the chicken flesh.

Put the rice on a serving dish, leaving a slight well in the centre. Put the chicken mixture on top of the rice and fill the well with washed lettuce. Chop the hard-boiled egg and use to decorate the chicken mixture.

Poulet Salade Chantilly—a sophisticated way to serve chicken

Macédoine Niçoise

Hotchpotch Niçoise

    225 g (8 oz) cold cooked chicken
    225 g (8 oz) cooked lean ham
    100 g (4 oz) mortadella or
      smoked sausage
    1 buckling, kipper or smoked
      mackerel (optional)
    1 green pepper
    1 head celery
    2 crisp eating apples
    3 cold cooked potatoes
    12 green olives
    1 lettuce heart
    3 hard-boiled eggs
    salt and pepper

For the sauce

    ½ bunch watercress
    2 x 15 ml spoons (2 tablespoons)
      chopped fresh herbs, e.g. chervil,
      parsley, tarragon, chives
    1 x 5 ml spoon (1 teaspoon)
      French mustard
    2 x 15 ml spoons (2 tablespoons)
      wine vinegar
    150 ml (¼ pint) mixed olive and
      ground nut oil
    pinch sugar
    salt and pepper

Cut all the chicken, ham and sausage into thin strips. If using the fish, discard all skin and bones and flake the fish.

De-seed and chop the pepper; blanch in boiling salted water for 2-3 minutes, then rinse under cold water and drain. Dice all the other vegetables, the apples and olives and mix with the meat and fish. Remove the yolks from the whites of the eggs, chop the whites and add to the meat and vegetables.

To prepare the sauce, put the washed watercress leaves, herbs and all other ingredients together in a liquidizer and liquidize for 1 minute. Taste and adjust the seasoning if necessary. Pour the sauce over the meat and vegetable mixture and turn out on to a flat dish.

Sieve the egg yolks and sprinkle over the top. Serve within 1 hour of dressing.

Egg Mousse

This mousse could also be made in a large soufflé dish and not turned out. In this case use only 20 g ($\frac{3}{4}$ oz. $1\frac{1}{2}$ sachets) gelatine.

> 12 hard-boiled eggs
> 30 g (1 oz, 2 sachets) gelatine
> 4-5 ml spoons (4-5 tablespoons) stock)
> 300 ml ($\frac{1}{2}$ pint) mayonnaise
> Worcestershire sauce, to taste
> anchovy essence, to taste
> 150 ml ($\frac{1}{4}$ pint) double cream
> salt and pepper

For the béchamel sauce

> 25 g (1 oz) butter
> 25 g (1 oz) flour
> 450 ml ($\frac{3}{4}$ pint) milk
> 150 ml ($\frac{1}{4}$ pint) stock

For the devil sauce

> 3-4 large tomatoes
> 2 x 15 ml spoons (2 tablespoons) oil
> 2 x 5 ml spoons (2 teaspoons) wine vinegar
> 1 x 5 ml spoon (1 teaspoon) sugar
> 2 x 15 ml spoons (2 tablespoons) tomato ketchup
> Worcestershire sauce to taste
> salt and pepper

For decoration

> 1 cucumber

Put the gelatine in a small bowl with the stock. Stand in a pan of hot water and leave until dissolved.

To make the bechamel sauce, melt the butter in a pan and, when foaming, stir in the flour. Cook for 1-2 minutes, stirring all the time, then gradually stir in the milk. Bring to the boil, stirring continuously to keep the sauce smooth, season well and beat in the stock and dissolved gelatine. Mix everything together well and leave to cool.

Chop the eggs and put one aside for decoration. Fold the chopped eggs into the mayonnaise and add the Worcestershire sauce, anchovy essence and seasoning to taste.

Whip the cream lightly. When the béchamel sauce is on the point of setting, fold it into the mayonnaise mixture with the whipped cream. Turn into an oiled 2-litre ($3\frac{1}{2}$ pint) cake tin or charlotte mould and leave for at least 4 hours or prefer-ably overnight in the refrigerator.

To make the devil sauce, skin and de-seed the tomatoes and combine with all the other ingredients. Liquidize thoroughly. When ready to serve, turn out the mousse and decorate with thin slices of cucumber and the reserved hard-boiled egg. Serve the devil sauce separately.

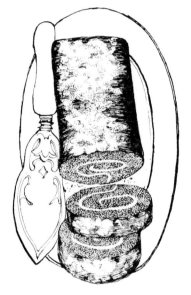

Roulade au Chocolat

Chocolate Roll

> 175 g (6 oz) plain chocolate
> 3-4 x 15 ml spoons (3-4 tablespoons) water
> 5 eggs
> 225 g (8 oz) castor sugar

For the filling

> 300-450 ml ($\frac{1}{2}$-$\frac{3}{4}$ pint) double cream
> brandy to taste
> icing sugar

Line a 30 x 20-cm (12 x 8-in) swiss roll tin with oiled greaseproof paper. Put the chocolate in a pan with the water and melt it gently to a thick cream. Separate the eggs and beat the yolks and sugar together until the mixture is thick and mousse-like. (Do this over a pan of hot water unless using an electric whisk.) Stir in the melted chocolate. Whisk the egg whites stiffly and fold into the chocolate mixture. Pour into the prepared tin and bake for 15-20 minutes at 180°C, 350°F/Gas 4, until the cake is firm.

Cool the roulade slightly in the tin. Then cover with a damp cloth and leave overnight in the refrigerator or other cool place.

To serve, whip the cream stiffly, flavouring with brandy. Dust a piece of greaseproof paper with icing sugar and turn the roulade on to it. Strip off the cooking paper and spread the flavoured cream over the under surface of the cake. Roll it up, using the greaseproof paper to help. Then lift it carefully on to a serving plate and sprinkle with more icing sugar. Decorate with extra whipped cream, if liked.

Almond and Raspberry Flan

For the pastry

> 175 g (6 oz) flour
> 75 g (3 oz) butter
> 25 g (1 oz) lard
> 40 g ($1\frac{1}{2}$ oz) ground almonds
> 40 g ($1\frac{1}{2}$ oz) castor sugar
> 1 egg yolk
> water
> 225 g (8 oz) fresh or frozen raspberries

For the meringue

> 3 egg whites
> 175 g (6 oz) castor sugar
> 175 g (6 oz) ground almonds

For decoration

> 150 ml ($\frac{1}{4}$ pint) double cream
> 25 g (1 oz) flaked, browned almonds

To prepare the pastry, sift the flour on to a board, make a well in the centre and put all the rest of the pastry ingredients into it. Using the fingers, work the fat, sugar, almonds, and egg together, gradually working in the flour. Use a little water if necessary to get a smooth, non-sticky paste. Set aside to relax for 20-30 minutes.

Roll out the pastry and line a 20-cm (8-in) flan ring. Prick the base and cover it with the raspberries (just thawed and drained if frozen).

To make the meringue, whisk the egg whites until stiff. Sift the sugar and ground almonds together and fold into the egg whites. Bake for 30-35 minutes at 180°C-

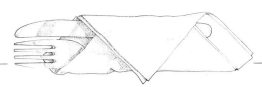

190°C, 350°-375°F/Gas 4-5. Then leave to cool. When the pie is quite cold, decorate with the cream, lightly whipped, and the almonds.

Gâteau Jalousie

pâte feuilletée made with 225 g (8 oz) flour (see Basic Recipes)
50 g (2 oz) mixed crystallized fruits
100 g (4 oz) apricot jam
1 x 15 ml spoon (1 tablespoon) rum or kirsch
beaten egg
icing sugar

Prepare the pastry in the usual way and leave wrapped in a clean cloth for 20 minutes. Chop the crystallized fruits finely and mix with the jam and the rum or kirsch.

Roll out the pastry into an oblong about 35 x 30 x 0·5 cm thick (14 x 12 x $\frac{1}{4}$ in). Cut in half lengthwise and put one half upside down on a dampened baking sheet. Brush round the edge to a depth of 2·5 cm (1 in) with beaten egg and spread the filling in the centre.

Lightly flour the second piece of pastry and fold in half lengthwise. Make cuts on the folded edge to a depth of 5 cm (2 in) about 1 cm ($\frac{1}{2}$ in) apart, leaving at least 2·5 cm (1 in) at the top and bottom. Unfold the pastry and place carefully on top of the other piece. Press lightly round the edges to seal, then scallop the edges with a knife. Leave for 20 minutes, then brush with beaten egg and bake for 30 minutes at 210°-230°C, 425°-450°F/Gas 7-8. Remove and dust with icing sugar, then return to the oven for 5 minutes. Cool on a rack and serve cold or just slightly warm.

Salade des Fruits

Fruit Salad
Always include a good variety of colours in a fruit salad. If using canned fruit, it is not usually necessary to make a syrup.

100 g (4 oz) sugar
300 ml ($\frac{1}{2}$ pint) water
2 oranges

Salade des Fruits—served chilled, this is a particularly delicious way to round off a meal and can be made from fresh or canned fruit

2 apples
1 lemon
2 pears
225 g (8 oz) grapes, black and white
strawberries
pineapple
cherries
raspberries
melon
peaches
2 bananas

Put the sugar and water in a pan and bring it to the boil to make a syrup. Pare 2-3 thin slices of orange peel and add to the syrup. Peel and core the apples and add the peel and cores to the syrup. Squeeze half of the lemon and add the juice. Simmer for 10 minutes, then strain and cool. (This syrup will keep for several days in the refrigerator.)

Prepare the fruit according to type: peel, core and dice the pears, dice the apples, and squeeze the juice from the remaining half lemon over these to stop the flesh discolouring. Cut the pith from the oranges and remove the segments of flesh, cutting them free from the skin. Skin and pip the grapes and mix all the fruit together, adding the strawberries and other fruit, suitably prepared. Finally, skin and slice the bananas and add them. Mix all the fruit together gently in a glass dish and pour the syrup over. Chill until required.

Side Salads, Vegetable Dishes and Salad Dressings

Pois à la Normande
Tomates Mousmées
Gratin de Pommes de Terre Crécy
Pommes de Terre Alphonse
Pommes de Terre Macaire
Ratatouille Niçoise
Potato Salad
Winter Salad
Salade Niçoise
Salade de Riz
Spanish Salad

French Dressing or Vinaigrette
Mayonnaise

Herb Bread
Hot Anchovy or Garlic Bread
Cheese Sablés

The cold salads all generally go best with cold buffet dishes, but some, such as Spanish salad, could be served with hot dishes too. *Ratatouille* is an extremely useful and versatile vegetable dish as it is delicious hot or cold. It also freezes well. The winter salad of cabbage, carrots, celery and apples is another great standby for times when green salads are prohibitively expensive and of poor quality.

The three potato dishes are all useful for adding substance and warmth to a winter party, while the recipe for a cold potato salad is a classic.

The flavoured breads are invaluable as extra fillers to appease the appetites of younger guests. Serve with bowls of steaming hot soup.

The cheese sablés are an ideal savoury and save the expense of producing a cheese board.

Pois à la Normande

Normandy peas
Triple these quantities for a buffet party of 25-30 people and serve another salad too.
225-350 g (8-12 oz) shelled peas
6 tomatoes

3 x 15 ml spoons (3 tablespoons) thick cream
2 x 15 ml spoons (2 tablespoons) chopped fresh mixed herbs
lemon juice
sugar
salt and pepper
Cook the peas for 3-4 minutes in boiling, salted water, rinse under the cold tap and drain well. Skin the tomatoes and slice thickly. Mix very gently with the peas and season well, adding a pinch of sugar. Put in a dish and chill.

Mix the cream with the chopped herbs, lemon juice, salt and pepper.

Pour the dressing over the tomatoes and peas at the very last minute before serving.

Tomates Mousmées

Allow one tomato per person.
6 large even-sized tomatoes
150-300 ml ($\frac{1}{4}$-$\frac{1}{2}$ pint) homemade mayonnaise
1 large dessert apple
3 sticks celery
1 hard-boiled egg

Pois à la Normande and Salade Niçoise, which can be served with tuna fish if desired

Here is a collection of side salads and vegetable dishes, plus recipes for herb, garlic and anchovy bread, mayonnaise and a basic French dressing. These last two have been used in many of the recipes throughout the preceding menus. When making them in large quantities for a number of different dishes, keep them fairly bland, then add more flavouring and seasoning as required for individual recipes.

Choose and prepare side-salad dishes that complement the main dishes you are serving. Most of those given here, however, depending a little on the time of year, would go with almost any of the previous menus.

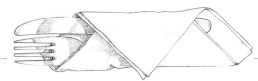

chopped parsley
salt and pepper

Cut a slice from the top of each tomato and carefully remove the inside flesh and seeds. Sprinkle the insides with salt and drain upside down on kitchen paper for 15 minutes.

Prepare the mayonnaise in the usual way, using lemon juice as well as vinegar. Season well. Peel and core the apple and chop it. Wash the celery and chop finely. Mix the apple and celery with enough mayonnaise to really moisten it and fill the tomatoes. Slice the hard-boiled egg and top each tomato with a slice. Sprinkle with chopped parsley and chill.

Gratin de Pommes de Terre Crécy

Carrot and Potato Gratin
Serves 6-8
This is an excellent vegetable dish for a winter party. It may be prepared in advance and the sliced potatoes left in a bowl of water until needed.

225 g (8 oz) carrots
1 large onion
butter
900 g (2 lb) potatoes
100 g (4 oz) grated Gruyère
*   cheese*
300 ml (½ pint) cream or top of milk
salt and pepper

Peel and slice the carrots and peel and chop the onion. Put in a pan with a knob of butter and salt and pepper. Just cover with water and bring to the boil. Cook very gently for 20-30 minutes, until the liquid has evaporated.

Butter a flameproof dish generously. Peel and slice the potatoes and arrange in layers with the carrots. Season well between each layer, dotting with butter and grated cheese as you go. End with a layer of potatoes and dot with butter and cheese. Pour the cream or milk on top. Bring just to the boil on the top of the stove, then bake for 1-1½ hours at 150°C, 300°F/Gas 2. (If using a china dish which cannot be heated before going into the oven, allow an extra 30 minutes cooking time.)

Pommes de Terre Alphonse

Potatoes Alphonse
Serves 6-8
900 g (2 lb) potatoes
100 g (4 oz) butter
2 x 15 ml spoons (2 tablespoons)
*   chopped parsley*
lemon juice
25 g (1 oz) Cheddar cheese
salt and pepper

Wash the potatoes and boil in their skins until just tender. Meanwhile, soften the butter and beat in the parsley, lemon juice, salt and pepper, to make *beurre maître d'hôtel*.

Peel the potatoes and slice thickly. Layer them in a fireproof dish and dot with butter. Continue in this way, ending with a layer of potatoes. Grate the cheese and sprinkle on top. Brown the potatoes at 200°C, 400°F/Gas 6 for 15-20 minutes.

Pommes de Terre Macaire

Potatoes Macaire
This is a useful potato dish for the winter. You can prepare it in advance and re-heat it when you require it. Two methods of cooking are given: the first is the classic one in which you do not add cheese; the second is easier for large numbers. Allow per person:

1 large old potato
25 g (1 oz) butter
25 g (1 oz) Cheddar cheese
salt and pepper

For both methods, first scrub the potato, prick well and rub the skin with a butter paper. Bake at 150°-160°C, 300°-325°F/Gas 2-3 until soft. Scrape out the potato flesh and beat with butter and seasoning.

For method 1, heat some butter in a shallow cake tin; press in the potato pulp and bake for 30 minutes at 200°C, 400°F/Gas 6 until golden and crisp. Turn out on to a warm dish and serve.

Alternatively, pile the potato pulp into a well buttered, fireproof dish, sprinkle with cheese and bake for 30 minutes at the same temperature.

Ratatouille Niçoise

This is useful for serving hot or cold and also makes a delicious supper dish with an omelette or fried eggs.

3-4 onions
1 green pepper
2 courgettes
1 aubergine
150 ml (¼ pint) olive oil
4 tomatoes
5 cloves of garlic
chopped parsley
salt and pepper

Peel and finely slice the onions; de-seed the peppers and slice the flesh. Dice the courgettes and thinly slice the aubergine. Heat the oil in a heavy pan and fry the onion gently until it is soft but not brown. Add the peppers, courgettes and aubergine and season well. Cook, covered, for about 10 minutes. Skin and de-seed the tomatoes and dice the flesh; crush the garlic with a little salt. Add these to the pan and continue to cook slowly for 10 minutes removing the lid for the last 5 minutes. Adjust the seasoning and sprinkle with chopped parsley.

Potato Salad

Serves 6-8
1-1·5 kg (2-3 lb) potatoes
2-3 shallots
French dressing
chopped fresh herbs, including
*   parsley*
salt

Wash the potatoes well and cook them in boiling salted water until they are just tender. Rinse under the cold tap and, while they are still hot, skin and slice them into a bowl. Peel and chop the shallot, sprinkle over the potatoes and moisten everything with French dressing. Sprinkle with the herbs just before serving.

Winter Salad

This is a very useful and popular salad when green salads are poor in quality and expensive. It can be prepared in advance and kept covered with cling-wrap in a cool place until required. Dress it just before serving. Quantities are given in cup measures, as it is the proportions of vegetables that is important—there should be twice as much cabbage as carrot, and twice as much carrot as celery and apple.

2 cups finely shredded white cabbage
1 cup coarsely grated carrot
$\frac{1}{2}$ cup finely chopped celery
$\frac{1}{2}$ cup finely chopped apple
currants
chopped blanched onion
orange ⎫ use all or
chopped blanched ⎬ any as
  pepper ⎭ you like
nuts
herbs

For the dressing
1 part vinegar
3 parts salad oil
sugar
French mustard ⎫
pepper and salt ⎬ to taste

Shake all the dressing ingredients together. Mix the prepared vegetables and fruit in a large bowl. Pour over the dressing as required.

Salade Niçoise

You can add tuna fish to this salad if you want to make it more substantial. Some people prefer to mix the French beans with mayonnaise instead of French dressing.

700-900 g (1$\frac{1}{2}$-2 lb) potatoes
1 shallot
350 g (12 oz) French beans
6-8 tomatoes
chopped fresh herbs
2 hard-boiled eggs
1 can anchovy fillets
10-12 black olives
capers
French dressing
salt and pepper

Wash the potatoes and cook in boiling, salted water until tender. Plunge into cold water, peel and slice coarsely. Peel and finely chop the shallot and sprinkle over the potatoes. Moisten slightly with French dressing while the potatoes are still warm.

Top and tail the beans and cut into 2·5-cm (1-in) lengths. Cook in boiling, salted water for 2-3 minutes, rinse under the cold tap and drain. Toss in French dressing. Skin the tomatoes and cut into quarters. Sprinkle with French dressing.

Pile the potatoes into a serving dish and sprinkle with the chopped herbs. Quarter the hard-boiled eggs and arrange around the potatoes with the beans and the tomatoes. Arrange the anchovy fillets over the top in a lattice pattern and decorate with black olives and capers.

Salade de Riz

Rice Salad
Do not be tempted to make too much rice salad—it always seems to be the most common leftover. This quantity feeds at least 6 people.

225 g (8 oz) Patna rice

Winter Salad—an excellent side dish which makes use of less expensive vegetables and which can be prepared in advance. Served with the dressing, it is most refreshing with a rich main dish

225 g (8 oz) shelled peas
1 cucumber
finely chopped fresh herbs
French dressing

Slowly tip the rice into boiling salted water and cook for 14-16 minutes. Drain well and rinse under cold water.

Cook the peas quickly in boiling salted water. Drain and rinse under cold water. Peel the cucumber, discard the seeds and dice the flesh. Mix the rice, peas, cucumber and chopped herbs together. Just before serving, mix in enough French dressing to moisten it.

Spanish Salad

1 large onion
1 green pepper
450 g (1 lb) tomatoes

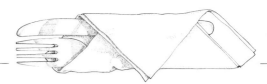

French dressing
chopped parsley, basil and tarragon
salt and pepper

Peel and slice the onion into fine rings. De-seed the pepper and slice the flesh into rings too. Plunge the onion into boiling, salted water and as soon as the water returns to the boil, add the peppers. Boil for 1 minute, then drain the vegetables and rinse under cold water. Drain and dry them on kitchen paper.

Skin the tomatoes and slice them. Mix all the vegetables together in a bowl. Season well and sprinkle with the French dressing and finely chopped herbs just before serving.

Vinaigrette

French dressing
Keep a quantity of basic dressing in a screw-top jar. It will always separate out, so should be well stirred or shaken before use.

1 part wine vinegar
3 parts oil (olive or a mixture of olive and other salad oils)
sugar
mustard
salt and pepper

Put the sugar, salt, pepper and a pinch of mustard in a bowl and add the vinegar. Stir in the oil gradually. Add chopped shallot or herbs to the basic dressing to vary it, if desired.

Mayonnaise

2 egg yolks
1 x 15 ml spoon (1 tablespoon) wine vinegar or lemon juice
300 ml (½ pint) oil
mustard (optional)
salt and pepper

Put the egg yolks in a bowl, add a pinch of salt and pepper and the mustard, if using, and mix together well. Stir in a few drops of vinegar or lemon juice. Add the oil, drop by drop, stirring all the time. (Use a wire sauce whisk or a wooden spoon.) As the mayonnaise begins to thicken, you can add the oil a little more quickly, but be careful. The final consistency when all the

oil is stirred in should be that of whipped cream; add a little water, or more vinegar or lemon juice, if it becomes too thick.

One egg yolk will absorb up to 300 ml (½ pint) oil at the maximum. If the mayonnaise curdles during making, put 1 x 5 ml (1 teaspoon) cold water in a clean basin and pour the curdled mixture on very slowly, whisking continuously.

Herb Bread

1 French loaf
butter
1 clove garlic
chopped fresh herbs
salt and pepper

Cut the loaf into thick slices, cutting not quite through to the bottom crust. Soften the butter. Crush the garlic and mix with the butter, herbs, salt and pepper. Spread the butter between the slices, then push the loaf back into shape. Wrap in foil and heat for 10 minutes in a medium oven before serving.

Hot Anchovy or Garlic Bread

2 French loaves
For garlic butter
100 g (4 oz) butter
2 cloves garlic

salt and pepper
For anchovy butter
100 g (4 oz) butter
anchovy essence
lemon juice
pepper

Slice the loaves thickly, cutting not quite through to the bottom crust.

Prepare both butters by pounding the ingredients for each until they are mixed thoroughly. (For the garlic butter, crush the garlic with a little salt first.)

Spread the loaves with the butters and press back into shape. Wrap each in foil and bake for 10 minutes at 200°C, 400°F/Gas 6. Unwrap and bake for a few more minutes. Serve hot.

Cheese Sablés

These store well and are ideal to serve instead of cheese at a buffet party—but they are very fragile.

225 g (8 oz) butter
275 g (10 oz) flour
100-125 g (3-4 oz) Cheddar cheese, grated
salt and pepper
For the topping
25-50 g (1-2 oz) Roquefort or Gorgonzola cheese
100 g (4 oz) cream cheese
2-3 x 15 ml spoons (2-3 tablespoons) cream
paprika
salt and pepper

Cream the butter, then work in the flour, Cheddar cheese and some salt and pepper. Work into a dough and chill until firm. Roll out quickly and cut into small circles. Put on grease-proof paper on a baking sheet and bake for 10-12 minutes at 160°-180°C, 325°-350°F/Gas 3-4. Leave to crisp before transferring to a wire tray to cool.

To make the topping, grate the Roquefort or Gorgonzola and beat with the cream cheese, cream, paprika, salt and pepper until smooth. Using a forcing bag and 1-cm (½-in) plain or star tube, pipe a little of the mixture on each biscuit. Dust with paprika.

Basic Recipes

Palmiers, sacristans and *langues de boeuf* are excellent ways of using up leftovers from a dish using puff pastry.

Pâte Sucrée

> *150 g (5 oz) plain flour*
> *75 g (3 oz) butter*
> *50 g (2 oz) castor or icing sugar*
> *2 egg yolks, or 1 yolk and*
>   *1 x 15 ml spoon (1 tablespoon)*
>   *water*

Sieve the flour on to a board or table and make a well in the centre. Into this put the slightly softened butter, the sugar, and egg yolks. With the fingers of one hand mix the butter, sugar and eggs together, gradually drawing in the flour to make a crumbly dough. Knead this lightly with the heel of your hand until the dough is of a smooth consistency. Leave in a cool place for 30 minutes before rolling out and using as required.

Pâte Feuilletée

Puff Pastry

> *225 g (8 oz) plain flour*
> *225 g (8 oz) butter*
> *150 ml ($\frac{1}{4}$ pint) water*
> *pinch salt*

Sift the flour on to a pastry board or marble slab. Make a well in the centre, add the salt and 75-100 ml (3-4 fl oz) ice-cold water. Draw the flour into the centre, little by little, with your fingers until you have a thick, sauce-like consistency. Rub the flour lightly between your fingers, until it is flaky and crumbly. Add the rest of the water gradually, kneading the dough lightly until soft and smooth. Wrap in a clean cloth and leave in a cool place for 20 minutes, or overnight.

Put the dough on a floured surface and roll out to the size of a tea plate. Tap the butter lightly with the rolling pin until it is the same consistency as the dough. Fold the edges of the dough over the butter to make a parcel. Make sure the edges meet and that no butter is showing. Tap the edges gently with a rolling pin to seal them and to elongate the dough slightly.

Keeping the edges straight and the ends as square as possible, roll out the dough in a long strip (but do not roll quite to the ends). Fold the strip into 3 (one end to the middle, the other end overlapping). Give the pastry a half turn, so that the fold is on the left side. Tap with the rolling pin to seal, then repeat the process. Fold again in the same way. Leave the pastry to relax in a cool place for 20 minutes. Then repeat the rolling and folding process twice more. Leave to relax for a further 20 minutes and then give the pastry 2 more rollings and foldings. (Each roll and fold is known as a turn, and 6 turns complete the pastry.) Leave it to relax for another 20 minutes and the pastry is then ready to use.

Sacristans and Langues de Boeuf

Sacristans are made with puff pastry rolled in sugar, as for palmiers. Roll out the pastry, cut into strips about 7.5 x 2 cm (3 x $\frac{3}{4}$ in), twist and put on a damp baking sheet lightly pressing each end down. Cook as for palmiers, but do not turn over.

For *langues de boeuf*, roll out trimmings of puff pastry thinly, cut into 5-cm (2-in) circles and sprinkle with a little sugar. Roll each one into an oval and put on a damp baking sheet. Bake for 5-10 minutes at 210°-230°C, 425°-450°F/Gas 7-8.

Rich Shortcrust Pastry

> *225 g (8 oz) flour*
> *1 egg yolk*
> *150 g (5 oz) butter*
> *1 x 5 ml spoon (1 teaspoon) sugar*
> *2-3 x 15 ml spoons (2-3*
>   *tablespoons) water, plus a squeeze*
>   *of lemon juice*
> *salt*

To prepare the pastry, sieve the flour on to a board and make a well in the centre. Put all the other ingredients for the pastry into this and, using the fingertips of one hand, work it up into a firm dough. Knead it lightly and then leave it in a cool place to relax for 20-30 minutes.

Palmiers

Make a quantity of puff pastry in the usual way but for the last 2 turns, dust the board with castor sugar instead of flour. Leave the pastry to relax for 10-15 minutes.

Roll it out 3-6 mm ($\frac{1}{8}$-$\frac{1}{4}$ in) thick in a rectangle of about 30 x 45 cm (12 x 18 in). Trim the edges, fold each long side into the middle, then fold once again. Cut the pastry into strips 6 mm ($\frac{1}{4}$ in) thick and put these, cut side up, on a baking sheet. Leave plenty of room for them to spread sideways. Bake for 5-10 minutes at 210°C, 425°F/Gas 7, turning them over when golden. Cook for another 3-4 minutes, keeping an eye on them all the time.

When making puff pastry for a particular dish, you can use up any leftovers by making small versions of palmiers. Sprinkle the trimmings heavily with sugar, roll out into a rectangle and proceed as above.

Fun...
and fine food

Picnics or alfresco garden meals and barbecues can be as simple or as lavish as you like. Two basic picnic menus are given here—one for bad-weather occasions when the food may have to be eaten in a car, and the other for hot summer days. All the picnic and barbecue recipes can be interchanged. Children's parties are dealt with separately and are divided into various age-groups.

Bad Weather Picnics

Much of the food included in this picnic would be suitable for any picnic-type occasion, but there are some special factors that make it a bad weather picnic. First of all it has a selection of hot soups, which would not be so welcome on a very hot day, and secondly it has been planned so that it could be eaten in a car if the weather turns really nasty.

The first consideration for any picnic which may have to be eaten in a car, railway carriage or some similarly cramped space is that you must be able to eat all the food with your fingers. Therefore it must not be too messy or sticky. Always take along a good supply of kitchen paper, good-sized paper plates, wide-based mugs (which will tip over less easily than those that taper towards the base), a damp cloth in a polythene bag and a hand towel.

The soups can all be drunk from a mug and include old favourites as well as some new ideas. If you do not want to take soup, but need something warming, try vacuum flasks of hot blackcurrant cordial for the young and mulled wine for the adults.

As far as picnic food is concerned, ordinary sandwiches seem to have faded in fashion and popularity, but they are convenient in that they can be made in advance. They can also be delicious, particularly if the bread is thinly sliced. Try ringing the changes by using granary or brown bread and make the fillings as moist as you can without them becoming messy. If you only need a packet of sustaining sandwiches to slip into a pocket until lunchtime, brown bread and homemade chicken liver or smoked mackerel pâté are hard to beat.

If children are coming to the picnic, a large packet of crisps will help to stave off the hunger pangs.

Mushroom Soup

225 g (8 oz) white mushrooms or
  mushroom stalks
50 g (2 oz) butter
40 g (1½ oz) flour
600 ml (1 pint) milk
300 ml (½ pint) stock
150 ml (¼ pint) single cream
salt and pepper

Wash the mushrooms and chop them very finely. Melt the butter in a pan, add the flour and cook gently for 2-3 minutes, stirring all the time. Add the milk gradually and bring to the boil, still stirring. Season well, then stir in the mushrooms. Add the stock, bring back to the boil and cook gently for 4-5 minutes. Pour a little of the boiling soup on to the cream, stir and return to the pan. Heat without boiling and pour immediately into a vacuum flask.

Velouté Indienne

Curried Velouté Soup
25 g (1 oz) butter
25 g (1 oz) flour
1 x 5 ml spoon (1 teaspoon) curry
  powder
1 litre (1¾ pints) chicken stock
1 strip lemon peel/juice of ½ a lemon
50 g (2 oz) desiccated coconut or
1 fresh coconut
2-3 x 15 ml spoons (2-3 tablespoons)
  single cream
salt and pepper

Melt the butter in a pan, add the flour and cook for 2-3 minutes, stirring all the time. Stir in the curry powder, then add the stock, lemon peel and lemon juice. Bring to the boil, stirring frequently. Season and simmer gently for 20 minutes. Put the desiccated or grated fresh coconut in a basin and cover with boiling water. Leave for 10 minutes, then strain liquid into the soup, squeezing the coconut well. Just before pouring into a vacuum flask, stir in the cream. (Do not let it boil after you have added the cream.)

Tomato Soup

900 g (2 lb) tomatoes or 1 x 700-g
  (1½-lb) can tomatoes
1 carrot
1 onion
1½ litres (2½ pints) chicken stock
grated rind of ½ orange
strip of lemon peel
bouquet garni
30 g (1¼ oz) butter
40 g (1½ oz) flour
tomato purée
sugar
150 ml (¼ pint) single cream
salt and pepper

Chop the tomatoes, and peel and chop the carrot and onion roughly. Put them in a pan with the stock, grated orange rind, lemon peel, bouquet garni, salt and pepper. Cook gently for 40-45 minutes, then pass through a sieve or fine vegetable mill.

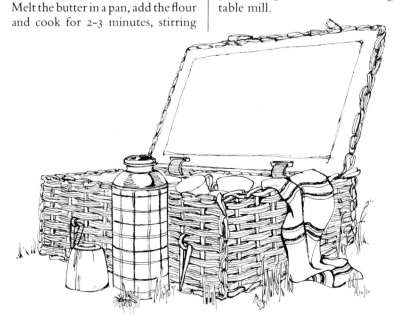

Melt the butter in a large pan, add the flour and cook for 2-3 minutes, stirring all the time. Add the tomato pulp, bring to the boil and taste for seasoning. If necessary add a little tomato purée and sugar. Simmer for a further 4-5 minutes. Finally, stir in the cream, re-heat without boiling and pour into a vacuum flask.

Note You could add paprika or other spices to this soup according to taste.

Lentil and Tomato Soup

350 g (12 oz) lentils
2 litres (3½ pints) stock or water
450 g (1 lb) tomatoes or
  medium-sized can tomatoes
75 g (3 oz) belly of pork or
  fat green bacon
1 onion
½ head celery
garlic
2 x 15 ml spoons (2 tablespoons) oil
chopped parsley
salt and pepper
Soak the lentils in cold water for

2-3 hours. Put them in a large pan with the stock or water. Bring to the boil and cook for 30-40 minutes. Chop the tomatoes roughly and dice the pork or bacon. Peel and chop the onion and wash and chop the celery. Crush the garlic with a little salt. Add to the pan, season well, then add the oil. Cook briskly for a further 30-40 minutes, then pass the soup through a vegetable mill. Re-heat, stir in the chopped parsley and pour quickly into a vacuum flask.

Note Be careful not to make the soup too thick if it is to be served from a vacuum flask.

Stuffed French Loaves or Rolls

Use small French or Vienna loaves and allow one between three people. Alternatively, use fresh individual rolls. In both cases, cut off the tops and scoop out the crumbs. Then butter the inside lightly, stuff with a filling and replace the top.

Fillings: cold hard-boiled eggs,

Tomato Soup is a family favourite which never fails and this recipe makes the most of it with a variety of tasty ingredients

chopped and mixed with cream cheese and chutney; chopped ham mixed with French mustard, cream cheese and celery or chutney; sardines blended with butter, lemon juice and tomato ketchup; corned beef mixed with butter, mayonnaise, pickles or chutney.

An omelette made with 2-3 eggs makes a good filling for a Vienna loaf. Cook the omelette in the usual way, adding chopped ham or mushrooms. While the omelette is still hot, slide it into the loaf, prepared as above, and replace the top. Slice the loaf when the omelette is cold and wrap in foil. Pack in a plastic container.

Similarly, both rolls and loaves can be filled with *piperade*. Cook it rather well so that the mixture is solid when cold, but fill the rolls or loaves while it is still warm.

Scotch Eggs—the tasty and infinitely superior home-made variety

Scotch Eggs

   8 eggs
   450 g (1 lb) pork sausage meat
   chopped parsley
   1 shallot
   salt and pepper

For coating

   1 egg plus an extra egg white
   1 x 15 ml spoon (1 tablespoon) oil
   flour
   dried crumbs
   deep fat or oil for frying

Put the eggs in cold water, bring to the boil and cook for 6-8 minutes, according to size and freshness. Plunge into cold water, shell and dry well.

Mix the sausage meat with the chopped parsley. Peel and finely chop the shallot and beat this in, adding salt and pepper. Divide into eight portions and flatten out each with a damp hand. Put an egg on to each and press up the sausage meat to cover the egg completely.

Beat the egg for the coating with the oil and a little salt and roll the Scotch eggs first in flour and then in the egg mixture. Coat with crumbs. Tap off any excess crumbs and leave for 15-20 minutes. Fry in hot fat or oil until golden brown, drain on kitchen paper and leave to cool. Serve cut in half.

Stuffed Sausages

Serve these as a simple alternative to Scotch eggs. If there are children on the picnic, take a small screw-topped jar of tomato ketchup in which to dip the sausages.

   450 g (1 lb) large pork sausages or chipolatas
   75-100 g (3-4 oz) cream cheese
   French mustard
   chutney or tomato ketchup

Fry the sausages gently until they are cooked. Drain and cool them. Beat the cheese with the mustard and chutney or ketchup, split the sausages lengthwise and fill with the cheese mixture.

Pipérade

   1 large red or green pepper
   2 large onions
   4 large tomatoes
   garlic
   40 g (1½ oz) butter or lard
   6 eggs

marjoram (optional)
salt and pepper

Slice the peppers finely, discarding the seeds, then blanch the flesh in boiling salted water for 1-2 minutes. Drain and refresh under cold water. Peel and finely slice the onions. Skin, de-seed and slice the tomatoes. Crush the garlic with a little salt.

Melt the butter or lard and cook the onion slowly until golden brown. Add the peppers and continue cooking gently until they are soft. Add the tomatoes, garlic, marjoram if you are using it, salt and pepper. When the mixture has reduced almost to a purée, lightly beat and season the six eggs and add them to the mixture. Cook gently, stirring all the time until they are the consistency of creamy scrambled eggs.

Picnic Tartlets

The quantities given here are sufficient for about twelve tartlets.

225 g (8 oz) flour
100 g (4 oz) butter and lard, mixed
75 g (3 oz) grated cheese
2-3 x 15 ml spoons (2-3 tablespoons) water

For the filling
100 g (4 oz) streaky bacon
1 large onion
4 small gherkins
1 egg
6 x 15 ml spoons (6 tablespoons) milk
mustard
extra beaten egg
salt and pepper

To make the pastry, sieve the flour and salt onto a board and make a well in the centre. Add the butter and lard and work with the flour to a crumbly consistency. Mix in the cheese and enough water to make a firm paste, then set aside to relax in a cool place for at least 30 minutes.

To prepare the filling, trim the rind from the bacon and cut it into small pieces. Fry gently until the fat runs. Peel and chop the onion and add to the bacon. Chop the gherkins and add to the pan. Mix the egg and milk together and season with mustard, salt and pepper.

Roll out the pastry and cut into 12 large and 12 smaller circles. Line tartlet tins with the large circles and prick the bases. Divide the bacon, onion and gherkin mixture between them, then spoon in the egg mixture on top. Cover with the remaining pastry circles, brush with beaten egg and bake for 30 minutes at 190°C, 375°F/Gas 5. Allow to cool slightly and then remove from the tin. Serve warm if possible.

Flavoured Breads

Herb or anchovy bread can be made in the same way as usual, heated through and taken on picnics. If you can keep the bread warm in an insulated picnic box, so much the better, but in fact these flavoured breads are still very tasty served cold.

Terrine de Lièvre

Hare Pâté

Serve this either straight from the dish, or slice it in advance and pack the slices in a box. Fresh bread rolls are an ideal accompaniment.

1 hare giving 700 g (1½ lb) meat (keep liver and blood)
700 g (1½ lb) belly of pork
100 g (4 oz) piece streaky bacon
1-2 x 15 ml spoons (1-2 tablespoons) chopped parsley and majoram
1-2 cloves garlic
2 x 15 ml spoons (2 tablespoons) brandy
1 wineglass white wine
pinch mace
225 g (8 oz) thin streaky bacon rashers
salt and pepper

Joint the hare, reserving the liver and blood. Roast the joints for 15 minutes at 180°C, 350°F/Gas 4. Remove all the flesh from the bones and pass through the coarse blade of a mincer with the belly of pork and the hare's liver. Cut the streaky bacon into cubes and add to the hare

flesh with the parsley and marjoram. Crush the garlic with a little salt and add, together with the hare's blood. Mix in well. Stir in the brandy, white wine and other seasonings. Make sure everything is well mixed together.

Line a terrine with the thin rashers of bacon and fill with the mixture. Cover with more bacon and a lid. Leave to stand for 1-2 hours before cooking, if possible, as this allows the flavours to blend together.

Stand in a baking tin of hot water and cook for about 1½ hours at 160°-180°C, 325°-350°F/Gas 3-4. Allow to cool slightly then put a 1·5-kg (3-lb) weight on top, until the terrine is cold.

Note Terrines are cooked when they shrink from the side of the dish and the liquid surrounding them is clear.

Pâté de Campagne

Country Pâté

450 g (1 lb) lean pork or veal
225 g (8 oz) pig's liver
100 g (4 oz) fat pork
1 shallot or small onion
50-75 g (2-3 oz) white bread
150 ml (¼ pint) sherry, port or red wine
3 eggs
225 g (8 oz) thin streaky bacon rashers
pinch allspice and marjoram
salt and pepper

Mince the pork or veal, liver and fat pork. Peel and chop the shallot or onion and soak the bread in the wine. Mix together. Beat the eggs and add to the mixture. Season well.

Line a loaf tin with the bacon rashers and fill with the pork mixture, pressing down well. Cover and cook for 1-1½ hours in a *bain-marie* at 180°C, 350°F/Gas 4. When cooked, press the pâté with a 1·5-kg (3-lb) weight and leave until cold.

Note If required, this pâté can be frozen either in slices or wrapped whole in foil. Thaw for 18-24 hours in a refrigerator before using.

Pork and Pear Loaf

2 large pears or firm apples
700 g (1½ lb) pork sausage meat
100 g (4 oz) fresh white
 breadcrumbs
1 large onion
grated rind of ½ lemon
2 eggs
chopped herbs, including sage
mustard
salt and pepper

Peel, core and chop the pears or apples. Mix them with the sausage meat and breadcrumbs. Peel and finely chop the onion and mix with all the remaining ingredients and the sausage-meat mixture. Season well.

Butter a 900-g (2-lb) bread tin and press the mixture into it. Cook for 45 minutes at 190°C, 375°F/ Gas 5. Then cool under a light weight of about 900 g (2 lb). Unmould the loaf before it is completely cold.

Note This is also good served hot with homemade tomato sauce on non-picnic occasions. In this case, leave it for 10-15 minutes when you first take it from the oven, then unmould on to a warm dish and serve.

Cumberland Rum Nicky

On non-picnic occasions, this is delicious served hot with cream.

For the pastry
 225 g (8 oz) flour
 150 g (5 oz) butter
 1 egg yolk
 squeeze of lemon juice
 2 x 15 ml spoons (2 tablespoons)
 cold water

For the filling
 100 g (4 oz) chopped dates
 50 g (2 oz) chopped ginger
 50 g (2 oz) butter
 25 g (1 oz) sugar
 rum to taste

To make the pastry, sift the flour on to a board and make a well in the centre. Add the butter, egg yolk and lemon juice. Using the fingers of one hand, work together, drawing in the flour to produce a crumbly consistency. Add the water and

knead to make a smooth dough. Leave in a cool place for at least 30 minutes.

Roll out two-thirds of the pastry and use to line a 17·5-cm (7-in) flan ring or pie dish. Prick the base and cover with dates and ginger. Beat the butter and sugar together, then beat in rum to taste. Spread over the fruit. Cover with the remainder of the pastry, then leave in a cool place for 15 minutes. Brush with egg white and sprinkle with sugar.

Bake for 10-15 minutes at 200°C, 400°F/Gas 6, then reduce the heat to 180°C, 350°F/Gas 4 and bake for a further 25 minutes.

Mrs Dixon's Chocolate Cake

Make this cake 24-48 hours before you want to eat it, or cook it whenever you have time and freeze it (allow 24 hours to thaw). It can be iced with butter icing, but for a picnic, it is best left plain.

 150 g (5 oz) butter
 150 g (5 oz) castor sugar
 4 eggs
 70 g (2½ oz) flour
 50 g (2 oz) ground almonds
 1 x 5 ml spoon (1 teaspoon) baking
 powder
 70 g (2½ oz) drinking chocolate
 powder

Butter and flour a 450-g (1-lb) bread tin or 17·5-cm (7-in) *moule à manqué* shallow cake tin. Line the base with greaseproof paper.

Cream the butter and sugar together until white and fluffy. Separate the eggs and beat in the yolks. Sift the flour, almonds, baking powder and chocolate powder together and fold into the butter mixture. Whip the egg whites stiffly, then fold in lightly, spoon the mixture into the prepared tin and bake for 40-60 minutes at 180°C, 350°F/Gas 4. Cool on a rack and dust with icing sugar.

Sticky Ginger Cake

Make this cake a few days before you want to eat it. It goes well with cheese or apples for a picnic.

 100 g (4 oz) butter
 100 g (4 oz) brown sugar
 225 g (8 oz) black treacle or golden
 syrup and treacle mixed
 2 eggs
 225 g (8 oz) flour
 1 x 5 ml spoon (1 teaspoon) ground
 ginger
 50 g (2 oz) sultanas
 50 g (2 oz) walnuts
 2 x 15 ml spoons (2 tablespoons)
 warm milk
 ½ x 5 ml spoon (½ teaspoon)
 bicarbonate soda

Butter and flour a 450-g (1-lb) bread tin and line the base with grease-proof paper. Melt the butter in a pan. Remove from the heat and add the sugar, treacle and eggs. Sift the flour and ginger together and stir in the sultanas. Chop the walnuts and add to the flour. Pour the treacle mixture (which should be only just warm) into the flour and beat everything together well. Finally, carefully stir in the milk and bicarbonate of soda. Pour into the prepared tin and bake for 1½ hours at 160°C, 325°F/Gas 3. Reduce the heat after 1 hour if necessary, then allow to cool partially in the tin before turning out the cake.

Guards' Cup

    1 bottle dry cider
    ½ bottle perry
    1 wineglass brandy
    300 ml (½ pint) medium sweet sherry
    1 litre (1¾ pints) water
    1 wineglass vermouth (optional)
    sugar to taste
    borage or mint

Chill all the ingredients for several hours before you make the cup. Put several ice cubes into a jug and then make up to 1 litre (1¾ pints) with cold water. Mix everything together, adding sugar to taste. Keep in a container in an insulated cold bag or pour into a vacuum flask.

Mulled Wine

This recipe is excellent if you want a spicy, warming drink.

    6-8 x 15 ml spoons (6-8 tablespoons)
      sugar
    600 ml (1 pint) water
    1 orange
    1 lemon
    nutmeg
    cinnamon
    1 litre bottle red wine
    1-2 wineglasses brandy (optional)

Put the sugar and water in a pan. Thinly pare the rind of the orange

Pork and Apple Loaf can be served cold or hot with tomato sauce

and lemon and add to the pan. Squeeze the juice from the lemon and add with the spices to taste. Bring to the boil, then simmer for 10 minutes and strain. Add the wine and heat gently until a white froth begins to form on top. Remove pan from the heat and add the brandy. Pour into vacuum flasks. Make sure the wine does not boil. If it does the alcohol will evaporate, making the flavour harsh.

Sticky Ginger Cake—rich and moist and simply delicious

Lemonade or Fruit Drink

This drink will keep for several weeks in the refrigerator. Dilute to taste. It is stronger than commercial squash, therefore less will be needed for each glass. In summer, the drink is particularly refreshing if served with plenty of ice.

    3 lemons
    4 oranges
    1 grapefruit (optional)
    1·75 kg (4 lb) sugar
    25 g (1 oz) tartaric acid
    25 g (1 oz) epsom salts
    50 g (2 oz) citric acid
    2 litres (3½ pints) water

Grate the rind and squeeze the juice from all the fruit. Put the sugar, tartaric acid, epsom salts and citric acid in a bowl. Add the fruit juice and rind to the bowl. Boil the water and stir it in until the solid ingredients have dissolved. Let the squash cool, then bottle and keep in the refrigerator.

The recipes that follow are for a more sophisticated type of picnic—one with plates and cutlery and preferably a table and folding chairs. The food could either be prepared and packed in insulated containers and baskets for a country picnic, or it could be served as a garden meal for a summer lunch or dinner.

The section is divided into cold soups and starters, main courses and puddings, so you can choose to suit the occasion. Unless otherwise stated, the quantities are sufficient for four to six people.

If the picnic is away from home, the preservation of the food en route is an important consideration. Cars can get very hot and any creamy or gelatinous dish, particularly if not kept in an insulated container, can quickly become unpalatable.

Another point worth remembering is that while most of the preparation can be done in advance, some dishes have to be finished off at the last minute before serving. Keep this in mind as you plan your menu. Dishes which need last-minute attention are more suitable for garden meals close to home than for picnics.

If you have a washing-up machine, it is often easier to take everyday crockery on the picnic, so that it can be put straight into the machine. Plastic items usually have to be washed by hand. Take a large plastic bag on the picnic to hold the dirty cutlery and another for the rubbish.

Cold Soups and Starters

The three cold soups given here are all delicious for a hot day, but they must be served really well chilled to be appetizing. Keep them in a wide-necked vacuum flask, or in a plastic container in an insulated picnic box, and serve in small bowls. The mushroom soup and the avocado and spinach soup should be made with jellied stock, otherwise they will be too liquid. If using a stock cube, make the stock up to half-strength, then add gelatine to it.

The sardine pâté, bacon pâté and terrine of chicken livers can all be made a few days before you need them. They all transport easily and the bacon pâté also freezes well.

The crab dish is tastiest made with fresh crab, although you can use frozen crab meat if fresh is unavailable. Make it the day before and put it in a plastic container. You need cool travelling conditions for this starter.

Whichever first course you choose to serve, remember to include something to eat with it. French bread, croûtes and dry savoury biscuits are all excellent with both soups and pâtés.

Chilled Mushroom Soup

225 g (8 oz) white button mushrooms
300 ml (½ pint) single or double cream
50 g (2 oz) butter
50 g (2 oz) flour
1·25 litres (2 pints) jellied chicken or veal stock
chopped parsley and tarragon
salt and pepper

Wipe the mushrooms, then liquidize with the cream. Melt the butter in a pan, add the flour and cook for 1-2 minutes, stirring all the time. Gradually add the stock and bring to the boil, stirring frequently. Season well and add the mushroom purée. Simmer for 5 minutes, then adjust the seasoning. Cool and chill. Add the parsley and tarragon as late as possible before serving.
Note If using stock cubes, add 20 g (¾ oz, 1½ sachets) dissolved powdered gelatine.

Avocado and Spinach Soup

This soup should be eaten on the day it is made, otherwise the spinach discolours and turns it a rather unpleasant brown. If using fresh spinach, 700 g (1½ lb) is needed to produce 350 g (12 oz) blanched. (This can be done the day before.)

2 avocado pears
350 g (12 oz) frozen or blanched spinach
450 ml (¾ pint) jellied chicken stock
150 ml (¼ pint) single or double cream
1 lemon
1 small onion
chopped chives
salt and pepper

Scoop the flesh from the avocados, including as much of the green part as possible. Put in a liquidizer with the well-drained spinach, the stock and cream. Grate the rind and squeeze the juice from the lemon, peel and grate the onion and add to the other ingredients in the liquidizer. Liquidize until smooth. Adjust the seasoning and chill the soup. Serve with a little extra cream and a sprinkling of chopped chives.
Note If using a stock cube, make the stock up to half-strength and add 1 x 5 ml spoon (1 teaspoon) dissolved powdered gelatine while it is still warm.

Gazpacho

8 large ripe tomatoes
2 cloves garlic
1 cucumber
½ onion
1 green pepper
6 x 15 ml spoons (6 tablespoons) olive oil
lemon juice to taste
1 x 400-ml (14-fl-oz) can tomato juice
salt and pepper
ice cubes

Chop the tomatoes roughly and peel the garlic. Place in a liquidizer and liquidize thoroughly. Skin and dice the cucumber. Peel and roughly chop the onion. De-seed and dice the pepper and add to the liquidizer. Liquidize again. Season well and rub the purée through a large sieve or vegetable mill. Chill well.

Just before serving, put the soup back in the liquidizer and add the oil gradually, liquidizing all the time. Add lemon juice to taste, and some ice. Mix in the tomato juice (pre-

Bacon Pâté—excellent with French bread or crackers, this is a good, chunky dish for a picnic and easily transportable wrapped in foil or sliced

viously chilled).

Note This soup is best served very cold. Small bowls of skinned, de-seeded and chopped tomatoes and cucumber, diced blanched pepper and croûtons of fried bread can be served as accompaniments, but this may not be very convenient on a picnic. As an alternative, sprinkle freshly chopped herbs over the soup, after pouring it into serving bowls.

Insulated Containers
These are now obtainable in both box and bag form, and are slightly more efficient at keeping food cool than hot. They are invaluable for summer picnics, particularly for creamy or gelatinous dishes which need to be kept cool. On a journey of more than an hour or so, the boot of a car can easily become hot enough to spoil a dish of this sort, unless kept in an insulated container. The temperature-maintaining sachets, which come with the bags, may be heated or cooled beforehand (depending on whether hot or cold food is being transported) and then tucked in between the food containers in the bag.

Bacon Pâté

*450 g (1 lb) green long back bacon
  rashers (no. 5 cut)*
4 eggs
450 g (1 lb) pork fillet or lean pork
1 onion
100–150 g (4–6 oz) fresh breadcrumbs
1 small glass sherry
nutmeg
chopped parsley
salt and pepper

Cut the rind from the bacon and flatten out 4 rashers. Line a 450-g (1-lb) loaf tin with these and set aside another 4 rashers. Hard-boil 2 eggs.

Mince the pork fillet with the rest of the bacon. Peel and chop the onion very finely. Chop the hard-boiled eggs roughly and add these to the meat together with the breadcrumbs, sherry, nutmeg, chopped parsley, salt and pepper. Beat the remaining 2 eggs and stir into the mixture thoroughly. Put a layer of the mixture into the bread tin, then cover with 2 rashers of bacon cut into large pieces. Continue layering in this way until the tin is full. Finish with a layer of minced meat.

Cover the tin with foil and put in a roasting tin of water. Bake for 1¼–1½ hours at 160°–180°C, 325°–350°F/Gas 3–4. When cooked, remove from the roasting tin and cool under a light weight of 1–1·5 kg (2–3 lb). Turn out when it is cold and either wrap whole in foil, or slice first.

Sardine Pâté

2 cans sardines
100 g (4 oz) cream cheese
garlic
lemon juice
Worcestershire sauce } *to taste*
Tabasco sauce
paprika
salt and pepper

Drain off a little of the oil from the sardines and remove the backbones. Put the sardines in a liquidizer with the cheese. Crush the garlic with a little salt and add with all the remaining ingredients. Liquidize well, season and put in a small terrine or pot. Sprinkle the top with paprika.

Crabe à la Façon des Pêcheurs

Crab Fisherman-style
Allow ½-1 crab per person, depending on the size of the crabs. For a party, this recipe looks attractive served in the crab shells, in small scallop shells or individual china soufflé dishes, but for a picnic it would be easiest to put it in one large soufflé dish.

1-2 cooked crabs (depending on size)
1 clove garlic
2-3 egg yolks
1-1½ x 5 ml spoons (1-1½ teaspoons)
  French mustard
1 x 5 ml spoon (1 teaspoon) wine
  vinegar
1-2 x 15 ml spoons (1-2 tablespoons)
  oil
½ lemon
salt and pepper

Crush the garlic with a little salt and put in a liquidizer with the crab meat, egg yolks, mustard, vinegar and oil. Squeeze the juice from the lemon and add with some salt and pepper. Liquidize at a *low* speed until everything is well mixed together. Season well and put in the crab or scallop shells or soufflé dish.
Note If you are serving this at a dinner party, decorate the surface with lines of sieved yolks and chopped whites from hard-boiled eggs mixed with chopped parsley.

Main Dishes

A variety of cold dishes is given here, all of which will transport well, although some certainly need to be carried in an insulated container. The mousses should be put in suitably-sized soufflé dishes as the consistency might soften on a warm day. If the occasion is special, the top of the mousses could be decorated with thinly sliced cucumber.

For those who like chicken, and want a fairly filling dish, the chicken and noodle salad is a more solid dish that would satisfy a hungry crowd. The chicken and avocado salad is particularly tasty, but needs rather more last-minute finishing off before serving. The prawn flan can be prepared in advance.

The ham roulades are tasty and a bit unusual and would make a good alternative to one of the chicken dishes. Provided they are well wrapped in cling wrap, they can be prepared a day in advance. The cold version of the *boeuf Stroganoff* is rather an extravagant dish and needs to be finished off on the day it is to be eaten.

Chicken and Ham Mousse

1·5 kg (3 lb) chicken (cooked)
100 g (4 oz) softened butter
100 g (4 oz) cooked tongue
2 x 15 ml spoons (2 tablespoons)
  cream
225 g (8 oz) cooked ham
salt and pepper
For the sauce
1 small onion
300 ml (½ pint) milk
1 bay leaf
25 g (1 oz) butter
25 g (1 oz) flour
2 x 5 ml spoons (2 teaspoons,
  1 sachet) gelatine
5 x 15 ml spoons (5 tablespoons)
  stock, white wine or water
salt and pepper

To prepare the sauce, peel and thinly slice the onion and put in a saucepan with the milk, bay leaf, salt and pepper. Bring gently to the

boil, then remove the pan from the heat, cover and leave to infuse for 10-15 minutes. Melt the butter in another pan, stir in the flour and cook for 2-3 minutes, stirring all the time. Strain the infused milk into the pan, bring to the boil, still stirring, and cook for a further 2-3 minutes. Cool.

Meanwhile put the gelatine in a small bowl with the stock, water or wine and stand the basin in a small pan of hot water until the gelatine has dissolved. Strain into the sauce.

Strip all the flesh from the chicken, discarding any skin. Mince or pound the flesh and gradually add the sauce, beating all the time. Add the softened butter. Finely chop the tongue and add to the sauce. Season the mixture to taste and fold in the cream.

Cut the ham into julienne strips, removing any fat. Put one-third of the chicken mixture into a soufflé dish and cover it with half the ham. Top with half the remaining chicken mixture, then the rest of the ham, finishing with a layer of chicken. Chill overnight.

Mousse aux Langues

Tongue Mousse
225 g (8 oz) tongue
50 g (2 oz) ham
2 x 5 ml spoons (2 teaspoons,
  1 sachet) gelatine
5 x 15 ml spoons (5 tablespoons) hot
  stock or water
1-2 x 15 ml spoons (1-2 tablespoons)
  Madeira, sherry or port
3-4 x 15 ml spoons (3-4 tablespoons)
  mayonnaise
150 ml (¼ pint) double cream
1-2 egg whites
salt and pepper
For the sauce
20 g (¾ oz) butter
20 g (¾ oz) flour
300 ml (½ pint) milk
1-2 x 5 ml spoons (1-2 teaspoons)
  tomato purée
salt and pepper

To prepare the sauce, melt the butter in a pan, stir in the flour and

cook for 2-3 minutes, stirring all the time. Add most of the milk and bring to the boil, stirring until the sauce thickens. Add the rest of the milk if the sauce is very thick. Season well and add the tomato purée. Leave to cool.

Mince the tongue and ham. Put the gelatine in a basin with the hot stock or water. Stand in a pan of hot water till the gelatine dissolves.

When the sauce is cold, stir in the dissolved gelatine and the Madeira, sherry or port. Beat in the minced tongue and ham. Fold in the mayonnaise. When the mixture is on the point of setting, whip the cream lightly and the egg whites stiffly. Fold into the mixture. Pour into a soufflé dish. Chill overnight.

Prawn Flan

For the pastry
225 g (8 oz) flour
150 g (5 oz) softened butter
1 egg yolk
squeeze lemon juice
2-3 x 15 ml spoons (2-3 tablespoons)
cold water

For the filling
4 hard-boiled eggs
225 g (8 oz) shelled prawns
2-3 x 15 ml spoons (2-3 tablespoons)
mayonnaise
½ cucumber
chopped fresh herbs
1 can anchovy fillets
milk
salt and pepper

To make the pastry, put the flour on a board and make a well in the centre. Into this, put the butter, egg yolk and lemon juice and work into a crumbly consistency, gradually drawing in the flour. Add the water and knead to a smooth dough. Leave in a cool place for at least 30 minutes, then roll out and use to line a 20-23-cm (8-9-in) flan ring. Prick the base, line with greaseproof paper and baking beans. Bake for 15-20 minutes at 200°C, 400°F/Gas 5. Remove the baking beans and paper and return the flan to the oven for a few more minutes. Allow to cool.

To prepare the filling, separate the yolks from the whites of the hard-boiled eggs. Sieve the yolks and put on one side. Chop the whites and mix with the prawns. Season well and fold in the mayonnaise. Dice the cucumber, discarding the seeds, and sprinkle the flesh with salt. Leave in a sieve for 15 minutes to drain, then dry well. Mix with the herbs and pepper. Divide the anchovies lengthwise and leave to soak in the milk for 10 minutes.

When the pastry case is quite cold, spoon the prawn and mayonnaise mixture into it. Arrange the cucumber around the edge in a thick border and fill the centre with the sieved egg yolk. Decorate with anchovies. Chill before serving.

Jambon Roulé aux Fines Herbes

Ham Rolls with Herbs
6 slices ham
450 g (1 lb) spinach or 1 packet
frozen leaf spinach
2-3 sorrel leaves
garlic
chopped chervil, tarragon, fennel
and parsley (as available)
6 x 15 ml spoons (6 tablespoons)
double cream
25 g (1 oz) softened butter or
cream cheese
salt and pepper

Wash the spinach and sorrel in 3 changes of cold water and pull out the centre stalks. Cook in boiling, salted water for 4-5 minutes, then refresh immediately under cold water. If using frozen spinach, defrost and drain well, then cook as directed. Squeeze well to remove all water. Chop roughly. Put in a bowl and add the garlic crushed with a little salt, the herbs, cream, salt and pepper. Beat in the butter or cheese gradually.

Divide this mixture between the slices of ham and spread evenly. Roll up the ham and chill.

Boeuf Stroganoff en Salade

Beef Stroganoff Salad
1 kg (2-2½ lb) boned sirloin or
fillet of beef
butter
white wine
350 g (12 oz) white button
mushrooms
2 lemons
3 large mild-flavoured onions
20 black olives
150 ml (¼ pint) soured cream
French dressing
chopped parsley
salt and pepper

Roast the meat for 30 minutes at 200°C, 400°F/Gas 6, basting it with a little butter and some white wine. Allow to cool.

Wash the mushrooms and put in a pan with 1 x 15 ml spoon (1 tablespoon) water, the juice of ½ a lemon, salt and pepper. Cover and cook briskly for 1-2 minutes, then allow to cool. (If the mushrooms are really white, there is no need to cook them — just sprinkle them with lemon juice.)

Peel and thinly slice the onions. Blanch in boiling salted water for 1 minute, then refresh under cold water. Drain well.

Slice half the mushrooms and chop 10 olives. Slice the meat, then shred it. Mix it with the mushrooms. Season well and stir in most of the cream. Put on a flat dish.

Mix the onions with the rest of the mushrooms and olives and sprinkle with French dressing. Stir in a little cream and arrange this around the meat. Sprinkle with parsley and serve with quartered lemons.

> **Soured Cream**
> Always buy cultured soured cream when this is stipulated in a recipe. Pasteurized cream that has been allowed to sour naturally has a bitter, bad taste and adding lemon juice to cream merely curdles or acidulates it, but will not sour it.

Chicken and Avocado Salad

If you want to serve this on a picnic, take the avocados along whole and add them to the salad at the last minute, otherwise they will discolour. You could use 300 ml (½ pint) mayonnaise instead of the boiled dressing.

1·5-kg (3½-lb) chicken
1 onion
1 carrot
lemon peel
salt and pepper
For the boiled dressing
1 x 15 ml spoon (1 tablespoon) castor sugar
2 x 5 ml spoons (2 teaspoons) flour
½ x 5 ml spoon (½ teaspoon) salt
2 x 5 ml spoons (2 teaspoons) made mustard
150 ml (¼ pint) water
150 ml (¼ pint) wine vinegar
1 egg
knob of butter
milk or single cream
For the salad
1 head celery
4 tomatoes
100 g (4 oz) walnuts
2-3 avocado pears
French dressing
chopped fresh herbs
Put the chicken in a pan and half cover with cold water. Bring to the boil and skim the surface. Peel the onion and carrot and add with the lemon peel, salt and pepper. Simmer gently for 1 hour, turning the bird once or twice. Leave to cool in the cooking liquid.

To make the boiled dressing, combine all the dry ingredients together and mix to a cream with a little of the water. Add the rest of the water and the vinegar, pour into a pan and cook, stirring continuously for 3-4 minutes. Beat the egg and the butter together and whisk into the hot mixture. Leave to cool and dilute with milk or cream to taste.

Wash and trim the celery and cut into 2·5-cm (1-in) pieces. Soak in very cold water for 30-40 minutes, then drain and dry. Skin and de-seed the tomatoes and cut into quarters.

Discard all the skin and bones from the chicken and cut the flesh into neat pieces. Mix with the celery, tomatoes and walnuts and pour the boiled dressing (or mayonnaise) over the top.

Place the chicken on a dish and just before serving, skin the avocados, cut into quarters, and arrange around the salad. Spoon some French dressing over the avocados at once and sprinkle with herbs.

Chicken and Avocado Salad—for an elegant summer meal

Chicken and Noodle Salad

Watercress and quartered tomatoes make an attractive garnish for this dish.

1·5-kg (3½-lb) chicken
sprig tarragon or thyme
butter
1 wineglass dry vermouth
300 ml (½ pint) stock
225 g (8 oz) green noodles
225 g (8 oz) button mushrooms
lemon juice
2 x 15 ml spoons (2 tablespoons) oil
300 ml (½ pint) mayonnaise
100 g (4 oz) sliced ham
100 g (4 oz) sliced tongue
salt and pepper
Put a sprig of tarragon or thyme inside the chicken and add seasoning. Rub the breast with butter and put the bird on its side in a roasting tin. Pour the vermouth and half the stock into the tin and roast for 1-1¼ hours at 200°C, 400°F/Gas 6, turning and basting regularly. Make sure the breast is uppermost for the last 20 minutes. Remove the bird from the tin and cool. Add the rest of the stock to the tin and deglaze it well. Strain this and cool.

Hazelnut Roulade—filled with double cream and black cherries, dusted with icing sugar—this is more than just a Swiss roll

Cook the noodles in boiling salted water for 10 minutes or so. Drain and wash under cold water. Slice the mushrooms and put in a pan with a little lemon juice. Cook briskly for 1 minute. Cool and sprinkle with oil and salt and pepper. Mix together well.

Dilute 2-3 x 15 ml spoons (2-3 tablespoons) mayonnaise with a little of the cooled stock and lemon juice. Put the noodles and mushrooms in a bowl and carefully fold in the diluted mayonnaise. Discard all the skin and bones from the chicken and dice the flesh into neat pieces. Add the remainder of the stock to the rest of the mayonnaise and mix enough of this with the chicken to moisten it well. Shred the ham and tongue. Put the noodles and mushrooms on to a dish and make a well in the centre. Pile the chicken in the middle and sprinkle with shredded ham and tongue.

Puddings

Most puddings are difficult to transport so only a small selection is given here. However, these can be varied in a number of ways. The *gâteau Bigarreau* could be finished off with any fruit in season, such as peaches, strawberries or raspberries, and you do not have to put nuts round the side, or top with the glaze. It is delicious with just fruit and cream. Leave out the praline if you are using fruit other than cherries (*Bigarreau* is a French variety of cherry). Leave the praline out of chocolate choux to make a change, or as an alternative to the praline, flavour the cornflour mixture with coffee and 1 x 15 ml spoon (1 tablespoon) sugar.

Meringues are always popular at picnics and alfresco meals. Take them unfilled together with a plastic container of whipped cream to serve with them.

Any pudding containing chocolate or butter cream risks becoming very sticky on picnics, but many cake-based puddings are suitable.

Meringues Chantilly

240 g (8½ oz) castor sugar
4 egg whites
icing sugar
300 ml (½ pint) double cream
1 x 15 ml spoon (1 tablespoon) icing sugar

Grease and flour 2-3 baking sheets, knocking off any excess flour. Sift the castor sugar on to a piece of paper.

Whisk the egg whites stiffly and whisk in 1 x 15 ml spoon (1 tablespoon) sugar. Fold in the rest of the sugar lightly. Pile the meringue into a forcing bag with a 1-cm (½-in) plain pipe and pipe shells or small baskets on to the baking sheets. Dust with icing sugar and bake for 1½-2 hours at 110°C, 200°F/Gas ¼-½. Reduce the heat as much as possible after the first half-hour and leave the meringues to cool in the oven when they are cooked.

Whip the cream lightly, fold in the sugar and whip until stiff. Sandwich the meringues together with the cream, or pipe it into the cases.

Note Meringues will store, unfilled, in a tin for 2-3 weeks.

Hazelnut Roulade

3 eggs
75 g (3 oz) sugar
75 g (3 oz) grilled ground hazelnuts
For the filling
1 x 400 g (14 oz) black or *morello* cherries
1 orange
1 x 5 ml spoon (1 teaspoon) arrowroot
300 ml (½ pint) double cream

Line a 30 x 17·5-cm (11 x 7-in) Swiss roll tin with oiled greaseproof paper.

Put the eggs and sugar in a bowl and beat until the mixture is thick and fluffy. (Do this over a pan of hot water unless using an electric mixer.) Fold in the hazelnuts and spread this mixture evenly in the prepared tin. Bake for 12-15 minutes at 200°C, 400°F/Gas 6. When the cake is cooked, turn it on to greaseproof paper sprinkled with sugar. Remove the oiled greaseproof paper from the underside of the cake. Cover the cake with a damp cloth. Leave to cool.

To prepare the filling, drain the cherries and put the syrup in a pan. Grate the rind and squeeze the juice from the orange and add to the syrup. Boil for 3-4 minutes to reduce slightly. Slake the arrowroot with a little cold water and stir into the fruit juice. Boil until the sauce thickens. Leave to cool, then stir in the cherries.

To finish off the cake, whip the cream stiffly and spread the cake with half of it. Cover with the fruit mixture. Roll up the cake starting from the long side. Put on a serving dish, dust the top with icing sugar and decorate with the rest of the cream.

Choux Pralinés au Chocolat

Almond Choux with Praline Cream
The choux buns and filling can be
made a day in advance. Do not fill
them or dust them with icing sugar
until just before they are wanted.

For the choux
> 50 g (2 oz) butter
> 100 ml (4 fl oz) water
> 65 g (2½ oz) flour
> 2 eggs
> 1 x 15 ml spoon (1 tablespoon)
>   almonds

For the filling
> 100 g (4 oz) praline, made with
>   100 g (4 oz) unblanched almonds
>   and 100 g (4 oz) castor sugar
> 1 x 15 ml spoon (1 tablespoon)
>   cornflour
> 150 ml (¼ pint) milk
> 75 g (3 oz) plain chocolate
> 200 ml (7 fl oz) double cream

To prepare the buns, cut up the
butter and put in a pan with the
water. Bring to the boil. Sift the
flour on to a piece of paper. When
the butter has melted, tip in all the
flour. Beat well to a smooth paste.
Beat in one egg, and when well
mixed, add the second gradually.
Reserve at least 1 x 5 ml spoon (1 teaspoon) egg for brushing the buns.
Put the mixture into a forcing bag
with a 1-cm (½-in) plain nozzle and
pipe small rounds about the size of
an apricot on a buttered baking
sheet. Brush with the reserved egg.
Chop the almonds finely and
sprinkle over the buns. Bake for
20-25 minutes at 200°-210°C, 400°-
425°F/Gas 6-7, reducing the heat if
they brown too quickly. Cool on a
rack.

To prepare the filling, make the
praline, put the almonds and sugar
in a strong pan and heat gently until
the sugar melts and begins to
caramelize. Stir once and cook until
the almonds begin to crack. Pour on
to an oiled baking sheet and leave to
cool. When quite cold, reduce to a
powder in a liquidizer or coffee mill.
Weigh out the required amount and
keep the rest in a screw-top jar.

Blend the cornflour and milk together until smooth, then bring to
the boil, stirring until the sauce
thickens. Cool in a covered bowl.
Break up the chocolate and put in a
basin. Cover with boiling water and
leave for 5 minutes. Pour off the
water and add the softened chocolate to the cornflour sauce. Leave to
cool. When quite cool, whip the
cream stiffly and fold into the
chocolate mixture with the praline.

When ready to serve, make a slit
in the side of each choux bun and fill
with the chocolate praline cream
using a forcing bag and plain nozzle.
Dust with icing sugar and serve at
once.

Drinks

Most people have their own
favourite picnic drinks, but
you will find that the Guards'
Cup and homemade fruit
drink (see car picnics) are
both very acceptable on hot
days. Iced coffee is also
popular. Make it quite strong
and strain carefully if using
ground coffee. Unless you are
sure of people's tastes, it is
better not to sweeten it.
Instead, take some icing sugar
or sugar syrup to add as
required.

Do remember to take a
bottle opener and a corkscrew
with you on picnics. They are
easy to forget and many a day
has been ruined by the lack of
them.

---

*Choux Pralinés au Chocolat—the
choux buns can be prepared in
advance and filled with rich
praline just before serving*

Gâteau Bigarreau

For the cake
> 3 eggs
> 120 g (4½ oz) castor sugar
> 75 g (3 oz) flour

For the filling
> 150-300 ml (¼-½ pint) double cream
> 2-3 x 15 ml spoons (2-3 tablespoons)
>   praliné (see recipe for choux pralinés
>   au chocolat)

For the topping and glaze
> 700 g (1½ lb) white or black cherries
> 3 x 15 ml spoons (3 tablespoons)
>   apricot jam
> 3 x 15 ml spoons (3 tablespoons)
>   redcurrant jelly
> 2 x 15 ml spoons (2 tablespoons)
>   water
> flaked browned almonds

Butter a shallow 20-cm (8-in) cake
tin and line the base with paper.
Sugar and flour the tin.

To make the cake, put the eggs
and sugar together in a bowl and
place over a pan of hot water, unless
using an electric mixer. Beat until
thick, white and fluffy, then remove
from the heat and continue beating
until the mixture is cool. Sift the
flour on to a piece of paper and fold
lightly into the eggs and sugar.
Turn the mixture into the tin and
bake for 25-30 minutes at 180°C,
350°F/Gas 4. Cool on a rack.

To prepare the topping and glaze,
stone the cherries, put the jam, jelly
and water in a pan and heat gently.
Simmer until smooth. Strain and
leave to cool.

To prepare the filling, whip the
cream and fold in the praline.

To finish the cake, split in half and
sandwich it with the cream and
praline. Brush the sides and top with
the jam and jelly glaze and press the
nuts round the sides. Arrange the
cherries on top of the cake and brush
lavishly with the rest of the glaze.

Barbecues

To barbecue basically means to cook outside over heated charcoal, but the equipment sold for barbecuing has become more and more sophisticated in recent years. As a result there is currently an enormous range on the market, from the simplest grills to elaborate models made for professional caterers.

This small section on barbecuing is to help you decide whether or not to launch yourself into the world of barbecues. By following the guidelines together with some of the recipes given here, you can experiment without too much initial outlay. If you find you enjoy it, you can go on to obtain more sophisticated equipment and try out some more unusual recipes.

Equipment

A barbecue can be either portable or built with bricks in a convenient place in the garden. The simplest one to construct takes about 20 household bricks and will need an oven shelf or grill tray. The portable barbecues come in all shapes, sizes and prices and the final choice will depend on what suits your need and pocket best.

If you are considering buying a small one, the square type is more practical than the round, as it gives a more effective cooking area. Look at all sorts before making a purchase in order to get as wide an idea as possible about what is available. A model with a grill that can be fixed in at least two different positions is preferable, the more practical ones will also have a wind shield.

There are all sorts of barbecue accessories, of which the only essential ones are a long-handled spoon and fork, a pair of tongs and some heavy gloves. A bubble syringe or well-washed squeezy bottle is useful for dampening down the flames during cooking.

Hand-grill A hand-grill consists of two hinged coarse-mesh grills with a long handle, and is particularly useful for food that breaks easily when handled or turned, such as fish, barbecued hot dogs and stuffed hamburgers. Hand-grills are available in different shapes and sizes.

Frying-pan A solid griddle is the best type of frying-pan to use, but failing this, a heavy frying- or sauté pan is useful for dishes that require a flat surface during cooking.

Skewers Long kebab skewers are useful and are obtainable from most stores that stock kitchen equipment.

Fuel Charcoal can be bought in bags from most coal merchants and suppliers of barbecue equipment. Solid-fuel tablets from chemists make useful firelighters. The fire for a barbecue needs to be kept fairly flat and should be fed from the edge. It will take at least 30-40 minutes after lighting before the charcoal either glows red, by night, or takes on the characteristic grey appearance noticeable during the day. These are the indications that it is ready for cooking.

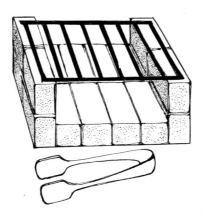

General points

In the right sort of weather, barbecues are tremendous fun, but there are a few points to bear in mind.

Barbecue lighting, tending and cooking is a technique, like any other, and therefore needs practice before you can confidently expect to entertain a large number of people in this way.

Food cooked over charcoal is delicious, but generally takes longer to cook through than it would in a conventional oven. Allow for this when planning the cooking schedule.

Most cheap barbecues are small and therefore it is impossible to cook for large numbers without considerable delays.

For a successful barbecue a great deal of food preparation, such as making marinades, sauces and side dishes, is necessary. Suitable storage and serving space that is within easy reach of the fire should be provided.

Quite a number of excellent indoor cooks find that exchanging their conventional cooker for the vagaries of the charcoal fire brings all sorts of unexpected problems. Try to persuade a responsible person to look after the barbecue. Most of the preparation will still have to be done by you, but at least you will have found someone who is prepared to do the actual cooking.

The Recipes

The recipes given here are all simple and do not take too long to prepare or cook. As you progress with your barbecueing technique, you will want to try more ambitious dishes. But it is much wiser to start with hamburgers and sausages and work up to spit-roast turkeys. Most meat needs basting regularly during barbecueing, otherwise it will scorch and dry out. For this, use one of the special barbecue bastes and marinades described here, because ordinary fat will make the charcoal flare and smoke.

Barbecued Sausages

Sausages are probably the best thing to cook at early barbecuing attempts. The large ones are best as they are least likely to dry out during cooking and do not need frequent basting owing to their high fat content.

Allow 20-30 minutes' cooking over a medium heat with the grill about 7·5 cm (3 in) from the charcoal. To prevent the meat sticking, always brush the grill with oil

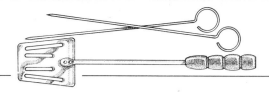

before putting meat on it.

Frankfurters

These can be grilled in the same way as sausages but they need less time.

Alternatives

Split the frankfurters down one side and insert a stick of cheese. Wrap each sausage in a thin rasher of bacon and secure with a cocktail stick. Grill as before.

Split the frankfurters as above and fill with chopped pineapple (fresh or canned). Wrap in bacon and grill as before.

Frankfurter Bun

These can be prepared in advance and frozen, but make sure they are fully thawed before cooking.

8 soft rolls
450 g (1 lb) frankfurters
2 hard-boiled eggs
garlic
4 x 15 ml spoons (4 tablespoons)
  soft, grated cheese
1 x 5 ml spoon (1 teaspoon)
  Worcestershire sauce
1 x 15 ml spoon (1 tablespoon)
  chutney or ketchup of your choice

2 x 15 ml spoons (2 tablespoons)
  mayonnaise
salt and pepper

Cut the rolls in half and scoop out the centres. Mince the frankfurters, chop the hard-boiled eggs and crush the garlic with a little salt. Mix all the filling ingredients together thoroughly and stuff into the rolls. Wrap each one in foil and grill for about 15 minutes, turning frequently.

Hamburgers

700-900 g (1-2 lb) bladebone or
  chuck steak
6 x 15 ml spoons (6 tablespoons)
  fresh breadcrumbs
1 egg
salt and pepper

Trim the meat, discarding any gristle but leaving some fat. Put through the coarse blade of the mincer or chop coarsely. Stir in the crumbs, egg, salt and pepper. Work as gently as you can into a flat cake and divide into 6-8 pieces. Form into rounds about 1 cm (½ in) thick and chill.

Grill over a medium to hot fire set about 7·5 cm (3 in) from the

coals. They will need 5-8 minutes on each side, depending on whether you want them medium or well cooked.

Cheeseburgers

3 x 15 ml spoons (3 tablespoons)
  grated mature cheese
1 small peeled and chopped onion
1 x 15 ml spoon (1 tablespoon)
  Worcestershire sauce

Add the above to the hamburger recipe. Cook in the same way.

Tomatoburgers

5-6 x 15 ml spoons (5-6 tablespoons)
  tomato ketchup
1 x 15 ml spoon (1 tablespoon) fresh
  chopped parsley
a shake of Tabasco sauce

Add the above to the hamburger recipe. Cook in the same way.

Mexican Hamburgers

1 small peeled and chopped onion
1 small chopped green pepper
a shake of Tabasco sauce

Add the above to the hamburger recipe. Cook in the same way.

(Left) A simple and easily transportable barbecue grill

(Right) A free-standing barbecue on a tripod with a wind shield

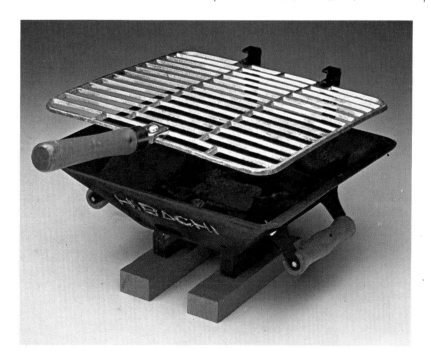

Corned Beefburgers

2 x 350 g (12 oz) cans corned beef
3 large potatoes
1 large onion
nutmeg
oil for grilling
salt and pepper

Chop the corned beef. Peel and dice the potatoes and cook in boiling salted water until tender. Drain well. Peel and chop the onion finely. Blanch in boiling water for 1 minute. Mix the meat, potatoes and onion together with the nutmeg, salt and pepper. Form into patties and chill. Brush with oil and grill for 5-6 minutes on each side. Serve with tangy barbecue sauce (see Sauces and Marinades).

Lamburgers

900 g (2 lb) shoulder or similar lamb
6 x 15 ml spoons (6 tablespoons)
 fresh breadcrumbs
3 x 15 ml spoons (3 tablespoons)
 chopped parsley and a little mint
1 clove garlic
2 eggs, beaten
salt and pepper

Trim away most of the fat from the lamb. Put the meat through the coarse blade of the mincer. Mix with crumbs, parsley and mint, the garlic crushed with a little salt, the 2 beaten eggs, salt and pepper. Work as gently as possible into a flat cake and cut into 6-8 pieces. Form these into rounds about 1 cm (½ in) thick. Chill.

Grill for 8-9 minutes on each side over a medium to hot fire, about 7·5 cm (3 in) from the coals. Serve with lemon, or with ranch barbecue sauce (see Sauces and Marinades).

Meat

Any piece of meat you would fry or grill in normal cooking can be barbecued. Some other cuts can also be used.

Steak

Rump or fillet are the best cuts. However, they are also the most expensive. Choose meat that has been well-hung, if possible, and have it cut at least 4-5 cm (1½-2 in) thick. Allow 175-300 g (6-12 oz) per head. It is better to err on the side of generosity when barbecuing —people are always hungrier outdoors.

To cook the steaks, make sure the fire is really hot, then brush the grill and the meat with oil. Cook steak that is 4 cm (1½ in) thick for 4-5 minutes on each side. It is usually ready for turning when the uncooked side looks redder and moister than at the start of cooking. Turn the steak and season the cooked side well with salt and black pepper, or use commercially prepared steak salt and pepper if preferred. Continue cooking until spots of juice appear on the cooked surface, at

which time the meat should still be pink inside. Obviously, if you like steak well done, it will need cooking for longer.

Variation for steak Roll the meat in crushed rosemary or black pepper before grilling.

Ham and Gammon

Ham or gammon steaks (the sort available in packets from supermarkets) grill well. They need 10-15 minutes on each side. Try basting them with sweet and sour sauce (see Sauces and Marinades) during cooking. This helps to keep them moist.

Lamb

Good-quality lamb chops can be grilled in exactly the same way as steak. The best ones are slightly pink and juicy.

Marinate poorer-quality meat in teriyaki or honey spice marinade (see Sauces and Marinades) for 2-4 hours. Then cook rather more slowly than for chops, allowing about 10-20 minutes on each side, depending on the thickness. Baste with the marinade during cooking.

Pork

Good-quality pork chops can be grilled on a barbecue, but make sure they are properly cooked. They should *not* be pink inside. The fire should be a little cooler and the chops will need at least 10-20 minutes on each side, depending on thickness. The honey spice marinade (see Sauces and Marinades) also goes well with pork. Baste the meat with it during cooking.

Chicken

Individual chicken joints are suitable for barbecuing. Drumsticks are particularly good as they are so easy to eat with the fingers. Marinate them in red wine marinade (see Sauces and Marinades) for at least 4 hours. Grill over a medium fire for 25-30 minutes, turning once or twice. Baste with the marinade during cooking and serve when the joints are really brown and crisp with tangy barbecue sauce (see Sauces and Marinades).

For a slightly more sophisticated party, boned chicken breasts can be stuffed before grilling. Mix together 50 g (2 oz) butter, 2 x 15 ml spoons (2 tablespoons) chopped parsley, 1 finely chopped shallot, 1 x 5 ml spoon (1 teaspoon) lemon juice, salt and pepper. Chill until hard. With a sharp knife, make small slits parallel to the skin in the breast meat and insert slices of the flavoured butter. Close them with a wooden cocktail stick. Brush the chicken with oil and place skin side down on a hot grill. Cook for 15 minutes, turning once.

Fish

If you are on a seaside holiday, a portable barbecue can be a boon, and provides an ideal way of cooking locally caught fish. A hand-grill is particularly useful for grilling mackerel, as this fish breaks up easily.

Clean the fish and trim the fins. Score the flesh on both sides if it weighs more than 275 g (10 oz). Make a thin paste of flour, salad oil, salt and pepper and brush over the fish. Barbecue for 6-8 minutes on each side, turning once.

Bread Rolls

All barbecued meat and fish need bread served with them. Frankfurters and hamburgers are usually served in soft bun-type rolls, but French or brown rolls can also be used. It is well worth keeping a supply of these in the freezer. Instead of always buying rolls, try making them yourself for a change. They will be well appreciated. The quantities given here make about 30 rolls.

900 g (2 lb) plain flour
1½ x 5 ml spoons (1½ teaspoons) salt
600 ml (1 pint) skimmed milk or
  milk and water mixed
100 g (4 oz) butter
1 x 15 ml spoon (1 tablespoon) sugar
25 g (1 oz) yeast

Sift the flour and salt into a bowl. Warm the milk and melt the butter. Mix with the sugar. Pour a little warm milk (it should be approximately blood heat) on to the yeast and cream well. Then add the rest of the milk.

Make a well in the centre of the flour and pour in the milk mixture. Mix together into a dough, then turn out of the bowl and knead until smooth. Put back in a clean bowl and cover with a cloth. Put in a warm place to rise. It should double in bulk within 2 hours, depending on the temperature.

Turn out the dough on to a floured board and knead well again. Divide into 30 portions and knead into small balls. Place on a greased baking sheet, flatten slightly and leave to rise again for 15-20 minutes in a warm place. Brush the tops with milk and bake for 15-20 minutes at 210°C, 425°F/Gas 7, reducing the heat if the tops brown too quickly. Cool on a rack.

Salads for Barbecues

On the whole it is best to keep

Kebabs make an interesting meal for a barbecue. However the food should be removed from the skewers before eating as they get very hot.

salads simple for barbecues. Just provide plenty of tomatoes or tomato salad and crisp lettuce.

Barbecuing on Skewers

Small pieces of meat threaded on skewers are known as kebabs and are ideal for barbecues. Different types of tender meat can be used and other ingredients, such as mushrooms, pieces of pepper and onions, can be threaded on to the skewer. It is usual to marinate the meat for several hours before skewering and cooking it. Any leftover meat can be refrigerated in screw-top jars in the marinade.

Make sure the grill and fire are really hot for kebabs. Serve with boiled rice.

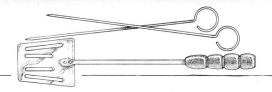

Kidney and Liver Kebabs

Serves 1

> *2 lamb's kidneys*
> *1 good slice lamb's liver*
> *2 rashers streaky bacon*
> *3-4 button mushrooms*
> *wine marinade (see Sauces and Marinades)*

Skin and split the kidneys, discarding the core. Trim the liver and cut it into 2·5-4-cm (1-1½-in) squares. Put the kidneys and liver in the wine marinade and leave for 2-3 hours.

Roll up the bacon rashers and plunge the mushrooms momentarily into boiling water. Thread the kidney and liver pieces on to skewers, alternating with the mushrooms and bacon rolls. Grill for about 10 minutes, brushing with the marinade and turning once or twice during cooking.

Oriental Kebabs

Serves 3-4

> *1 large can pineapple chunks*
> *450 g (1 lb) rump or sirloin beef*
> *large stoned olives*
> *teriyaki marinade (see Sauces and Marinades)*

Make the marinade using the juice from the pineapple. Cut the meat into 4-cm (1½-in) cubes and leave to

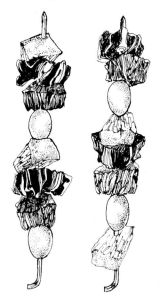

marinate in the teriyaki marinade for at least 3-4 hours.

Thread the meat on the skewers, alternating with pineapple and olives. Grill over a hot fire for about 15 minutes, basting with marinade.

Pork and Pepper Kebabs

Serves 6-8

Serve these kebabs with plain boiled rice and barbecue sauce (see Sauces and Marinades)

> *900 g (2 lb) pork fillet or tenderloin*
> *2 green peppers*
> *1 large can pineapple chunks*
> *8 small firm tomatoes*
> *wine marinade, made with white wine instead of red (see Sauces and Marinades)*

Cut the pork into 4-cm (1½-in) cubes and leave them to marinate for 2-3 hours in wine marinade. De-seed the pepper, cut the flesh into neat pieces and add to the marinade for the last 30 minutes.

Thread the meat, pineapple chunks and pepper alternately on skewers and cook over a hot fire for about 20 minutes, turning and basting frequently with the marinade. Thread the tomatoes on a skewer and grill for 5-7 minutes.

Note If preferred, use the honey spice marinade (see Sauces and Marinades).

Family Kebabs

Serves 1

> *2-3 sausages*
> *2 rashers streaky bacon*
> *3 mushrooms*
> *1 onion*
> *1 tomato*
> *wine marinade (see Sauces and Marinades)*

Cut the sausages in half and marinate for 2 hours in the wine marinade. Remove the rind from the bacon and roll the rashers up neatly. Plunge the mushrooms into boiling water for a moment. Peel and quarter the onion and divide it into pieces. Thread the sausages, bacon rolls, mushrooms and onion pieces

alternately on the skewer and grill for 15 minutes, brushing with the marinade. Thread the tomatoes on to a separate skewer and grill for 5 minutes.

Devilled Poultry Kebabs

These kebabs are made of cooked meat, which has been previously grilled in the kitchen. They are eaten either cold, or re-heated over the barbecue. They are particularly useful for novice barbecuers, as re-heating over a barbecue is quicker and easier than cooking from raw.

> *16-20 good-sized pieces chicken or turkey*
> *1 green pepper*
> *12 mushrooms*
> *8 rashers thin cut streaky bacon*
> *1 onion*
> *oil*
> *salt and pepper*

For the marinade

> *1 x 5 ml spoon (1 teaspoon) oil*
> *1 x 15 ml spoon (1 tablespoon) Worcestershire sauce*
> *2 x 15 ml spoons (2 tablespoons) tomato or fruit sauce*
> *1 x 5 ml spoon (1 teaspoon) French mustard*
> *salt and pepper*

Make the marinade by mixing all the ingredients together. Pour over the pieces of poultry. De-seed the pepper, cut into bite-sized pieces and blanch in boiling salted water for 1-2 minutes. Drain and refresh under cold water. Dry well. Trim the mushroom stalks and plunge the mushroom caps into boiling water for a few seconds. Drain and dry them. Remove the rind from the bacon and flatten out the rashers with a knife. Cut each one in half and wrap the pieces of meat in the half rashers of bacon. Cut the onion into quarters and divide into pieces.

Thread all the kebab ingredients equally on to 8 skewers, alternating the meat and vegetables. Brush with oil. Grill or cook in a hot oven until the bacon is crisp. Leave to cool, then re-heat over the barbecue when needed.

Basting Sauces

The sauces given here are used to baste a variety of meats during the cooking period. Basting sauces that contain a good deal of tomato should be used only for those dishes that need less than 15 minutes' cooking time. Alternatively, use the sauce only in the last 15 minutes of cooking. Tomato-based sauces will burn and discolour if cooked for longer.

Savoury Basting Sauce

1 shallot
1 small glass sherry
4 x 15 ml spoons (4 tablespoons) salad oil
2 x 5 ml spoons (2 teaspoons) brown sugar
1 x 5 ml spoon (1 teaspoon) French mustard
1 x 5 ml spoon (1 teaspoon) dried thyme and marjoram
salt and pepper

Peel and chop the shallot, then combine with all the other ingredients in the liquidizer. Liquidize thoroughly and store in a screw-top jar in the refrigerator. Shake well before using.

Bar-B-Q Basting Sauce

150 ml ($\frac{1}{4}$ pint) salad oil
200 ml (7 fl oz) wine vinegar
75 ml (3 fl oz) water
3 x 15 ml spoons (3 tablespoons) brown sugar
3-4 shakes Tabasco sauce
1 x 5 ml spoon (1 teaspoon) Worcestershire sauce
1 bay leaf
salt and pepper

Put all the ingredients in a small saucepan. Bring to the boil and simmer for 5 minutes. Use at once, keeping it warm while using.

Sweet and Sour Basting Sauce

1 green pepper
1 clove garlic
2 x 15 ml spoons (2 tablespoons) salad oil
150 ml ($\frac{1}{4}$ pint) concentrated orange or pineapple juice
5 x 15 ml spoons (5 tablespoons) soft dark brown sugar
150 ml ($\frac{1}{4}$ pint) wine vinegar
1 x 15 ml spoon (1 tablespoon) soy sauce
salt

De-seed the pepper and chop the flesh finely. Crush the garlic with a little salt, then gently fry with the pepper in the oil until soft. Add the rest of the ingredients and simmer for 5-10 minutes. Use this sauce warm.

Barbecue Sauces

These sauces are designed to accompany grilled or barbecued foods, and could be used as dips. If you have no time to make your own sauces, use tomato ketchup or other bottled sauces.

Ranch Barbecue Sauce

1 small onion
300 ml ($\frac{1}{4}$ pint) mayonnaise
1 x 175 g (6 oz) tomato purée
5 x 15 ml spoons (5 tablespoons) wine vinegar
3 x 15 ml spoons (3 tablespoons) Worcestershire sauce
1 x 15 ml spoon (1 tablespoon) horseradish sauce
few drops Tabasco sauce
salt and pepper

Peel and chop the onion, then liquidize it with all the other ingredients. Keep the sauce in the refrigerator and serve cold.

Lemon Barbecue Sauce

1 onion
1 clove garlic
5 x 15 ml spoons (5 tablespoons) oil
8 x 15 ml spoons (8 tablespoons) lemon juice
good pinch ginger
salt and pepper

Peel and chop the onion finely and crush the garlic with a little salt. Put with all the remaining ingredients in a screw-top jar, shake well and refrigerate overnight.

Tangy Barbecue Sauce

1 onion
1 x 175 g (6 oz) tomato purée
1 x 5 ml spoon (1 teaspoon) mustard
5 x 15 ml spoons (5 tablespoons) brown sugar
1 x 15 ml spoon (1 tablespoon) Worcestershire sauce
4 x 15 ml spoons (4 tablespoons) wine vinegar
2 x 15 ml spoons (2 tablespoons) water
2 x 5 ml spoons (2 teaspoons) lemon juice
salt and pepper

Peel and finely chop the onions and put with all the other ingredients in a saucepan. Bring to the boil, stirring occasionally, and simmer for 5 minutes. Cool, then leave the sauce for at least 4 hours before serving to allow the flavours to blend together.

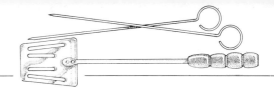

Marinades

A marinade is a combination of ingredients, usually including wine or vinegar, in which meat is soaked for some time before cooking. This helps to make the meat more tender as well as flavouring it. Do not rely exclusively on the marinade ideas provided here: experiment by trying out your own tasty marinades as well.

Wine Marinade

150 ml (¼ pint) salad oil
150 ml (¼ pint) red wine
1 large onion
1 clove garlic
1 x 5 ml spoon (1 teaspoon) salt
Tabasco sauce
salt and pepper

Put the salad oil and wine in a liquidizer. Peel and finely chop the onion and crush the garlic with the salt. Add to the liquidizer with a few drops of Tabasco sauce, salt and pepper. Liquidize everything together.

Store the marinade in the refrigerator in a screw-top jar and shake well before using.

Note This could also be used as a basting sauce. Try making it with white wine on some occasions as an alternative.

Teriyaki Marinade

300 ml (½ pint) pineapple juice
2 x 15 ml spoons (2 tablespoons) soy sauce
2 x 15 ml spoons (2 tablespoons) lemon juice
2 cloves garlic
pinch ground clove and nutmeg
pepper
1 bay leaf

Put all the ingredients in a liquidizer, having first crushed the garlic with a little salt. Liquidize, then store and use as for wine marinade.

Note This is particularly good for kebabs. If you are including chunks of pineapple on the skewers, use some of the syrup from the canned pineapple instead of pineapple juice.

The traditional hamburger is best served with a piquant sauce

Honey Spice Marinade

2 x 15 ml spoons (2 tablespoons) honey
2 x 5 ml spoons (2 teaspoons) ground ginger
2 x 5 ml spoons (2 teaspoons) dry English mustard
2– 3 cloves garlic
2 x 5 ml spoons (2 teaspoons) salt
2 x 15 ml spoons (2 tablespoons) soy sauce
150 ml (¼ pint) oil
5 x 15 ml spoons (5 tablespoons) lemon juice

Combine all the ingredients in a liquidizer, having first crushed the garlic with the salt.

Tarragon Marinade

300 ml (½ pint) salad oil
150 ml (¼ pint) red wine
5 x 15 ml spoons (5 tablespoons) tarragon vinegar
5 x 15 ml spoons (5 tablespoons) lemon juice
½ x 5 ml spoon (½ teaspoon) mustard
½ x 5 ml spoon (½ teaspoon) salt
2–3 cloves garlic
pepper
bay leaf
1 large onion

Combine all the ingredients, except the onion, in the liquidizer, having first crushed the garlic with the salt. Pour into a screw-top jar. Peel the onion, cut into thin rings and add to the jar. Keep this marinade for at least 6-8 hours before using and store in the refrigerator.

Puddings for Barbecues

Fruit and ice cream with a sauce are often sufficient. However, toasted marshmallows are fun to do, and are particularly popular with the young. Impale the marshmallows on skewers and toast them over a cooling fire. Dip them in sauce.

Sauces for Ice Cream or Toasted Marshmallows

Chocolate Sauce

175 g (6 oz) plain chocolate
50 g (2 oz) sugar
150 ml (¼ pint) water
15 g (½ oz) unsalted butter

Put the chocolate, sugar and water in a saucepan. Heat very gently, until the chocolate has dissolved. Simmer for 10 minutes, then beat in the butter. Add a little more water if the sauce is too thick. Serve hot.

Fruit Sauce

Purée fresh raspberries or strawberries in a vegetable mill or liquidizer. Add a little lemon juice and icing sugar to taste.

Blackcurrants, stewed with a tiny amount of water, then sweetened and put through a vegetable mill, make a delicious sauce for ice cream. Serve hot or cold.

Hot Fudge Sauce

This goes very well with coffee ice cream.

300 ml (½ pint) milk
50 g (2 oz) butter
vanilla sugar
75 g (3 oz) soft brown sugar
1 x 15 ml spoon (1 tablespoon)
  golden syrup
2 x 5 ml spoons (2 teaspoons)
  arrowroot
2 x 15 ml spoons (2 tablespoons)
  water

Warm the milk and butter together with the vanilla sugar. In another pan, melt the brown sugar and syrup, then boil until it is a rich caramel. Remove from the heat and pour in the milk and butter. Beat until smooth. Bring back to the boil. Slake the arrowroot with the water and add enough to the sauce to make a good coating consistency.

> **Camp-fire Cookery**
> If you do not want to launch yourself headfirst into the barbecue scene but would still like to be able to produce a hot dish at a picnic using a portable gas stove, consider these ideas for such occasions.

Pan Pizza

Prepare the dough and filling at home before the picnic, take them in separate containers and combine them at the picnic.

For the dough

175 g (6 oz) flour
salt
2 x 5 ml spoons (2 teaspoons)
  baking powder
25 g (1 oz) butter
6–8 x 15 ml spoons (6–8 tablespoons)
  water
1 x 15 ml spoon (1 tablespoon) oil

Marshmallows—delicious toasted

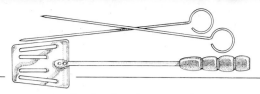

For the filling

1 onion
25 g (1 oz) butter
garlic
5-6 large tomatoes
2 x 5 ml spoons (2 teaspoons)
  tomato purée
pinch marjoram
100 g (4 oz) ham
grated cheese
salt and pepper

To prepare the dough, sift the flour, salt and baking powder together and rub in the butter. Add enough water to make a scone dough.

To prepare the filling, peel and slice the onion and fry in the butter until soft. Crush the garlic with a little salt and add to the onion. Skin and pip the tomatoes and chop the flesh roughly. Add to the pan with the tomato purée, herbs, salt and pepper. Cook for 5-10 minutes. Dice the ham and stir into the tomato mixture. Continue cooking until the mixture is a fairly thick purée.

To make the pizza, pat out the dough to fit in a 23-25 cm (9-10-in) diameter frying-pan. Heat the oil in the pan and put in the dough. Cook for about 5 minutes. Turn the dough over. Pile the filling on top of the cooked side and sprinkle with grated cheese. It will heat through as the underside cooks.

Croque Monsieur

Fried Ham and Cheese Sandwiches
Prepare the sandwiches at home and fry them just before serving. They also make an excellent savoury, cut in quarters, or an emergency supper dish.

8 thin slices stale white bread
butter
8 slices Gruyère or processed cheese
4 slices ham
oil
salt and pepper

Butter the slices of bread generously and put a slice of Gruyère on each. Put a piece of ham on 4 slices and season well. Cover the ham with the remaining bread and cheese slices and press firmly together. Trim the crusts and cut into triangles.

To cook the sandwiches, heat some butter and oil in a pan and fry on both sides until they turn a golden brown.

Picnic Fondue

Eat this at once by spearing chunks of French bread on forks and dunking in the pan.

300 ml (½ pint) cider
2 x 5 ml spoons (2 teaspoons)
  French mustard
50 g (2 oz) Danish blue cheese
225 g (8 oz) Dutch cheese
225 g (8 oz) soft Cheddar cheese
1 x 15 ml spoon (1 tablespoon)
  cornflour
garlic (optional)
salt and pepper

Heat the cider, mustard, salt and pepper in a heavy pan. Grate all the cheeses. Stir in the blue cheese and continue cooking until it has melted. Remove the pan from the heat and stir in the remainder of the cheese. Slake the cornflour with a little water and stir it in. Cook gently until the mixture is thick and creamy.

Picnic Cakes

The following two cakes are particularly good for picnics. They transport well and are moist and filling.

Baked Cheesecake

60 g (2½ oz) butter
150 g (5 oz) sugar
275 g (10 oz) curd or cream cheese
1 lemon
50 g (2 oz) raisins (optional)
50 g (2 oz) semolina
50 g (2 oz) ground almonds
2 eggs

Grease and flour a 20-cm (8-in) *moule à manqué* or shallow cake tin. Line the base with buttered greaseproof paper.

Cream the butter and sugar and sieve in the cheese. Beat well together. Grate and squeeze the lemon. Stir the rind and juice into the cheese mixture with the raisins, semolina and ground almonds. Separate the eggs and beat in the yolks. Whip the egg whites stiffly and fold into the mixture. Turn into the prepared tin and bake for 45-60 minutes at 180°C, 350°F/Gas 4. Allow to cool for 10-15 minutes before turning out on to a rack.

Brownies

50 g (2 oz) plain chocolate
100 g (4 oz) butter
225 g (8 oz) sugar
vanilla sugar
2 eggs
100 g (4 oz) walnuts
90 g (3½ oz) flour
½ x 5 ml spoon (½ teaspoon)
  baking powder

Put the chocolate on a plate and melt over a pan of hot water. Do not let the chocolate overheat. Cream the butter and sugars together. Beat in the eggs. Chop the walnuts and stir in with the chocolate. Fold in the flour and the baking powder. Turn the mixture into a buttered 20-cm (8-in) square tin and bake for 30-35 minutes at 150°C, 300°F/Gas 2. Cool in the tin, then cut into squares. **Note** An alternative method is to melt the butter and chocolate together in a pan. Beat the eggs and sugar together until white and fluffy. Fold in the flour, nuts and baking powder and finally the chocolate mixture. Bake as above.

Children's Parties

Formal tea-parties for children are fast becoming relics of a bygone era. Party teas have changed completely and where the accent used to be on sweet dishes—jelly, trifle and ice cream—it is now on snack-type food, mainly savoury rather than sweet. Nowadays an ordinary tea-party without some variety is not very enterprising and both the food and the entertainments need to be chosen according to the age-group.

For practical purposes, children's parties may be divided into the following groups: pre-school, 5-8-year-olds, 8-11-year-olds and 11 years upwards (including teenagers).

Obviously the groups will overlap a little. Many of the recipes are suitable for more than one age-group.

Pre-school

Children of this age usually come to a party accompanied by an adult. Amusement is easy: all that is needed is plenty of floor space, toys and some adult help to build towers for knocking down.

Ideas for food

Keep it simple and as non-messy as possible. The important factors are to keep everything small and to have plenty of colourful food on the table. Some ideas are:

marmite finger sandwiches
tiny drop scones (see recipe)
chocolate finger biscuits
sponge cake—either a birthday cake with candles, or one baked in a square tin and cut into very small fingers covered with glacé icing. Make a Victoria or a Genoese sponge (see Cakes) and use Smarties for decorations.
tiny, fancy-shaped biscuits (see Biscuits)
milk, orange and blackcurrant cordial to drink
ice cream for the 4-5 year olds. Serve it towards the end of the party rather than at tea. Jelly is not very popular with any age-group and is therefore best omitted.

Teddy Bear's Picnic – an irresistible treat for a children's party

5-8-year-olds

This age-group really enjoys afternoon tea-parties and to give such a party can be very rewarding. You will find that a lot of children, sometimes the whole class from school, just have to be invited, so organization is essential. Entertainment is important and children are generally not too blasé to enjoy playing some of the old favourites such as musical bumps or hunt-the-thimble. Always prepare too many games rather than too few. To run out is disastrous and it is impossible to predict how soon children will tire of any game.

The food can be more adventurous for this group. No child under fifteen wants to sit for very long at a meal. However, they do like to come back and pick at the leftovers.

Food

small bridge rolls, split and topped with salmon or egg
drop scones (see recipe)
sausages—on sticks
cheese and pineapple on sticks
tiny sausage rolls
small pink and white meringues
small Magda biscuits (see Biscuits)
crisps and other cocktail biscuits
birthday cake
milk shakes, orange and homemade squash to drink
ice cream or lollies for the end of the party.

Birthday cakes for 5-8 year olds

This is the age that really appreciates a special birthday cake such as Dougal or a train or house. If you can get hold of a numeral cake tin, a cake that says the child's age is always popular.

Clock Cake Make a round sponge. Ice and decorate it like a clock face with the hands pointing to the age of the child.

Maypole Cake Make a Genoese or Victoria sponge (see Cakes). Split it and fill with butter cream. Sandwich together again and brush with hot apricot glaze, then let it cool (this helps the icing to cover the cake smoothly and prevents crumbs mixing with the icing). Sift 450 g (1 lb) icing sugar, add the juice of half an orange and about 2-3 x 15 ml spoons (2-3 tablespoons) water to make a thick icing. Warm to blood heat, but do not overheat or it will go dull. Pour quickly over the cake, standing on a rack, and tap the rack to make the icing fall smoothly

down the cake. Allow to set before moving to a cake board. Colour a little butter cream with some pink and some green colouring. Pipe a decorative star border round the edge of the cake and round the base of the board. Wind four different-coloured narrow ribbons about 50 cm (20 in) long around a 23-cm (9-in) knitting needle, stopping 5 cm (2 in) from the pointed end. Fix the ribbons at the top with glue and a little bow and push the needle into the middle of the cake. Let the ends of the ribbons fall round the cake on to the board.

8–11-year-olds

Most parents, however enthusiastic,

Maypole Cake—a novel way of decorating a sponge cake

find giving parties for this age-group something of a responsibility. It is generally wiser to segregate the sexes at this age and have either a girl's party or a boys' party, unless there is some special theme, such as a swimming gala. Little girls rather like to dress up and enjoy playing games that are well organized by an adult. Boys of this age, on the other hand, tend to judge a party by the opportunity it gives them for letting off steam. The hallmark of a good party is whether it has crisps and fighting! An outdoor party can often save a lot of wear and tear on carpets and furniture and if it has a theme, so much the better. It could be a cavemen's party, for example, where the food might include cold roast chicken legs, or a tramp's party, where everyone has their food in individual bags.

If there is not a theme, it is essential (for your own sanity) to have plenty of fairly energetic, well-organized games. The planning of these warrants more time than that given to decorating the food, especially for a crowd of boys.

Boys' parties

small bridge rolls, split and topped with salmon, cheese or Marmite
drop scones
pineapple and cheese on sticks
cheese straws
sausages
crisps and twiglets
a selection of biscuits
cake—make a square sponge and decorate it as a football or cricket field, using plastic figures.
Coca-Cola and squash to drink
ice cream—for the end of the party.

Girls' parties

Girls are often a little more sophisticated than boys at this age, particularly at ten-plus. An early evening party from 6 to 9 pm is popular as they can really dress up for it. A well-planned programme is still important—the young hostess will be full of her own ideas, but chaos may take over unless an adult is nearby to control proceedings.

Food may be as for a boys' afternoon party or as given below:

Evening buffets

open sandwiches or hamburgers
fried chicken joints with chips or baked potatoes
savoury choux with chicken or ham filling
Hawaiian Beans (see Buffet Food)
big meringue cake or ice-cream cake (see Cakes)
brandy snaps (see Biscuits)
chocolate crispies (see Biscuits)
Coca-Cola and orange to drink
ice-cream shakes (see Drinks) for the end of the evening.
Do keep the food easy to manage, so it can be eaten with the fingers or just a fork. Have lots of paper napkins and a damp cloth handy, as spills will be inevitable.

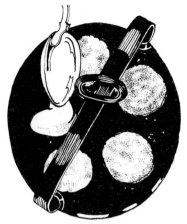

11-years upwards

In most instances, particularly if catering for young teenagers, it is still best to segregate the sexes. A barbecue makes a good party for this age-group, particularly if it follows some organized event such as a swimming gala or treasure hunt. Joining with other parents and hiring a hall can be a good way of holding such a party, but in any case a good master of ceremonies is essential.

For a smaller number of boys, the coward's way out for parents is to organize a party when there is some suitable spy or thriller movie showing locally and follow this with a buffet supper and one or two games.

Food

follow suggestions for the 8-11 age-group, but add pizzas (see Buffet Food) and perhaps hot dogs as well. The devilled poultry kebabs from the barbecue section would also be popular. Coca-Cola is generally the most popular or favourite drink for this age-group.

Bridge Roll Toppings

Cut the bridge rolls in half and top with a selection of the following:
100 g (4 oz) butter blended with 1 can sardines, tomato ketchup and lemon juice;
100 g (4 oz) butter blended with canned salmon and lemon juice;
cream cheese mixed with Marmite;
100 g (4 oz) butter mixed with chopped ham and tomato;
scrambled egg and tomato;

chopped chicken mixed with butter, cream, salt and pepper.

Drop Scones

225 g (8 oz) flour
1 x 15 ml spoon (1 tablespoon) sugar
½ x 5 ml spoon (½ teaspoon) bicarbonate of soda
½ x 5 ml spoon (½ teaspoon) cream of tartar
½ x 5 ml spoon (½ teaspoon) baking powder
pinch salt
12 g (½ oz) butter
1 x 15 ml spoon (1 tablespoon) golden syrup
1 egg
300 ml (½ pint) milk

Sift the flour, sugar, salt, bicarbonate of soda, cream of tartar and baking powder together. Rub in the butter. Add the syrup, the egg and enough milk to make the batter so that it will just drop from a spoon. Stand for 10-12 minutes.

Heat a griddle or heavy frying-pan and drop small spoonfuls of the batter on to it. Cook for about 3 minutes on each side. Wrap in a cloth to keep warm and butter when ready to be served.
Note These are best when freshly made, but they can be frozen and re-heated.

Biscuits
Vanilla Biscuits

65 g (2½ oz) butter
35 g (1¼ oz) sugar
vanilla sugar
1 egg yolk
90 g (3½ oz) flour

Cream the butter and sugars together and beat in the egg yolk. Work in the flour gradually to make a light dough. Chill slightly, then roll out thinly and cut into small fancy shapes (or use an animal cutter). Put on buttered baking trays and bake for 10-12 minutes at 150°C, 300°F/Gas 2 until golden. Cool on a rack and decorate with glacé icing and Smarties.
Note These keep well in a tin, but

should not be decorated until wanted.

Chocolate Crispies

225 g (8 oz) plain chocolate
50-75 g (2-3 oz) cornflakes or Rice Krispies

Melt the chocolate in a bowl over hot water and stir in the cornflakes or Rice Krispies. Put in small rough heaps in paper, cake cases and leave to set in a cool place.

Magda Biscuits

You can sandwich these together with coffee or chocolate cream or serve them plain.

225 g (8 oz) butter
vanilla sugar
100 g (4 oz) sugar
40 g (1½ oz) drinking chocolate
15 g (½ oz) cocoa
225 g (8 oz) flour
1 x 5 ml spoon (1 teaspoon) baking powder

Cream the butter and sugars together, sift the drinking chocolate, cocoa, flour and baking powder together and gradually beat into the butter mixture. Work into a paste and divide into pieces the size of a walnut. Put on a buttered baking sheet and flatten each with a wet fork, leaving a space between each. Bake for 10-12 minutes (watch carefully to make sure they do not burn) at 160°C, 325°F/Gas 3. Leave for a few minutes before removing from the trays and cooling on a rack.

Brandy Snaps

100 g (4 oz) flour
1 x 5 ml spoon (1 teaspoon) ground ginger
100 g (4 oz) sugar
100 g (4 oz) butter
100 g (4 oz) golden syrup
juice of 1 lemon
whipped cream

Sift the flour and ginger together and warm in an oven. Sift again. Melt the sugar, butter and syrup together and add the lemon juice.

Stir in the warmed flour. Put small spoonfuls of the mixture, very well spaced, on to buttered baking sheets and bake for 8-10 minutes at 160°-180°C, 325°-350°F/Gas 3-4. Leave to cool for a few seconds, then remove from the baking sheet and roll round a wooden spoon handle. When quite cold and ready to serve, fill with whipped cream, piped from a forcing bag.

Note Brandy snaps will keep for a few days in a tin, unfilled, but they are very fragile and must be handled with care.

Flapjacks

100 g (4 oz) butter
50 g (2 oz) demerara sugar
100 g (4 oz) porridge oats
65 g (2½ oz) plain flour
¼ x 5 ml spoon (¼ teaspoon)
  bicarbonate soda
salt

Melt the butter and stir in the rest of the ingredients. Press firmly into a well-buttered 15 x 23 cm (6 x 9 in) tin. Cook for 45 minutes at 160°C, 325°F/Gas 3. Cut into fingers while still hot and turn out of the tin when just warm.

Cakes

However you intend to decorate a birthday cake for a children's party, it is best to use a simple sponge cake as the base and use plain, not-too-rich fillings.

Genoese Sponge

This cake freezes well and can be used as a base for many fancy cakes. If you want to make a chocolate cake, replace 12 g (½ oz) of the flour with 25 g (1 oz) cocoa.

4 eggs
125 g (4½ oz) sugar
50 g (2 oz) cooled melted butter
100 g (4 oz) flour

Butter and flour a 20-cm (8-in) shallow square cake tin or a 17·5-20-cm (7-8-in) shallow circular tin, such as a *moule à manqué*.

Put the eggs and sugar in a bowl and whisk together until thick and fluffy. If you are not using an electric mixer, the easiest way is to put the bowl over a pan of hot water and beat with a hand rotary whisk. Do not let the mixture get warmer than blood heat.

Sift the flour (and cocoa if using it) and fold as lightly as you can into the eggs and sugar with the cooled melted butter. Pour the mixture into the tin and bake for 25-30 minutes at 190°C, 375°F/Gas 5, reducing the heat if the top browns too quickly. Allow the cake to stand in the tin for 3-4 minutes, then turn out and cool on a rack.

Victoria Sponge

175 g (6 oz) butter
175 g (6 oz) castor sugar
3 eggs
175 g (6 oz) flour
2 x 5 ml spoons (2 teaspoons)
  baking powder

Grease 2 x 17·5-cm (7-in) round sandwich tins or a 20-cm (8-in) square tin and line the base with greaseproof paper.

Cream the butter and sugar together until white and fluffy, then

beat in the eggs one at a time. Sift the flour and baking powder together and fold into the mixture. Divide equally between the tins (or put into the square tin). Level the surface with the back of a spoon. Bake for about 25 minutes at 180°C, 350°F/Gas 4 until the top is golden and the surface light and springy to touch. Turn the cakes out of the tins and cool on a rack.

Note Flavour the sponge with grated lemon or orange rind or a few drops of vanilla essence, if required.

Chocolate Log

This is particularly suitable for a Christmas birthday party, when the log can be topped with a sprig of holly and a small robin. On other occasions, push candles into piped stars of butter cream.

25 g (1 oz) flour
1 x 15 ml spoon (1 tablespoon) cocoa
3 eggs
100 g (4 oz) sugar
pinch cream of tartar
chocolate-flavoured butter cream,
  (use either recipe but use 250-300 g/
  9-10 oz butter)
icing sugar

Grease and flour a 20 x 30-cm (8 x 12-in) Swiss roll tin and line the base with buttered greaseproof paper. Sift the flour with the cocoa. Separate the eggs and cream the yolks with half the sugar until the mixture is thick (use an electric whisk if possible). Fold in the flour and cocoa. Whisk the egg whites with the cream of tartar until stiff, then beat in the rest of the sugar. Fold the egg yolk mixture into the whites and turn into the prepared tin. Bake for 20-25 minutes at 160°C, 325°F/Gas 3. Turn the roll out on to a sugared tea-towel and remove the paper. Trim the edges and roll up, using the tea-towel to help. Leave to cool.

When cold, unroll the cake and spread with half the butter cream mixture. Roll up again and put on a cake board. Cover the outside with the rest of the butter cream and, using a fork or a forcing bag with a star nozzle, draw lines along it to represent the lines in bark. Cut off one end diagonally to make it look more realistic.

Butter Cream

75 g (3 oz) sugar
2 egg yolks
150 g (5 oz) unsalted butter

Put the sugar in a pan with 2-3 x 15 ml spoons (2-3 tablespoons) water. Bring to the boil and cook until the syrup forms a thread in cold water (125°C/240°F). Pour the syrup on to the egg yolks, beating all the time, and continue to beat until the mixture becomes thick and fluffy. Cream the butter until soft, then add the cold egg mixture and beat very thoroughly. Flavour the cream to taste.

Note If the finished butter cream curdles, stand the bowl in hot water for 2-3 minutes and beat the mixture well.

Alternative method

If you have some surplus egg whites, make butter cream by putting 2 egg whites in a bowl with 150 g (5 oz) icing sugar and beat over hot water until you have a thick meringue-type mixture. Remove from the heat and continue beating until cold. Soften 250 g (9 oz) unsalted butter and cream it without oiling it. Add the cold meringue mixture to it and beat well. Flavour as you like.

Railway Cake

Bake a Genoese or Victoria sponge mixture in a 20-cm (8-in) square cake tin. Split the sponge and fill with jam or butter cream, then ice with pale green glacé icing. Put on a cake board and leave to harden.

Colour another portion of glacé icing brown and, using a paper forcing bag, pipe two parallel circles round the top of the cake about 2·5 cm (1 in) apart, to represent a railway line. Pipe in sleepers and use candles with a piece of coloured paper attached to represent the signals. To make a tunnel, roll out 25 g (1 oz) marzipan to a rectangle measuring 7·5 x 4 cm (3 x 1½ in). Leave it to harden over a rolling pin. Put a miniature engine on the track.

Glacé Icing

At least 350 g (12 oz) icing sugar will be needed to ice a 20-cm (8-in) cake. This amount gives sufficient for pouring over the cake. Stand the cake on a rack over a clean tray, so that surplus icing can be scraped up and used again.

icing sugar
water
flavouring and colouring as preferred

Sift the icing sugar and add just enough water to get a pouring consistency. Heat to 38°C, 100°F and flavour as required.

Meringues and eclairs

Recipes for meringues and eclairs (choux pastry buns) are given in the pudding section of Summer Picnics. Make meringues very small for children's parties and colour some of them pink by adding a drop of red food colouring to the basic mixture before cooking.

To make éclairs, make up the choux pastry as in *choux pralines au chocolat* and pipe small strips on to buttered baking sheets. Omit the the nuts, but cook in the same way as the choux buns. When quite cold, fill with a tiny amount of whipped cream and top with chocolate-flavoured glacé icing.

Meringue Cake

5 egg whites
300 g (10½ oz) sugar
icing sugar

For the filling

4-5 peaches or 450 g (1 lb)
strawberries or raspberries or
1 large can pineapple or white
peaches

450 ml (¾ pint) double cream
sugar

Line 3 baking sheets with non-stick paper and draw a 23-cm (9-in) circle on each.

Make the meringue in the usual way (see *meringue Chantilly*, in the Summer Picnics section) and put a third of it in a forcing bag with a star tube. Pipe a trellis in one circle, outlining it round the edge with stars. Divide the rest of the meringue evenly between the other two circles, spreading it over the area.

Dust with icing sugar and bake for 2 hours at 130°C, 250°F/Gas ½, reducing the temperature as low as you can after 30-40 minutes. (If you find piping a trellis too difficult, just spread the meringue evenly over the 3 circles.)

To prepare the filling, if using fresh peaches, skin and slice into a bowl. Sprinkle with sugar and leave for 10-15 minutes. If using strawberries, cut them in half, place in a bowl and sprinkle with sugar. Put raspberries straight into a bowl.

Drain canned fruit well and cut into smaller pieces.

Whip the cream and as it thickens add the juice from the drained fruit. Continue whisking until thick. Put aside a quarter of the cream for decoration and fold the fruit into the rest. Also keep a little fruit for decoration.

Put one layer of the meringue on a serving dish and spread half the fruit and cream on it. Cover with the second layer and the rest of the fruit and cream. Put the trellis meringue

Meringue Cake—a dessert fit for the most elegant table and the most refined taste

on top and decorate with the reserved fruit and cream.

Note The meringue circles will keep in a large storage box for a week or so. The cake could also be filled with flavoured ice cream, in which case put the whole cake in the freezer until it is needed—but for no longer than 5 hours. Decorate with cream at the last minute.

Ice-cream Cake

Make this with as many different-flavoured ice creams as you like, either bought or homemade. If using homemade ice creams, make sure they are not too hard to spread. If using bought, buy the ordinary type, not the soft-scoop variety.

1 litre (1¾ pints) ice cream
(vanilla, chocolate and strawberry)

Chill a 23-cm (9-in) cake tin with a loose base and line the base with greaseproof paper.

Spread the ices neatly in layers in the tin and put it in the freezer for 24 hours to harden. Keep in the freezer until you need it. Before serving, cover the top with fruit, meringues and whipped cream.

Note The cake could also be decorated with thin slices of Swiss roll or sponge fingers pressed around the side. Alternatively, make a Swiss roll, let it cool, and instead of filling it, cut strips and wrap these around the cake to encircle it.

Buffet Food
Hawaiian Beans

2 large cans baked beans
1 large can pineapple rings (12 rings)
brown sugar
few cloves

Chop 8 pineapple rings into small pieces and mix with the beans. Tip into a casserole, and top with the remaining 4 pineapple rings, studded with a few cloves. Sprinkle with sugar and bake for 25 minutes at 190°C, 375°F/Gas 5.

Tarte à l'Oignon

Onion Tart
For the pastry
225 g (8 oz) flour
1 egg yolk
150 g (5 oz) butter
1 x 5 ml spoon (1 teaspoon) sugar
2-3 x 15 ml spoons (2-3
tablespoons) water, plus a
squeeze of lemon juice
salt

For the filling
700 g (1½ lb) onions
50 g (2 oz) butter
1 x 15 ml spoon (1 tablespoon) oil
3 egg yolks
150 ml (¼ pint) double cream or
creamy milk
grated nutmeg
salt and pepper

To prepare the pastry, sieve the flour on to a board and make a well in the centre. Put all the other ingredients for the pastry into this and using the fingertips of one hand, work it up into a firm dough. Knead it lightly and then leave it in a cool place to relax for 20-30 minutes.

To prepare the filling, peel and slice the onions very finely and cook gently in the butter and oil until soft and golden. Remove from the heat and stir in the beaten egg yolks and cream or milk. Season well with nutmeg, salt and pepper.

Roll out the pastry and line a 17.5-20-cm (7-8-in) flan ring. Prick the base, leave to stand for 10 minutes and then pour in the filling. Bake at 200°C, 400°F/Gas 6 for 30 minutes.

To freeze, first cool then open-freeze until hard. Wrap, label and put in the freezer. Thaw for 6-8 hours and reheat for 20-25 minutes at 180°-190°C, 350°-375°F/Gas 4-5.

Drinks
Raspberry or Strawberry Milk Shake

300 ml (1 pint) milk
150 ml (¼ pint) fruit purée
2 x 15 ml spoons (2 tablespoons)
sugar
2-3 scoops ice cream or 2-3 x 15 ml
spoons (2-3 tablespoons) double
cream

Liquidize the milk, fruit purée and sugar in a liquidizer until frothy. Add the ice cream or cream and blend for a second. Serve chilled.
Note If you are using frozen fruit purée, let it thaw before liquidizing.

Milk Shakes

Alternative flavours

For a chocolate milk shake, make in the same way as raspberry milk shake, but add chocolate sauce instead of the fruit purée.

For a banana milk shake, omit the fruit purée and add 3 bananas instead.

Fruit Punch

This quantity makes 16-18 glasses
225 g (8 oz) sugar
150 ml (¼ pint) water
2 lemons
2 grapefruit
5 oranges
150 ml (¼ pint) pineapple juice
600-900 ml (1-1½ pints) soda water
orange and lemon slices
sprigs of mint

Boil the sugar and water together for 5 minutes with 2-3 strips of lemon rind. Strain and cool. Squeeze the juice from all the fruit and strain it. Add to the sugar syrup with the pineapple juice and put in the refrigerator to chill. Just before serving, pour in the soda water and garnish with orange and lemon slices and sprigs of mint.

Let your freezer lend a helping hand

Freezer Cookery deals with one important aspect of the home freezer—the ways in which it can be used to simplify entertaining. This does not mean only formal entertaining but includes emergency dishes, dishes which can be cooked in large quantities for family use and some basic sauces and recipes to make a plain meal more exciting.

Freezer Cookery

After the initial acquisition of a freezer, it can take up to a year to discover how to use it in the most effective way. This could mean keeping a mixture of garden produce, uncooked meat and poultry, home-prepared dishes and commercial products, such as beefburgers and fish fingers, or storing mainly one type of item, such as garden vegetables or made-up dishes to save work later. The quantities and proportions will vary according to individual needs and circumstances, but there are three cardinal rules to remember:

no food is actually improved by freezing (ices excepted);

ideally, *nothing* should remain in a freezer more than ten months and most food items much less;

cooked dishes and frozen fish should generally be used within weeks rather than months.

Most freezer-owners fall into one of two groups. There are the squirrels, who, having stocked the freezer, cannot bear to take anything out; and those who, having bought a forequarter of beef or 500 skinless sausages cheaply, insist that the family live exclusively on this bargain. Try to maintain a happy medium between the two.

Stocking the freezer with cooked dishes needs considerable thought and care. For most people, it is not helpful to have too many such meals in the freezer at any one time, unless specific use is planned for them. Bear this in mind and look ahead to future special occasions when planning cooked dishes for the freezer.

The recipes that follow divide into five sections: Soups and Starters, Main Dishes, Sweets and Puddings, Emergency Dishes and Ices, and Basic Recipes (which include stocks and sauces). It is best to avoid taking a whole meal from the freezer. Dishes which freeze really well have a tendency to resemble each other, so it would be wiser to prepare at least one of the courses from fresh ingredients.

Very few prepared dishes can be taken from the freezer and served without any further additions or finishing. For this reason, it is most important to label everything carefully, not just with the name of the dish, the date it was made and the number of people it will serve, but also with any instructions for finishing it off after thawing.

Soups and Starters

Many soups, particularly smooth or sieved ones, are suitable for freezing. However, those given here are a little out of the ordinary. All would be suitable for serving at a dinner party, as well as on more mundane occasions.

As a general rule, add cream or egg yolks to soup on re-heating rather than before freezing. Do not be worried by the appearance of soup when it first comes out of the freezer: it will resume its proper consistency on re-heating. If it does seem to have thinned a little, re-thicken it by adding arrowroot or potato flour, slaked with water. Allow approximately 200 ml (7 fl oz) per person when serving soup as a starter.

While many starters use fresh (as opposed to cooked) ingredients, and are therefore not suitable for freezing, those given in this section will all freeze well. They include savoury mousses, pizzas and flans as well as some fish recipes. Nearly all of these starters would make good supper dishes as well.

Apple and Cabbage Soup

½ large firm green cabbage
3 large green apples
3 medium onions
50 g (2 oz) butter
2 litres (3 pints) stock
chopped parsley or green ginger
salt and pepper

Shred the cabbage finely. Peel, core and slice the apples and peel and finely slice the onions. Melt the butter in a large pan and cook the onion gently until it is transparent. Add the cabbage and apples and cook gently until they are all soft. Add the stock and seasoning and simmer gently for a further 15-20 minutes. Cool slightly and either liquidize the soup or pass it through a vegetable mill. Season to taste and leave to cool. Pour into suitable container and freeze.

To serve Thaw the soup, then reheat it and sprinkle with chopped parsley or green ginger.

Celery and Almond Soup

1 head celery
1 medium onion
1 medium carrot
1 medium leek
25 g (1 oz) butter
1 litre (1¾ pints) chicken stock
bouquet garni
25 g (1 oz) ground almonds
150 ml (¼ pint) milk
2 x 5 ml spoons (2 teaspoons)
  potato flour or arrowroot
4 x 15 ml spoons (4 tablespoons)
  double cream
12 g (½ oz) browned flaked almonds
salt and pepper

Chop all the vegetables finely, peeling and washing first as necessary. Melt the butter in a heavy pan and cook the vegetables gently until they are soft. Add the stock, bouquet garni and seasoning. Simmer for 20 minutes. Cool slightly then liquidize or pass through a vegetable mill. Stir in the ground almonds and milk, pour into a suitable container and freeze.

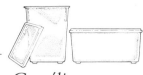

To serve Thaw the soup, then bring to the boil and thicken as required with the potato flour, slaked with a little stock or water. Adjust seasoning to taste and stir in the cream and flaked almonds just before serving.

Crème Agnès Sorel

Agnès Sorel Soup

Agnès Sorel (1422-50) was mistress to Charles VII of France. This soup was presumably named in her honour.

 100 g (4 oz) button mushrooms
 50 g (2 oz) butter
 3 x 15 ml spoons (3 tablespoons) water
 lemon juice
 1 litre (1¾ pints) chicken stock
 25 g (1 oz) flour
 1 slice cooked chicken
 1 slice tongue (optional)
 2 egg yolks
 2 x 15 ml spoons (2 tablespoons) double cream
 salt and pepper

Wipe the mushrooms and put them in a pan with 15 g (½ oz) butter, the

water and a squeeze of lemon juice. Season, cover, bring to the boil and cook for 1 minute. Strain off the liquor and add to the chicken stock. Put the mushrooms on one side.

Melt 25 g (1 oz) of the remaining butter in a large pan and stir in the flour. Cook for 2-3 minutes, then add the stock. Bring to the boil and season well. Cool, then pour into a suitable container and freeze. Freeze the mushrooms separately or, alternatively, with the garniture.

To serve Thaw the soup and bring to the boil. Slice the chicken, tongue (this adds colour, but can be omitted) and mushrooms into julienne strips and warm them in a little soup. Mix the egg yolks with the cream and the remaining butter in a basin and pour a little boiling soup on to it. Pour into the pan and stir well. Re-heat the soup but do not let it boil. Add the chicken, tongue and mushrooms and serve the soup at once.

Note The garniture (of chicken, tongue and mushrooms) can be prepared in advance and frozen separately in a small container, or prepared at the time of serving.

Crème Camélia

Cream of Pea Soup with Mint

 1 litre (1¾ pints) light stock
 sprig of mint
 450 g (1 lb) shelled peas or 2 large packets frozen peas
 2 x 5 ml spoons (2 teaspoons) arrowroot
 150 ml (¼ pint) single cream
 25 g (1 oz) butter
 2 x 15 ml spoons (2 tablespoons) cooked chicken (optional)
 salt and pepper

Put the stock in a pan with the sprig of mint and bring to the boil. Add the peas and cook gently until they are tender. Sieve or liquidize the soup or pass through a vegetable mill. Return to a clean pan and, if necessary, thicken with arrowroot slaked with water. Cool and freeze.
To serve Thaw the soup and bring to the boil. Mix the cream with the butter in a basin and pour a little boiling soup on to it. Stir well and return to the pan. Season. Re-heat without boiling. Add diced chicken.

Simple ingredients for Apple and Cabbage Soup

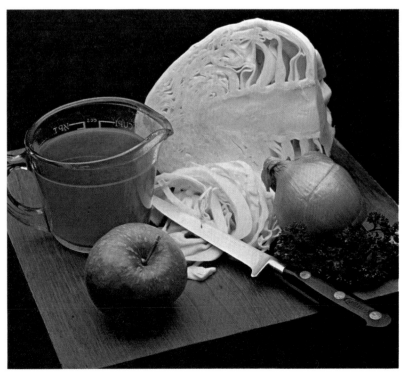

Crème Doria

Cream of Cucumber Soup
This is almost the only satisfactory way of freezing surplus cucumbers. The soup may be served hot or cold.

2 cucumbers
1 medium onion or 2 shallots
1 litre (1¾ pints) light chicken stock
65 g (2½ oz) butter
40 g (1½ oz) flour
green food colouring
2 egg yolks
2 x 15 ml spoons (2 tablespoons)
  double cream
sprig of mint
salt and pepper

Peel the cucumbers and put half of one aside for garnish. Slice the remainder. Peel and finely slice the onion or shallots. Put the cucumber and onion in a saucepan with the stock and a mint leaf. Bring to the boil, add seasoning and simmer for 10-15 minutes. Liquidize or rub through a sieve. Melt 40 g (1½ oz) butter in a pan, stir in the flour and cook for 2-3 minutes. Stir in the cucumber stock and bring to the boil. Check for seasoning and colour the soup a delicate green with the colouring. Cool, then pour into a suitable container and freeze.

To serve hot Thaw the soup and bring to the boil. Mix the egg yolks, cream and remaining butter together in a basin and pour a little of the boiling soup on top. Stir well, return to the pan and re-heat without boiling. Just before serving, garnish with the remainder of the cucumber, either grated or diced, and 1 x 5 ml spoon (1 teaspoon) chopped mint.

To serve cold Freeze the soup after liquidizing it, omitting the roux. Thaw and bring to the boil and thicken with 1 x 15 ml spoon (1 tablespoon) arrowroot, slaked with single cream. Allow to cool again. Chill and stir in the double cream just before serving. Garnish as for hot soup.

Potage Crécy

Carrot and Onion Soup

2 large onions
700 g (1½ lb) carrots
50 g (2 oz) butter
2 large potatoes
1·25 litres (2 pints) chicken stock
2 x 5 ml spoons (2 teaspoons)
  crème de riz
150 ml (¼ pint) double cream or
  50 g (2 oz) butter
chopped parsley
salt and pepper

Peel and finely slice the onions and carrots. Melt the butter and gently cook the onions and carrots until soft. Do not let them brown. Peel and finely slice the potatoes, add to the pan and cook for a further 5 minutes. Add the stock and bring to the boil. Add seasoning and simmer until the vegetables are tender. Liquidize or pass through a vegetable mill. Cool and then freeze.

To serve Thaw the soup, bring to the boil and thicken with the crème de riz, slaked with a little cold water if necessary. If the soup is too thick, dilute with more stock. Adjust seasoning and, just before serving, stir in the cream or butter. Sprinkle with chopped parsley.

Crêpes Ripieni

Stuffed Pancakes
For the batter

100 g (4 oz) flour
1 egg and 2 extra yolks
300 ml (½ pint) milk
knob of butter
salt

For the stuffing

1 large onion
50 g (2 oz) butter
1 x 15 ml spoon (1 tablespoon) oil
175 g (6 oz) mushrooms
½ green pepper
100 g (4 oz) ham
50 g (2 oz) grated cheese
1 egg
1 x 5 ml spoon (1 teaspoon)
  tomato purée
2 x 15 ml spoons (2 tablespoons)
  fresh breadcrumbs
salt and pepper

For the sauce

40 g (1½ oz) butter
40 g (1½ oz) flour
500 ml (¾-1 pint) milk
50 g (2 oz) grated cheese
salt and pepper

For the topping

25 g (1 oz) Gruyère cheese

First prepare the batter. Put the flour and a generous pinch of salt in a large bowl. Make a well in the centre and put the beaten egg and yolks into it. Mix to a smooth batter with the flour, adding the milk gradually. Leave to stand for 30-40 minutes. Melt the butter and add to the batter just before cooking.

To prepare the stuffing, peel and finely chop the onion and fry gently in the butter and oil until soft. Wipe and finely chop the mushrooms and add these. Chop the pepper, discarding the seeds, and blanch the flesh for 2-3 minutes in boiling water. Chop the ham roughly. Remove the onion and mushroom mixture from the heat and stir in the pepper and ham, together with the grated cheese, egg, tomato purée and breadcrumbs. Season to taste and leave on one side.

To prepare the sauce, melt the butter and add the flour. Cook for 2-3 minutes, stirring all the time.

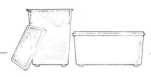

Pizza can be frozen without the filling which can be added when the flan has thawed. Heat from cold at 210°C, 425°F/Gas 7 for 35-40 minutes. This Pizza Napolitana is a classic recipe

Add most of the milk and bring to the boil, stirring to produce a thick, creamy sauce. Add the remainder of the milk if you think it is too thick. Season well, remove from the heat and add the grated cheese (reserve the Gruyère).

Cook the pancakes individually in a tiny amount of hot fat. Put a little of the sauce in a fireproof dish, put a spoonful of the stuffing on each pancake and roll up. Put in the dish and cover with the rest of the sauce. Grate the Gruyère and sprinkle it on top. Freeze.

To serve Thaw overnight in the refrigerator or for 6-8 hours at room temperature. Cover the dish with buttered paper and foil and heat at 180°C, 350°F/Gas 4 for 30-40 minutes. Remove the foil and paper and brown under the grill. Serve at once.

Note You can also use this stuffing and sauce for cannelloni. Prepare stuffing and sauce in the same way and fill about 8-10 cannelloni, cooked in boiling salted water for 12-14 minutes. Freeze, thaw and re-heat in the same way.

Crêpes aux Epinards
Spinach Pancakes
For the batter
  as for crêpes ripieni
For the filling
  1·5 kg (3 lb) fresh spinach or 700 g (1½ lb) frozen leaf spinach
  100 g (4 oz) butter
  50 g (2 oz) grated cheese
  salt and papper
For the sauce
  1 large onion
  2 x 15 ml spoons (2 tablespoons) oil
  225 g (8 oz) minced beef
  1 x 15 ml spoon (1 tablespoon) flour
  garlic
  1 x 400-g (14-oz) can tomatoes
  2 x 5 ml spoons (2 teaspoons) tomato purée
  300 ml (½ pint) stock
  bouquet garni
  salt and pepper
For the topping
  grated cheese

Prepare the batter in exactly the same way as for *crêpes ripieni* and leave to stand for about 40 minutes.

To prepare the filling from fresh spinach, remove the tough, central stalks, then wash the leaves well in several changes of cold water. Cook in boiling, salted water for 2-3 minutes. Drain, rinse under cold

water and squeeze well to remove all water. If using frozen spinach, thaw it thoroughly and squeeze it dry.

Heat the butter in a pan until golden and add the spinach. Cook it until it is dry, stirring regularly. Season well and stir in the grated cheese. Leave to cool.

To prepare the sauce, peel and chop the onion and fry in the oil until soft. Add the minced beef and cook until golden. Stir in the flour and cook for 3-4 minutes. Crush the garlic with a little salt and add, then stir in the rest of the ingredients. Season well and simmer for 25-30 minutes. Leave to cool.

Butter a fireproof dish. Cook the pancakes and put a spoonful of cold spinach mixture on each one. Roll up and arrange in the dish. Cover with the cold sauce and sprinkle with cheese. Cover with foil and freeze.

To serve Thaw overnight in the refrigerator or for 6-8 hours at room temperature. Re-heat for 35-40 minutes at 180°C, 350°F/Gas 4.

Pizza Napolitana

This is the classic recipe for *pizza napolitana*, although there are a host of other versions in existence.

For the dough
  225 g (8 oz) flour
  1 x 5 ml spoon (1 teaspoon) salt
  50 g (2 oz) butter or lard
  7-15 g (¼-½ oz) yeast
  2 x 15 ml spoons (2 tablespoons) warm water
  1 egg
For the filling
  450 g (1 lb) ripe tomatoes
  100 g (4 oz) Bel Paese or moist Cheddar cheese
  olive oil
  chopped basil, marjoram and oregano
  1 small can anchovies
  salt and pepper

To prepare the dough, sift the flour and salt into a warm bowl and rub in the butter or lard with your fingertips. Dissolve the yeast in the warm water. Make a well in the centre of the flour mixture and add the yeast and the beaten egg. Mix everything together to form a firm dough, adding a little more warm water if necessary. Knead the dough well and put it in a clean bowl. Cover it with a clean cloth and leave in a warm place to rise for 1½-2 hours.

To prepare the filling, skin and de-seed the tomatoes and slice them roughly. Slice the cheese finely.

Break down the dough by kneading it to knock out the air bubbles, then roll it out into a circle. Put in an oiled 20-cm (8-in) flan ring on a baking sheet and pat it out to the edge. Cover the top with the tomatoes, sprinkle with olive oil and herbs and arrange the anchovies on top. Season well. Cover with the slices of cheese and bake for 20-25 minutes at 200°C, 400°F/Gas 6. Cool and freeze. (If the cheese is very soft, only put it over the pizza for the last 10 minutes of cooking.)

To serve Thaw for 6-8 hours in the kitchen, then re-heat for 15-20 minutes at 190°C, 375°F/Gas 5.

Pissaladière

This is the French version of pizza. There is rather more filling and less base.

For the pastry
225 g (8 oz) flour
1 egg yolk
150 g (5 oz) butter
1 x 5 ml spoon (1 teaspoon) sugar
2-3 x 15 ml spoons (2-3 tablespoons) water, plus a squeeze of lemon juice
salt

For the filling
700 g (1½ lb) onions
olive oil
2 large tomatoes
2 cloves garlic
1 x 5 ml spoon (1 teaspoon) tomato purée (optional)
1 small can anchovies
12-18 stoned black olives
salt and pepper

To prepare the pastry, sieve the flour on to a board and make a well

in the centre. Put all the other ingredients for the pastry into this and, using the fingertips of one hand, work it up into a firm dough. Knead it lightly and then leave it in a cool place to relax for 20-30 minutes.

To prepare the filling, slice the onions finely and fry them in the oil until they are soft and golden (not brown). Skin and roughly chop the tomatoes and crush the garlic with a little salt. Add to the onions. If the tomatoes are not a good colour, add the tomato purée. Stir and season well, and cook gently until the onions and tomatoes are amalgamated and the mixture is fairly dry. Leave to cool.

Roll out the pastry and use it to line a 17·5-20-cm (7-8-in) flan ring. Prick the base well and spread the onion and tomato mixture over it. Arrange the anchovies in a lattice pattern over the filling and put the olives in between. Bake for 10 minutes at 210°C, 425°F/Gas 7, then reduce the heat to 190°C, 375°F/Gas 5 and cook until the pastry is golden (about another 20 minutes). Cool and open-freeze on a plate until hard. Wrap, label and put back in the freezer.

To serve Thaw for 6-8 hours at room temperature and re-heat for 20-25 minutes at 180°-190°C, 350°-375°F/Gas 4-5.

Savoury Mousses

The savoury mousses which freeze best are those with a fairly large amount of white sauce and not too much egg white. These are considerably less 'wet' when thawed than a lighter-textured mousse. Ham mousse and tongue mousse made following the same principles as the mousses given here would freeze well.

Tuna Fish Mousse

Serves 8-10
3 x 200-g (7-oz) cans tuna
20 g (¾ oz, 1½ sachets) gelatine
juice of half a lemon
150 ml (¼ pint) water
300 ml (½ pint) mayonnaise
2 x 15 ml spoons (2 tablespoons) double cream
2 egg whites
salt and pepper

For the béchamel sauce
1 onion
600 ml (1 pint) milk
40 g (1½ oz) butter
25 g (1 oz) flour

For the garnish
1 cucumber or 1 head celery
4 firm tomatoes
French dressing mixed with
1 x 5 ml spoon (1 teaspoon) chopped, fresh herbs
watercress

Oil a 1·5-litre (2½-pint) ring mould and leave to drain. To prepare the béchamel sauce, peel and finely slice the onion and put it in a pan with the milk. Bring slowly to the boil, remove from the heat and leave for 15 minutes to infuse. Melt the butter in a clean pan, add the flour and cook for 2-3 minutes, stirring all the time. Strain the milk gradually into the butter and flour roux, stirring all the time. Bring to the boil and cook for 1-2 minutes. Season well and cool.

Soak the gelatine in the lemon juice and 3 x 15 ml spoons (3 tablespoons) cold water, taken from the 150 ml (¼ pint). Stand bowl in a pan of hot water until the gelatine has dissolved, then add rest of water.

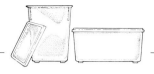

Drain the tuna. Using an electric mixer, beat the fish on a low speed, gradually adding the cold béchamel sauce. Stir in the dissolved gelatine and the mayonnaise. Leave in a cool place to set. Whip the cream and the egg whites stiffly. When the tuna mixture is nearly set, fold these in, adjust the seasoning, and pour the mixture into the ring mould. Put in the refrigerator for 3-4 hours or overnight to set.

When the mousse has set, turn it out on to a foil plate. Open-freeze until hard, then wrap, label and re-place in the freezer.

To serve Remove the wrapping from the mousse and place on a serving dish. Thaw overnight in the refrigerator. Just before serving, peel the cucumber and remove the seeds. Cut into thick strips, salt these lightly and leave them to drain for 15-20 minutes. Alternatively, trim the celery, wash and dry it well and cut it into neat strips. Skin and de-seed the tomatoes and cut into quarters. Mix the cucumber or celery and the tomatoes together and moisten with the French dressing. Fill the centre of the mousse with this mixture. Decorate with watercress.

Infusing Milk
Be careful not to keep milk simmering when infusing it with onion and herbs for a white sauce. Bring it slowly to the boil, then take it off the heat altogether and leave it, covered, for 10-15 minutes. Strain, and make it up to the original quantity with more milk. If you leave milk to simmer, it acquires a very cooked flavour.

Fresh Haddock Mousse
Serves 6-10
450 g (1 lb) fresh haddock fillet
lemon juice
300 ml (½ pint) milk
½ finely sliced onion

1 bay leaf
15 g (½ oz, 1 sachet) gelatine
25 g (1 oz) butter
25 g (1 oz) flour
1 x 5 ml spoon (1 teaspoon) paprika
1 x 5 ml spoon (1 teaspoon) tomato purée
4 x 15 ml spoons (4 tablespoons) double cream
1-2 egg whites (depending on size)
salt and pepper
For the sauce garnish
300 ml (½ pint) mayonnaise
150 ml (¼ pint) tomato juice
few drops Tabasco sauce
½ cucumber

Wash and skin the haddock fillet and put it in a buttered dish. Sprinkle with lemon juice, salt and pepper. Cover with buttered paper and cook for 15-20 minutes at 180°C, 350°F/Gas 4. Leave to cool.

Put the milk in a pan with the onion, bay leaf and some salt and pepper. Bring slowly to the boil, remove from the heat and leave to stand for 5-10 minutes. Soak the gelatine in 3 x 5 ml spoons (3 tablespoons) cold water in a small basin, then stand this in a pan of hot water until the gelatine has dissolved.

Melt the butter in a pan and stir in the flour and paprika. Cook, stirring for 2-3 minutes, then gradually strain in the milk. Bring to the boil, stirring all the time and cook for 1-2 minutes. Season and add the tomato purée. Strain in the dissolved gelatine and leave to cool.

Drain the fish and pound it in a mixer, gradually adding the sauce. Put in the refrigerator to set. Whip the cream and the egg white(s) stiffly.

When the haddock mixture is on the point of setting, fold in the cream and the egg whites. Turn into a 1-litre (1½-pint) oiled mould and leave in the refrigerator to set. Either freeze it in the mould or turn it out when set on to a foil plate and open-freeze until hard. Wrap, label and put back in freezer.

To serve Thaw the mousse over-night in the refrigerator and turn

out on to a serving dish if necessary. Thin the mayonnaise to a coating consistency with the tomato juice and add a few drops of Tabasco. Coat the mousse with this and decorate with slices of cucumber.

Pâtés
Most pâté recipes do not freeze very well as they tend to be 'wet' on thawing. If you want to freeze pâté, look for a recipe that contains either white sauce or bread-crumbs. Always thaw pâtés for at least 24 hours in the refrigerator. The slower they thaw, the better. The recipe given here for Danish liver pâté really does freeze well.

Danish Liver Pâté
Serves 8-10
300 ml (½ pint) milk
1 onion
bay leaf
25 g (1 oz) butter
25 g (1 oz) flour
450 g (1 lb) pig's liver
175 g (6 oz) fat bacon
3-4 anchovy fillets or 2 x 5 ml spoons (2 teaspoons) anchovy essence
garlic
225 g (8 oz) thinly sliced fat bacon
salt and pepper

Put the milk in a pan with the peeled and sliced onion, bay leaf and salt and pepper. Heat until nearly boiling, then remove from the heat, cover and leave to infuse for 20 minutes.

Melt the butter in a clean pan, add the flour and cook for 2-3 minutes, stirring all the time. Add the strained milk gradually and bring to the boil, stirring. Leave to cool.

Trim the liver and bacon and mince together with the anchovy fillets (or alternatively, stir in the essence). Crush the garlic with a little salt and stir it into the meat mixture. Blend the sauce into the meat mix-

*Coquilles de Poisson au Cidre—
this dish freezes well and looks
very good served in the shells*

---

ture, using a mixing machine if possible. Season well. Line a terrine
dish with the thinly sliced bacon and
pour the pâté mixture into this.
Cook in a baking dish of boiling
water for 1½-2 hours at 170°-180°C,
325°-350°F/Gas 3-4. Cool under a
light weight and turn out of the dish
when cold. Wrap and freeze.

To serve Thaw overnight in the
refrigerator and serve cut in slices.

Coquilles de Poisson au Cidre

Fish in Cider
>   700 g (1½ lb) fresh haddock or cod
>   fillet
>   1 onion or shallot
>   150 ml (¼ pint) dry cider
>   150 ml (¼ pint) water
>   milk
>   25 g (1 oz) butter
>   25 g (1 oz) flour
>   50 g (2 oz) grated cheese

Skin the fish fillets and cut each one
into 3-4 pieces. Chop the onion or
shallot finely and spread on the
bottom of a buttered fireproof dish.
Put the fish pieces on top, pour over
the cider and water and season well.
Cover with a buttered paper and
cook at 190°C, 375°F/Gas 5, for 20-
25 minutes. Remove fish and keep
warm. Strain the liquor and make it
up to 450 ml (¾ pint) with a little
milk.

Melt the butter in a pan, add the
flour and cook for 2-3 minutes, stirring all the time. Gradually add the
fish liquor and bring to the boil, stirring. The sauce should be a good
coating consistency—add a little
more milk if necessary. Remove
from the heat, season well and stir in
most of the grated cheese.

Put a little sauce in the base of 6
coquille shells and divide the fish
between them, putting it on top of
the sauce. Cover with the rest of the
sauce and sprinkle the remaining
cheese on top. Cool, wrap each shell
in foil and freeze.

To serve Thaw for 2-3 hours, then

re-heat the shells for about 20 minutes at 180°C, 350°F/Gas 4. Brown
under the grill if necessary.

Crabe Diablé

Devilled Crab
This is a good recipe for when crabs
are plentiful. It also freezes well.
>   225 g (8 oz) crabmeat, fresh or
>   canned
>   1 small onion
>   1 shallot
>   25 g (1 oz) butter
>   1 x 15 ml spoon (1 tablespoon)
>   brandy
>   2 x 5 ml spoons (2 teaspoons) Dijon
>   mustard

For the béchamel sauce
>   25 g (1 oz) butter
>   25 g (1 oz) flour
>   300 ml (½ pint) milk
>   salt and pepper
>   browned breadcrumbs

Peel and chop the onion and shallot
finely and fry in the butter until
soft and golden. Remove the pan
from the heat and stir in the brandy
and mustard.

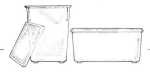

To make the sauce, melt the butter, stir in the flour and cook for 2-3 minutes. Gradually add the milk, stirring all the time until the sauce boils. Season well. Stir the onion mixture and crabmeat into the sauce and pour into six coquille shells (or use the crab shells, if using fresh crab). Sprinkle with browned crumbs. Cover with foil and freeze.

To serve Thaw for 1-2 hours, then re-heat for 15-20 minutes at 200°C, 400°F/Gas 6. Finish off by browning under the grill, if necessary.

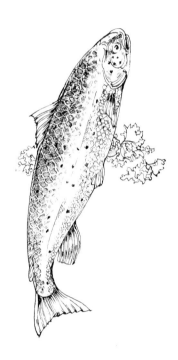

Tourte au Saumon

Salmon Flan
This is tastiest if it is made with Scotch salmon, but failing this, the Pacific variety is quite acceptable.

*225 g (8 oz) rich shortcrust pastry
  (see recipe for pissaladière)*

For the filling

*450 g (1 lb) salmon
4 × 15 ml spoons (4 tablespoons)
  white wine
100 g (4 oz) mushrooms
50 g (2 oz) butter
2 egg whites
150 ml ($\frac{1}{4}$ pint) double cream
salt and pepper*

For the herb butter

*50 g (2 oz) butter
juice of half a lemon
finely chopped parsley, tarragon
  and chives
salt and pepper*

Remove the skin and bone from the salmon and cut it into 3-4 neat slices. Put these (with the trimmings) into a bowl with the white wine and some salt and pepper. Leave to marinate for 30 minutes.

Prepare the pastry as in the recipe for pissaladière and leave in a cool place for about 40 minutes.

To prepare the filling, wipe the mushrooms and chop finely. Put two-thirds of the salmon in a mortar or bowl of an electric mixer with the liquid from the marinade, the mushrooms and butter. Pound, or beat at a low speed, until smooth. Add the egg whites little by little and then the cream. Season the mixture well.

Roll out the pastry and use half to line a deep flan ring. Prick the base and spread a layer of salmon mixture over it. Put the reserved slices of salmon on top and cover with the remainder of the filling. Cover with pastry, seal the edges and brush with beaten egg. Make a small hole in the centre and bake for 40 minutes—1 hour at 200°C, 400°F/Gas 4. Cool and freeze.

To serve Thaw at room temperature for 6-8 hours and re-heat for 25-30 minutes at 190°-200°C, 375°-400°F/Gas 5-6. To make the herb butter, melt the butter and add lemon juice, herbs and seasoning and serve separately from the tourte.

Moules aux Herbes

Mussels with Herbs
Mussels can be frozen in their liquor and then finished off as required. As they are time-consuming to scrape and clean, but quick to finish off, it can help to get the cleaning and scraping done in advance.

*3.5 kg (8 lb) mussels
2 shallots
25 g (1 oz) butter
1 stick celery*

*1 wineglass white wine
sprig of parsley
salt and pepper*

For the sauce

*2 large onions
40 g (1$\frac{1}{2}$ oz) butter
1 × 15 ml spoon (1 tablespoon)
  flour
1 × 15 ml spoon (1 tablespoon)
  tomato purée
garlic
bouquet garni
1 small can tomatoes
chopped fresh thyme, parsley and
  marjoram
100 g (4 oz) mushrooms
salt and pepper*

Scrub the mussels well and wash thoroughly until clean. Peel and finely chop the shallots and fry them in the melted butter until soft. Chop the celery and add it to the pan with the wine, parsley and salt and pepper. Bring to the boil and add the mussels. Cook briskly in a covered pan, shaking occasionally, for about 4 minutes, at which time the mussels will open. Strain them, and reserve the liquor. Remove the shells and beards and keep the mussels on one side. Strain the liquor into a clean pan and reduce to 450 ml ($\frac{3}{4}$ pint).

To prepare the sauce, peel and finely chop the onions and cook them gently in the butter until tender. Stir in the flour and cook for a few minutes, then add the reserved mussel liquor. Bring to the boil, stirring all the time. Stir in the tomato purée, the garlic crushed with a little salt and the bouquet garni. Drain the tomatoes, press out the seeds, chop the flesh and add it to the mussels. Add the drained tomato juice to the sauce and let it simmer for another 10-15 minutes. Put the sauce through a vegetable mill or sieve and add the chopped herbs. Stir in the mussels and tomato. Wipe and finely chop the mushrooms and add. Cool and freeze.

To serve Thaw at room temperature for 6-8 hours, then re-heat gently in a saucepan over a low heat.

Main Dishes

All the dishes in this section freeze, thaw and re-heat with no noticeable difference between the frozen version and one freshly prepared and cooked. It is always better to thaw any stew, casserole or other meat dish overnight and then re-heat it slowly. If you have an emergency on your hands—people suddenly arriving at a mealtime—and you have to heat a dish directly from the freezer, choose one such as a goulash or carbonnade, in which the meat has been cut in fairly small pieces and frozen in plenty of sauce.

There are many poultry dishes that freeze well, and these are well represented here. Incidentally, it is quite safe to re-freeze frozen chickens, provided they have been thoroughly cooked first.

Instructions are given at the end of each recipe for finishing off the dish and serving it. Besides putting the name of the dish and the date it was made on the label, also make a note of any additions to be made on re-heating.

Unless otherwise stated, quantities given here are generally sufficient for about six people, but you will have to make allowance for individual appetites.

Meat and Chicken
In nearly all the following recipes, the meat or chicken joints are browned in fat and removed from the pan. Then the vegetables are browned in the same fat. As always, the secret of a rich, well-flavoured dish lies in the proper browning of the meat. The fat used, usually butter and oil or dripping, must be really hot so that the meat is sealed immediately by the heat. Do not stir, or turn the pieces over too quickly, as this will lower the temperature of the fat appreciably. The meat should always be removed from the pan before the vegetables are added, allowing them to be properly browned too. Add the flour just before the liquid, to guard against it burning.

If the fat used is butter, a golden rather than brown result will be achieved, as butter burns at too low a temperature to brown well.

It is better to cook all these dishes for a longer period at a slower temperature than to try to hurry them by turning up the heat. A heavy enamelled iron casserole is ideal for this type of dish as it can be used on top of the stove or in the oven.

Coq au Vin
Serves 4-6
1 x 1·5-kg (3½-lb) roasting chicken
50 g (2 oz) butter
2 x 15 ml spoons (2 tablespoons) oil
1 large onion
1 clove garlic
1 x 15 ml spoon (1 tablespoon) flour
2 x 15 ml spoons (2 tablespoons) brandy
½ bottle red wine
stock
bouquet garni
arrowroot
salt, pepper and paprika
For the garniture
20 small onions
225 g (8 oz) green bacon in one piece
225 g (8 oz) mushrooms
50 g (2 oz) butter
slices of bread

Joint the chicken. Heat the butter and oil and brown the joints evenly. Peel and slice the onion and add to the pan. Brown well. Crush the garlic with a little salt and add it with the flour, stirring well. Pour in the brandy and flame it. Add the wine and enough stock to cover. Add the bouquet garni and seasoning, cover and simmer for 40-60 minutes.

To prepare the garniture, peel the onions and cook gently until just soft, in boiling, salted water. Cut the bacon into pieces, place in a pan of cold water and bring to the boil. Drain. Wipe the mushrooms, cut into quarters, and fry in the butter until golden. Remove the mushrooms and fry the drained onions and bacon until golden.

Remove the chicken from the pan and put in a container for freezing. Strain the sauce, skim and boil to reduce slightly. Thicken with a little slaked arrowroot if necessary. Add a little sauce to the onion garniture and mix. Let the remaining sauce cool slightly before pouring it over the chicken. Seal and freeze. Freeze the garniture separately.

To serve Thaw both chicken and garniture overnight and re-heat separately for 40-60 minutes at 180°C, 350°F/Gas 4. Cut slices of bread into triangular croûtons and fry them in hot butter. Put the chicken in a serving dish, pour the sauce over and surround with the garniture and croûtons. Sprinkle the top with chopped parsley.

Poulet Sauté à la Basquaise
Basque Fried Chicken
Serves 4-6
Plain boiled rice or mashed potatoes, instead of the pilaff, make a perfectly acceptable accompaniment to this chicken dish.
1 x 1·5-kg (3½-lb) chicken
oil
2-3 red peppers or 1 green pepper and 1 can red pimentos
4 large onions
10 tomatoes
4 cloves garlic
175 g (6 oz) rasher green gammon
2 x 5 ml spoons (2 teaspoons) flour
4 x 5 ml spoons (4 teaspoons) tomato purée
150 ml (¼ pint) stock or water
bouquet garni
parsley
salt and pepper
For the rice pilaff
225 g (8 oz) Italian rice
1 onion
25 g (1 oz) butter
600 ml (1 pint) stock
salt and pepper
Joint the chicken and fry the joints until brown in 3-4 x 15 ml spoons (3-4 tablespoons) oil. Reduce the heat, cover and cook gently for another 10 minutes.

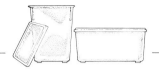

De-seed and chop the peppers and blanch for 1 minute in boiling, salted water. Refresh under cold water and drain. Peel and chop the onions finely. Skin and pip the tomatoes and chop the flesh coarsely. Crush the garlic with a little salt and cut the gammon into strips.

Remove the chicken joints from the pan and add a little more oil to it. Fry the onions until golden, then stir in the flour and cook for 1-2 minutes. Add all the remaining ingredients (except the chicken and pilaff). Season well and let the mixture simmer for 5 minutes. Replace the chicken joints, cover the pan and cook gently for 30 minutes or until the chicken is tender. Cool, put in a suitable container and freeze.

To serve Thaw the chicken overnight and re-heat in a casserole for 40-60 minutes at 180°C, 350°F/Gas 4. To prepare the pilaff, peel and chop the onion and fry in the butter until it is soft. Add the rice and fry for 2-3 minutes. Pour in the boiling stock and season well. Cover and cook for about 18-20 minutes at 180°C, 350°F/Gas 4. Arrange the pilaff round the edge of a deep fireproof dish with the chicken and sauce in the middle. Sprinkle with chopped parsley.

Poulet Sauté à la Basquaise—succulent chicken cooked in a delicious mélange of peppers, onions, tomatoes and gammon with plenty of garlic

Jointing a chicken
For this job a sharp knife is essential. First remove all trussing string and put the bird on a board on its side, head end pointing to the right. Lift the right leg well away from the body, take the knife and cut through the skin. Pull the thigh joint out of its socket and remove the entire leg by cutting through the sinews and tendons. Turn the bird over and remove the left leg in the same way. Put the bird on its back, head end towards you, and balance by pulling out the wings. Remove the right wing with a good slice of breast meat attached. The knife should 'fall' on the wing joint—search for this point to ensure that you cut through the joint. Remove the left wing in the same way. Then, with a good strong pair of kitchen scissors remove the top section of the carcass from the bone and cut the breast piece in two. Divide each leg into two pieces by cutting through the joint, leaving the piece of the lower leg on the drumstick until the bird is cooked. This helps to prevent the flesh shrinking up the drumstick.

A 1·4-1·8 kg (3-4 lb) bird is the best weight for jointing and divides into 8 good-sized joints. An appreciably bigger bird gives rather large pieces, while a smaller one should really be halved or quartered. Frozen or fresh birds can both be jointed, but frozen ones may tend to be wet and stick to the pan when fried.

Poulet au Currie

Curried Chicken
Serves 4
Serve this dish with plain boiled rice
and the chutney of your choice.

1 x 1·5-kg (3½-lb) chicken
1 x 15 ml spoon (1 tablespoon) oil
50 g (2 oz) butter
1 large onion
1 x 15 ml spoon (1 tablespoon)
  curry powder
1 x 5 ml spoon (1 teaspoon) curry
  paste
1 x 15 ml spoon (1 tablespoon)
  flour
450 ml (¾ pint) stock
garlic
2 x 5 ml spoons (2 teaspoons)
  tomato purée
1 x 15 ml spoon (1 tablespoon)
  desiccated coconut
lemon juice
1 x 15 ml spoon (1 tablespoon)
  redcurrant jelly
4 x 15 ml spoons (4 tablespoons)
  double cream
salt and pepper

Joint the chicken and fry in the oil
and butter until golden. Remove
from the pan. Peel and chop the
onion and fry until golden. Then
add the curry powder and paste.
Cook for 2-3 minutes, then stir in
the flour and cook for another
minute. Add the stock, the garlic
crushed with a little salt, the tomato
purée and salt and pepper. Replace
the chicken joints and simmer for
30-40 minutes.

Meanwhile, put the coconut in a
basin and pour a teacup of boiling
water over it. Leave to soak.

When the chicken is cooked, remove it from the pan and put in
a suitable container for freezing.
Strain the liquid from the coconut
and add to the sauce. Let the sauce
cool, then pour it over the chicken,
wrap and freeze.

To serve Thaw the chicken overnight and re-heat it for 40-60 minutes at 180°C, 350°F/Gas 4. Add the
lemon juice, jelly and cream and
heat through just before serving.

Boning Poultry

Any bird, from a quail to a
turkey, can be boned. The
method is the same in all
cases. First have the bird
plucked and drawn, then lay
it breast down on a board.
Using a small sharp knife, cut
the skin down the back from
the neck to the parson's nose.
Holding the knife like a pen,
cut the flesh from the carcass,
keeping close to the bones all
the time. Cut through the
wing and thigh joints and
continue cutting carefully to
remove the meat from the
breast bone. Finish one side,
then repeat the process on the
other. When both sides are
clear of flesh, cut along the top
of the breast bone, taking
great care not to break the
skin (there is very little flesh
along the top of the bone
here). Remove the carcass.

Working from the inside,
remove the thigh bones. You
can stuff the bird at this stage,
before sewing up the back
with a trussing needle and fine
string. Reform the bird and
truss so that it returns to its
original shape. Alternatively,
you can bone out the drum
sticks and wing bones too,
splitting the skin on the inner
side of the pockets formed.
Then spread the bird out flat,
stuff it and roll it up like a
large sausage. Tie at intervals.

If you like, you can slice the
breast meat and spread it
evenly over the bird before
stuffing. Do not overstuff or
the bird will split during
cooking.

Boning out poultry is not
nearly as complicated as it
sounds, and it is well worth
mastering.

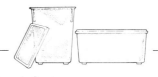

Ballotine of Chicken and Apricots

Stuffed Boned Chicken with Apricots

    1 x 2-kg (4½-lb) chicken

For the stuffing

    1 medium onion
    75 g (3 oz) butter
    175 g (6 oz) dried apricots, soaked
      overnight in water
    50 g (2 oz) stoned raisins
    100 g (4 oz) fresh breadcrumbs
    1 lemon
    chopped parsley
    1 egg
    garlic
    salt and pepper

For the braise

    1 large onion
    225 g (8 oz) mushrooms
    6 tomatoes
    2 x 15 ml spoons (2 tablespoons)
      oil
    1 x 5 ml spoon (1 teaspoon)
      curry powder
    4 x 15 ml spoons (4 tablespoons)
      white wine or brandy

To finish

    150 ml (¼ pint) stock
    lemon juice
    150 ml (¼ pint) double cream
    ½ x 5 ml spoon (½ teaspoon) potato
      flour or arrowroot

Bone out the chicken, leaving in the drumsticks and wing bones. To make the stuffing, peel and chop the onion finely and fry in 25 g (1 oz) butter until soft. Leave to cool. Cut up the apricots and mix with the raisins, breadcrumbs and the onion. Grate the rind from the lemon and squeeze the juice, then add to the mixture with salt and pepper. Add enough beaten egg to bind. Cream the remaining butter with a little crushed garlic and some more chopped parsley and salt and pepper.

Rub the interior of the chicken with half the seasoned butter. Pile the stuffing on top, sew up, re-shape the bird and truss it. Rub the outside with the rest of the seasoned butter.

To prepare the braise, peel and chop the onion, wipe and chop the mushrooms. Skin and de-seed the tomatoes, and chop the flesh. Fry the onion in a large pan in the oil until soft, then add the mushrooms. Add the curry powder and cook for 2-3 minutes. Add the tomatoes, season well and add the wine or brandy. Put the chicken on the top of this mixture, cover and roast for 60-75 minutes at 200°-210°C, 400°-425°F/Gas 6-7. Remove the lid for the final 15 minutes to brown the bird slightly. (An oval cast-iron pan is ideal for this dish.)

Remove the chicken and leave to cool. Skim the sauce, then add the stock and a good squeeze of lemon juice and bring to the boil. When the chicken is cold, wrap it and freeze. Cool the sauce and put it into a separate container and freeze.

To serve Thaw the chicken and sauce overnight. Remove strings from the chicken, wrap it in foil and cook for 40-50 minutes in a casserole or roasting tin at 180°C, 350°F/Gas 4. Add the cream to the sauce and boil for 3-4 minutes, thickening sauce first with the potato flour or arrowroot, slaked with water, and serve separately.

Galantine de Volaille

Chicken Roll in Jelly

    1 x 2-kg (4½-lb) chicken
    75 g (3 oz) slice ham
    75 g (3 oz) slice tongue
    2-3 x 15 ml spoons (2-3
      tablespoons) brandy
    2-3 x 15 ml spoons (2-3
      tablespoons) white wine or
      Madeira
    12 g (½ oz) pistachio nuts
      (optional)
    350 g (12 oz) sausage meat
    1 shallot
    1 x 15 ml spoon (1 tablespoon)
      finely chopped parsley
    salt and pepper

To finish

    600 ml (1 pint) aspic jelly
    black olives
    hard-boiled egg white

Bone the chicken, then remove the flesh from the skin, keeping the skin intact. Put on one side. Make stock with the chicken bones.

Cut the breast and the flesh from the top of the legs into thin strips, and put in a bowl. Cut the ham and tongue into similar strips and add to the chicken. Pour the wine and brandy into the bowl and leave to marinate for 30-60 minutes. Blanch and peel the pistachio nuts, if using them. Mince the remainder of the chicken flesh and mix it with the sausage meat. Peel and finely chop the shallot and add this to the chicken with the chopped parsley. Season well and stir in the brandy and wine from the marinade.

Spread the skin out on a board and put a layer of the chicken and sausage meat in the centre, keeping this rectangular in shape. Put half the chicken, ham and tongue strips on top and sprinkle with half the pistachio nuts. Cover with another layer of sausage meat etc., then the rest of the meat strips and nuts. Finish with a layer of sausage meat. Fold the skin over to form a neat roll and sew to keep secure.

Wrap the galantine tightly in a clean pudding cloth and tie the ends securely. Poach it gently in chicken stock for 1½-2 hours (depending on the size). Remove the galantine, untie the ends, but leave wrapped in the cloth. Put on another clean cloth roll this up rightly and put it on a dish. Cover with another dish and put a 1·5-kg (3-lb) weight on top. Leave to cool. Remove cloths, wrap in foil and freeze.

To serve Thaw the galantine overnight, then slice it neatly and arrange on a dish. Make up the aspic jelly and, when partially set, brush some over the galantine slices. Dip the black olives and the egg white into the remaining jelly and decorate with these. Spoon the jelly over to cover. (Aspic jelly is not essential: it merely helps to keep the meat moist if it is sliced and arranged some hours in advance of serving.)

Venison Ardennaise

Baked Venison with Chestnut Purée
Serves 4-6
The celeriac croquettes make an excellent accompaniment to this tasty venison dish, although they are by no means an essential part of it. They do not freeze so must be made before serving.

1-1·5-kg (2½-3-lb) haunch or shoulder of venison
450 g (1 lb) onions
1 x 15 ml spoon (1 tablespoon) dripping
300 ml (½ pint) brown ale
300 ml (½ pint) stock
1 x 5 ml spoon (1 teaspoon) red wine vinegar
garlic
1 x 5 ml spoon (1 teaspoon) sugar
2 x 5 ml spoons (2 teaspoons) French mustard
1 x 15 ml spoon (1 tablespoon) double cream
1 x 15 ml spoon (1 tablespoon) flour
1 x 225-g (8-oz) can unsweetened chestnut purée
salt and pepper
For the celeriac croquettes
1 large head celeriac
flour
egg
breadcrumbs
butter and oil for frying

Peel and slice the onions and brown well in the hot dripping. Add the venison and brown it. Pour over the ale, stock, vinegar, garlic (crushed with a little salt) and the sugar. Season well. Cover with a lid and cook for 1½ hours at 180°C, 350°F/ Gas 4. Remove the lid and cook for a further 15 minutes.

Put the meat on a baking dish. Mix the mustard with the cream and spread this on the surface. Return to the oven for a further 15-20 minutes.

Strain the gravy from the pan, reserving the onions. Skim the fat from the gravy and mix it with the flour. Return this to the gravy and bring to the boil, stirring all the time. Cool and freeze. Mix the chestnut purée and the onions and season to taste. Freeze in a separate container. Wrap the meat and freeze it.

To serve Thaw the venison and purée overnight and re-heat for 40-60 minutes at 180°C, 350°F/Gas 4. Thaw the gravy.

To make the celeriac croquettes, peel the celeriac and cut into wedges. Cook in boiling, salted water until just tender, then drain and refresh under cold water. Roll in flour, then in beaten egg and crumbs and fry in butter and oil until golden. Spread the hot purée on a serving dish, slice the meat and arrange on top. Re-heat the gravy and spoon on top of the venison. Arrange the croquettes at each end of the dish.

Faisan aux Marrons

Pheasant with Chestnuts
Serves 3-4
This dish can be completely finished, except for the parsley, before freezing. It is better to carve the pheasant when it has cooled and then freeze it in slices—it will then thaw and re-heat more easily.

1 pheasant, drawn and trussed
25 g (1 oz) butter
20 small onions
225 g (8 oz) chestnuts (weight after peeling and skinning)
1 x 15 ml spoon (1 tablespoon) flour
1 wineglass red wine
450-600 ml (¾-1 pint) stock
2 x 5 ml spoons (2 teaspoons) redcurrant jelly
1 orange
bouquet garni
chopped parsley
salt and pepper

Brown the pheasant all over in the butter in a heavy pan, then remove. Peel the onions and chestnuts and add to the pan. Brown well, then stir in the flour and cook for 1-2 minutes. Add the wine, stock and redcurrant jelly. Grate the rind from the orange and squeeze the juice. Add to the pan with the bouquet garni, salt and pepper. Bring to the boil. Replace the pheasant and cover and cook gently for 1-1½ hours over a low heat. Remove the pheasant from the pan and place on a dish. Leave to cool, then carve it and put in a container for freezing. Strain and skim the sauce and pour over the pheasant. Freeze. Freeze the onions and chestnuts for the garnish separately.

To serve Thaw the pheasant and garnish overnight and heat together for 40-60 minutes at 180°C, 350°F/ Gas 4.

Carbonnade de Boeuf Flamande

Flemish Beef Casserole
Serves 4
This casserole goes well with boiled potatoes and vegetables such as sprouts or carrots.

700 g (1½ lb) braising beef
40 g (1½ oz) dripping
6 large onions
2 cloves garlic
1 x 15 ml spoon (1 tablespoon) brown sugar
1 x 15 ml spoon (1 tablespoon) flour
600 ml (1 pint) brown ale
300 ml (½ pint) water or stock
salt and pepper

Cut the meat into large cubes and brown them quickly in very hot dripping, then remove from the pan. Peel and thinly slice the onions and add to the pan. Cook briskly,

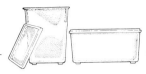

stirring all the time, until they are evenly browned. Pour off any excess fat and return the meat to the pan. Crush the garlic with a little salt and add it with the brown sugar and flour. Stir well and cook for 2-3 minutes. Add the ale and water or stock and season well. Bring to the boil, then simmer very gently for at least 1½ hours. Skim the surface, cool and freeze.

To serve Thaw overnight and re-heat in a casserole for 40-50 minutes at 180°C, 350°F/Gas 4.

L'Estouffat Gascon

Gascon Steak Casserole
900 g (2 lb) chuck steak
100 g (4 oz) streaky bacon in one piece
75 g (3 oz) lean slice ham
50 g (2 oz) dripping
10-20 small onions
2 x 5 ml spoons (2 teaspoons) flour
½ bottle red wine
stock
3-4 tomatoes
3-4 cloves garlic
bouquet garni
salt and pepper

For the garnish
225 g (8 oz) haricot beans
bicarbonate of soda
1 large onion
1 large carrot
2 x 15 ml spoons (2 tablespoons) oil
chopped parsley

Cut the steak into 5-cm (2-in) cubes, removing any excess fat or gristle. Cut the bacon and ham into cubes.

L'Estouffat Gascon—a meaty casserole of chuck steak

Heat the dripping in a heavy pan and brown the steak quickly on all sides. Remove and brown the bacon and ham in the same pan. Remove. Peel the onions and brown them, then return the steak, bacon and ham to the pan. Sprinkle in the flour and cook for 2-3 minutes. Add the wine and enough stock to cover the meat. Skin and de-seed the tomatoes and chop the flesh. Crush the garlic with a little salt and add to the pan with the bouquet garni and some salt and pepper. Cover and simmer gently for 1½ hours. Cool and freeze.

To serve Soak the haricot beans and thaw the casserole overnight. (It is not necessary to re-heat the beef at this stage.) Put the beans in a pan and cover with cold water. Add a pinch of bicarbonate of soda and bring to the boil. Simmer for 10 minutes. Drain and wash the beans and put them back in the pan with fresh water. Simmer for 1 hour, then season and continue cooking until tender. Peel and finely chop the onion and carrot and fry in the oil. Drain the beans and add to the carrot and onion, mix well. Then add to the beef, with a little extra stock if necessary. Cook gently for a further hour and serve with parsley.

Note The casserole can be frozen completed, with the haricot beans added. However, the beans tend to go mushy when frozen so it is more satisfactory to freeze at the stage recommended above.

Bitkis

100-175 g (4-6 oz) stale white bread
cold water
1 medium onion
450 g (1 lb) lean minced beef
chopped parsley
seasoned flour
dripping or oil and butter for frying
salt and pepper

For the tomato sauce
15 g (½ oz) butter
15 g (½ oz) flour
150-300 ml (¼-½ pint) stock
1 x 400-g (14-oz) can tomatoes
1 x 5 ml spoon (1 teaspoon) sugar
bouquet garni
salt and pepper

To finish
1 small carton soured cream

Cut the crusts off the bread and cover with just enough cold water to soak. Peel and finely chop the onion and beat into the minced beef with the parsley and some salt and pepper. Squeeze the bread well and crumble it into the meat. Work together well (preferably using an electric mixer), adding sufficient water to keep the mixture smooth and 'short' in texture. Turn out on to a damp board and shape into small round cakes about 6 x 2·5 cm deep (2½ x 1 in). Roll these in seasoned flour and fry them in dripping or oil and butter until they are brown on both sides. Arrange in a buttered fireproof dish.

To make the tomato sauce, melt the butter in a pan, stir in the flour and cook for 2-3 minutes. Add 150 ml (¼ pint) of the stock gradually. Add the tomatoes, sugar, the bouquet garni and some salt and pepper. Simmer gently for 20-30 minutes, then put through a vegetable mill. Adjust seasoning and thin with a little more stock, if necessary. Pour half the sauce over the fried cakes and cook for 25-30 minutes at 180°-190°C, 350°-375°F/Gas 4-5. Cool and freeze. Freeze the rest of the sauce in a separate container.

To serve Thaw. Re-heat for 40-50 minutes at 180°-190°C, 350°-375°F/ Gas 4-5. Spoon on soured cream.

Côtes de Porc Niçoise

Pork Chops Niçoise
Serves 4

    4 pork chops
    2 x 15 ml spoons (2 tablespoons)
     olive oil
    2 large onions
    1–2 green peppers
    450 g (1 lb) tomatoes
    1 x 5 ml spoon (1 teaspoon)
     tomato purée
    2 cloves garlic
    1 x 5 ml spoon (1 teaspoon)
     potato flour
    chopped parsley
    salt and pepper

Heat the oil in a heavy pan and brown the chops on all sides. Remove from the pan. Peel and chop the onions finely and cook them in the oil until soft. De-seed and chop the peppers and blanch the flesh for 1 minute in boiling salted water. Refresh under cold water and drain. Skin and de-seed the tomatoes and chop the flesh roughly. When the onions are soft, add the tomatoes, peppers, tomato purée and the garlic, crushed with a little salt. Bring to the boil and season well. Replace the chops, cover and cook for 30–40 minutes at 160°–180°C, 325°–350°F/Gas 3-4. Remove the chops and thicken the juice in the pan if necessary, using the potato flour slaked with water. Cool, then put the chops and sauce in a container and freeze.

To serve Thaw overnight and reheat for 40–60 minutes at 180°C, 350°F/Gas 4. Put the chops on a serving dish, spoon the sauce on top and sprinkle with parsley.

Elizabethan Casseroled Pork

Serves 6-8

    2 kg (4½ lb) boned shoulder of pork
    2 x 15 ml spoons (2 tablespoons)
     oil
    3 large onions
    3 large apples

    1 x 15 ml spoon (1 tablespoon)
     flour
    1 head celery
    6 dates
    100 g (4 oz) grapes (optional)
    ½ bottle red wine
    bouquet garni
    1 orange
    1 x 5 ml spoon (1 teaspoon)
     potato flour
    salt and pepper

Skin the pork and tie up neatly. Heat the oil in a large pan and brown the meat quickly on all sides. Remove from the pan. Peel and slice the onions and apples and add to the pan. Rub the pork with the flour and when the apples and onions are brown, put the pork on top of them. Season well. Chop the celery and the dates and skin and pip the grapes (if used). Add all these to the pan with the wine and the bouquet garni. Pare the skin from the orange with a potato peeler and cut into fine julienne strips. Remove the orange segments, discarding all the pith. Add to the casserole and cook for 3 hours at 150°C, 300°F/Gas 2.

Remove the pork, skim the sauce and thicken it slightly if necessary, using the potato flour slaked with a little water. Either slice the meat and freeze it with the sauce poured over it, or freeze the meat whole and the sauce separately.

To serve Thaw overnight and reheat in a casserole for 40–60 minutes at 180°C, 350°F/Gas 4.

Goulash d'Agneau

Lamb Goulash
Serves 6
Boulangère potatoes and broccoli go well with this goulash dish.

    1·5 kg (3 lb) shoulder, scrag end or
     chump end of loin of lamb
    2 x 15 ml spoons (2 tablespoons)
     dripping
    2–3 large onions
    1 x 15 ml spoon (1 tablespoon)
     paprika
    1 x 15 ml spoon (1 tablespoon)
     flour
    600 ml (1 pint) stock
    1 x 15 ml spoon (1 tablespoon)
     tomato purée
    garlic
    1 wineglass white wine
    1 bay leaf
    2–3 large tomatoes
    1 carton yoghurt or soured cream
    chopped parsley
    salt and pepper

Cut the meat into convenient-sized pieces and brown them quickly on all sides in the dripping in a heavy pan. Remove the meat. Peel and thinly slice the onions and brown in the dripping. Stir in the paprika and cook for 2–3 minutes, stirring all the time. Add the flour and continue to cook, stirring, for a further few minutes. Add the stock, tomato purée, garlic crushed with a little salt, wine, bay leaf and salt and pepper. Replace the meat and bring gently to the boil. Simmer gently for 1–1¼ hours or cook for the same

Côtes de Porc Niçoise—a new look for pork chops

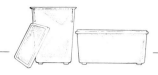

time at 180°C, 350°F/Gas 4.

Skin and de-seed the tomatoes and chop the flesh roughly. When the meat is tender, remove the bay leaf, skim the sauce if necessary and add the tomatoes. Cook for a further 5 minutes. Cool and freeze.

To serve Thaw overnight and re-heat for about 50 minutes at 180°C 350°F/Gas 4. Thicken the sauce with a little slaked potato flour if necessary, then spoon over the yoghurt or soured cream and sprinkle with chopped parsley, just before serving.

Lamb Chops Provençal

4-8 lamb cutlets or chops
2 x 15 ml spoons (2 tablespoons)
 olive oil
2 large onions
3-4 cloves garlic
1 x 15 ml spoon (1 tablespoon)
 flour
700 g (1½ lb) tomatoes, or 1 large
 can tomatoes
1 wineglass white wine
300-450 ml (½-¾ pint) stock
2 x 5 ml spoons (2 teaspoons)
 tomato purée
bouquet garni
chopped parsley
salt and pepper

Trim the cutlets or chops of any excess fat and brown them quickly in the oil. Remove from the pan. Peel and chop the onions and crush the garlic with a little salt. Cook these in the oil until they are golden, then stir in the flour. Cook for 2-3 minutes, stirring. Skin and de-seed the tomatoes and roughly chop the flesh. Add to the pan. If using canned tomatoes drain them and squeeze out the pips, then add to the pan (use the drained juice as part of the cooking liquid with the stock). Cook for a few more minutes, then add the wine, stock and tomato purée. Season well and add the bouquet garni. Replace the meat and simmer gently for 30-40 minutes, either on the hob or in a low oven. Remove the bouquet garni, cool the casserole and freeze.

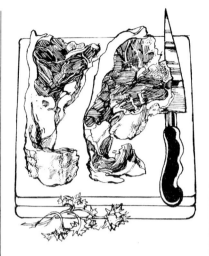

To serve Thaw overnight and re-heat for 40-50 minutes at 180°C, 350°F/Gas 4. Sprinkle with chopped parsley.

Note Try varying this casserole by substituting red wine and 350 g (12 oz) mushrooms for the white wine and tomatoes. The mushrooms should be quartered and added after the stock.

Langue de Boeuf Braisé aux Raisins

Braised Ox Tongue with Raisins
Serves 6-8
Serve glacé carrots and onions and mousseline potatoes with this dish.

1 unsalted ox tongue
25 g (1 oz) butter
1 x 15 ml spoon (1 tablespoon) oil
1 large carrot
1 large onion
1 stick celery
water or stock
1 x 5 ml spoon (1 teaspoon)
 tomato purée
bouquet garni
salt and pepper
For the sauce
100 g (4 oz) stoned raisins
150 ml (¼ pint) red wine
1 carrot
1 onion
bacon rinds
25 g (1 oz) lard or dripping
25 g (1 oz) flour
600 ml (1 pint) stock
mushroom peelings

1 x 5 ml spoon (1 teaspoon)
 tomato purée
bouquet garni
2 x 15 ml spoons (2 tablespoons)
 port or sherry
salt and pepper

Put the raisins for the sauce to soak in the red wine.

Wash the tongue well in cold water. Put it in a large pan and cover with fresh water. Bring to the boil, cook for 5 minutes, then drain. Put in fresh water and bring to the boil again. Season and simmer for about 1 hour, or until the skin peels off easily. Skin the tongue.

Melt the butter and oil in a strong pan and brown the tongue well on all sides. Remove from the pan. Peel and roughly chop the carrot and onion and brown in the butter. Replace the tongue, chop the celery and add to the pan with enough water or stock to come halfway up the tongue. Add the tomato purée, bouquet garni, salt and pepper and cook gently for 3 hours, turning occasionally. Leave to cool.

To prepare the sauce, chop the carrot and onion and fry with the bacon rinds in the lard or dripping until the vegetables are golden brown. Add the flour and cook, stirring all the time, until it browns. Add the stock taken from the tongue, and the wine strained from the raisins. Bring to the boil. Season and add the mushroom peelings and the tomato purée. Add a small bouquet garni and simmer gently for at least 1 hour, skimming frequently, and adding more stock if necessary. Strain into a clean pan, skim, add the port or sherry and the raisins.

When the tongue has cooled, trim the root away, then slice the rest of the flesh diagonally across the grain. Put in a suitable container for freezing, pour the cooled sauce over it and freeze altogether.

To serve Thaw overnight and re-heat in a casserole for 40-60 minutes at 180°C, 350°F/Gas 4.

Note You can mince the trimmed root of the tongue and use it in a spaghetti sauce.

Sweets and Puddings

Apart from the various types of ices, sweets and puddings for freezing tend to divide into three main categories:

rather solid creamy charlottes and mousses, and chocolate puddings; pastry flans and pies;

sponge-cake bases which may be finished off in a variety of ways.

All cream- or chocolate-based puddings which are to be eaten cold should be thawed overnight in the refrigerator. Check the consistency two to three hours before serving. Puddings with a large proportion of butter or chocolate may be too hard, and therefore rather flavourless, if served straight from the refrigerator. They should be served at room temperature. All the puddings marked with a star (★) come into this category.

For storage convenience, it is usually easier to turn puddings out of their moulds or containers before freezing. In such cases, open-freeze (unwrapped on a dish) until they are hard. This type of pudding should be unwrapped and placed on a serving dish immediately after being removed from the freezer.

Pastry dishes need less time to thaw than the more solid types of pudding. Six to eight hours is generally sufficient, and most pastry dishes taste better if they have been warmed through before serving.

The one fruit mousse recipe given in this section could be made with any other fairly thick fruit purée, such as gooseberry, blackcurrant or apricot. It is particularly good for freezing as it contains no stiffly beaten egg white, which is the ingredient that tends to go 'wet' on thawing. Avoid freezing *any* dish that contains more than two beaten egg whites. It is best to choose dishes incorporating no more than one.

Charlotte Louise★

Chocolate Charlotte

175 g (6 oz) unsalted butter
75 g (3 oz) castor sugar
100 g (4 oz) plain chocolate

100 g (4 oz) ground almonds
200 ml (7 fl oz) double cream
16-18 sponge finger biscuits
For decoration
extra cream
pistachio nuts
crystallized violets

Cream the butter and beat in the sugar until the mixture is fluffy and white. Soften the chocolate by covering it with boiling water and letting it stand for 5 minutes. Pour off the water and add the chocolate to the butter and sugar. Mix in the ground almonds. Whip the cream and fold this into the butter mixture.

Cut a circle of greaseproof paper to fit the base of a 1-1.25-litre (1½-1¾-pint) cake tin or charlotte mould. Oil it lightly. Trim the sponge biscuits and stand them round the sides of the mould. Spoon the chocolate mixture into the middle, levelling the top neatly. Stand in a cool place for 1-2 hours. Trim the biscuits to the level of the filling and turn the charlotte on to a dish. Open-freeze and when hard, wrap, label and put it into the freezer.

To serve Thaw overnight in the refrigerator, then remove 1-2 hours before serving. This recipe makes a rather solid pudding, and will therefore be a better texture if served at room temperature. Remove the oiled paper and decorate the top with whipped cream, pistachio nuts and crystallized violets.

Charlotte Malakoff★

Kirsch Charlotte

This recipe is similar in principle to *charlotte Louise*, except that the flavouring is provided by kirsch instead of chocolate, to give a rather more sophisticated taste. The result is very rich, but very good. Incidentally, never decorate with crystallized violets until the last minute as they are inclined to 'weep', spreading an unsightly purple stain.

175 g (6 oz) unsalted butter
175 g (6 oz) castor sugar
175 g (6 oz) ground almonds

1 x 5 ml spoon (1 teaspoon)
vanilla sugar
3 x 15 ml spoons (3 tablespoons)
kirsch
300 ml (½ pint) double cream
16-18 sponge finger biscuits
For decoration
150 ml (¼ pint) double cream
crystallized violets

Cream the butter until it is soft, then beat in the sugar until the mixture is light and fluffy. Stir in the ground almonds, vanilla sugar and kirsch. Whip the cream lightly and fold it into the mixture.

Prepare the charlotte tin in the same way as for *charlotte Louise*, lining it with trimmed sponge fingers. Pour the almond mixture into the middle and leave in the refrigerator for 2-3 hours. Trim the sponge fingers level with the filling and turn the pudding out on to a flat dish. Open-freeze until hard, then wrap, label and put it into the freezer.

To serve Thaw overnight in the refrigerator. When ready to serve,

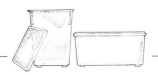

Charlotte Malakoff—the delicate flavour of this charlotte is heightened by a drop of kirsch

 50 g (2 oz) castor sugar
 50 g (2 oz) chopped walnuts
 50 g (2 oz) glacé cherries
 small sherry glass of brandy or rum

Line the base of a 450-g (1-lb) bread tin with oiled greaseproof paper and oil the sides.

 Crush the digestive biscuits roughly with a rolling pin. Put the chocolate in a large bowl and pour boiling water over it. Leave for a few minutes, then pour off the water. Soften the butter and beat it into the melted chocolate. Put the eggs and sugar in a bowl and beat with an electric whisk until thick, white and fluffy. Fold into the chocolate mixture, together with three-quarters of the walnuts and cherries and the brandy or rum. Stir in the crushed biscuits and pour the mixture into the tin. Cover with foil and put in the refrigerator overnight. Dip the mould in hot water and turn the pudding on to a dish. Open-freeze until hard, then wrap, label and return to the freezer.

To serve Thaw overnight and decorate with the remainder of the nuts and cherries. Add some whipped cream, if liked.

decorate with the remaining cream, stiffly whipped, and the crystallized violets.

Le Turinois★

Chestnut and Chocolate Mould
 900 g (2 lb) chestnuts
 vanilla pod
 150 g (5 oz) unsalted butter
 150 g (5 oz) castor sugar
 225 g (8 oz) plain chocolate
 rum or brandy to taste

For decoration
 whipped cream

Skin the chestnuts, by making a nick in the top of each one, plunging them into boiling water a few at a time, for 2-3 minutes, then removing both inner and outer skins. Put the peeled nuts in a pan of cold water with the vanilla pod and simmer until tender. Drain and rub nuts through a sieve or put through a fine vegetable mill.

 Cream the butter and sugar together until white and fluffy. Put the chocolate in a bowl and cover with boiling water. When the chocolate is soft, pour off the water and add the melted chocolate to the butter and sugar with the chestnuts and the brandy or rum. Mix together thoroughly.

 Line the base of a 450-g (1-lb) loaf tin with greaseproof paper and lightly oil both the paper and the sides of the tin. Press the mixture into the tin and leave in a cool place for 6-8 hours. Turn out and open-freeze until hard, then wrap, label and return to the freezer.

To serve Thaw overnight in the refrigerator and serve, cut in slices, with whipped cream.

Chocolate Brandy Cake★

Serves 8-10
This is an excellent pudding for a large party as a little goes a long way.
 225 g (8 oz) digestive biscuits
 225 g (8 oz) plain chocolate
 225 g (8 oz) unsalted butter
 2 eggs

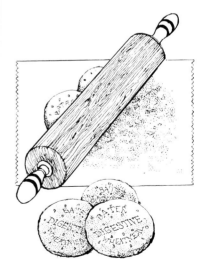

Délice au Chocolat★

Chocolate Delight

As this is a very rich pudding, it would be a good idea to offer fresh fruit as an alternative if serving it at a dinner party.

100 g (4 oz) unshelled almonds
100 g (4 oz) sugar
350 g (12 oz) plain chocolate
100 ml (4 fl oz) boiling water
75 g (3 oz) unsalted butter
1-2 x 15 ml spoons (1-2
tablespoons) rum or brandy
200 ml (7 fl oz) double cream

For decoration
150 ml (¼ pint) double cream

To make the praline, put the almonds and sugar together in a heavy pan and set it over a gentle heat. Stir occasionally until the sugar has melted and turned into a rich caramel. Turn out on to an oiled plate and leave to go cold. Reduce to a powder in a coffee mill or with a pestle and mortar. Weigh out 100 g (4 oz) for this recipe and store the remainder in a screw-top jar.

Break up the chocolate and melt it gently with the water. Cool this, then cream the butter and add the chocolate, praline and rum or brandy. Whip the cream lightly and fold it into the chocolate mixture. Pour into an oiled 1 litre (1½-pint) mould and leave in the refrigerator for at least 4 hours or overnight for use the next day.

Unmould and open-freeze until hard, then wrap, label and return to the freezer.

To serve Thaw overnight and serve the pudding at room temperature, decorated with stiffly whipped cream, piped with a star pipe.

Gâteau Alix★

Rich Chocolate Cake
4 eggs and their weight in unsalted
butter, castor sugar and plain
chocolate
2 x 15 ml spoons (2 tablespoons)
flour

For decoration
300 ml (½ pint) double cream

Melt the butter without browning it. Melt the chocolate in a large bowl over a pan of hot water and, when soft, stir in the butter and sugar. Beat together well, remove from the heat and stir in the flour. Separate the eggs and beat the yolks into the chocolate mixture. Whisk the egg whites stiffly and fold them into the mixture. Pour into a well-greased shallow tin or a 20-cm (8-in) *moule à manqué*. Stand in a bain-marie or baking tin of boiling water and cook for 1-1½ hours at 190°C, 375°F/Gas 5, until the top is crusty and the interior moist. Cool in the tin. As the cake is cooling it will fall to its original level in the tin.

Liqueurs and Spirits
General rules for adding alcohol to a dish are :
for hot dishes, add at a time when the alcohol will be well boiled and thereby reduced and concentrated in flavour ; the alcohol will evaporate, but will enhance the taste ;
for cold dishes, add the alcohol when the dish is cold so that the flavour remains unaltered.

A custard-based pudding should be allowed to cool before alcohol, or any other flavouring, such as nuts or fruit, is added. The flavour of any liqueur will be altered by heating.

Make sure that the crisp top falls back inside the tin too, and does not lodge on the edge. It may be necessary to crack it slightly to make it do this. Leave for at least 4 hours or preferably overnight, and when it has cooled, dip the tin into hot water and unmould on to a dish. Open-freeze until hard, then wrap, label and put back in the freezer.

To serve Thaw overnight and decorate with whipped cream before serving.

Gâteau Chocolat Suisse

Swiss Chocolate Cake

This is more of a cake than a pudding, but it freezes excellently so is good for an emergency.

100 g (4 oz) unsalted butter
100 g (4 oz) plain chocolate
4 eggs
100 g (4 oz) castor sugar
25 g (1 oz) flour
25 g (1 oz) fine white
breadcrumbs
50 g (2 oz) ground almonds

Grease a 17·5-cm (7-in) *moule à manqué* tin and dust it with flour. Line the bottom with paper.

Melt the butter gently and melt the chocolate on a plate placed over a pan of hot water. Separate the eggs and cream the yolks with the sugar until the mixture is white, thick and fluffy. Mix together the flour, breadcrumbs and ground almonds and sieve them.

Add the melted butter gradually to the egg yolk mixture, then stir in the melted chocolate. Whip the egg whites very stiffly and fold them into the chocolate mixture alternatively with the flour, breadcrumbs and ground almonds. Be careful not to overfold at this stage. Just mix sufficiently for everything to be well combined. Pour into the prepared tin and bake for 1 hour at 180°C, 350°F/Gas 4. Turn out and cool on a rack. When cold, freeze the cake.

To serve Thaw overnight and serve in slices.

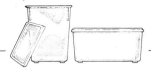

Bonnet Russe

Russian Chocolate Mousse

    15 g (½ oz 1 sachet) gelatine
    3 x 15 ml spoons (3 tablespoons)
      cold water
    4 egg yolks
    75 g (3 oz) castor sugar
    450 ml (¾ pint) milk
    100 g (4 oz) chocolate vermicelli
    150 ml (¼ pint) double cream

For the chocolate sauce

    175 g (6 oz) plain chocolate
    50 ml (2 fl oz) water
    1 x 15 ml spoon (1 tablespoon)
      sugar
    25 g (1 oz) unsalted butter

For decoration

    150 ml (¼ pint) double cream

Soak the gelatine in the water in a small basin. Stand this in a pan of hot water until the gelatine has dissolved.

Beat the egg yolks and sugar together. Bring the milk to the boil and pour it on the egg mixture. Stir well and return to the pan. Cook gently, stirring all the time, until the custard thickens, then remove from the heat and add the dissolved gelatine. Stir well and strain into a clean bowl. Cool, stirring occasionally, until the custard is on the point of setting. Add the chocolate vermicelli. Lightly whip the cream and fold this in too. Pour into a bombe mould and allow to set in the refrigerator for at least 4 hours or overnight. Turn out the mousse on to a dish and open-freeze until hard. Wrap, label and put back in the freezer. Alternatively, freeze the pudding in the mould.

To serve Thaw the mousse overnight in the refrigerator. Whip the cream and pipe on as a decoration. To make the chocolate sauce, break up the chocolate and put it in a pan with the water and sugar. Bring to the boil, stirring frequently and simmer for 5-10 minutes. Cool, then beat in the butter. Leave to go cold. If it is too thick, beat in a little more water. Pour a little round the mousse and serve the rest separately.

Bramble Mousse—a dish with a country ring to its name

Bramble Mousse

    15 g (½ oz, 1 sachet) gelatine
    5 x 15 ml spoons (5 tablespoons)
      cold water
    450 g (1 lb) blackberries
    2 cooking apples
    2 x 15 ml spoons (2 tablespoons)
      sugar
    1 x 15 ml spoon (1 tablespoon)
      water
    3 eggs
    75 g (3 oz) sugar
    150 ml (¼ pint) double cream

For decoration

    150 ml (¼ pint) double cream

Soak the gelatine in the cold water in a small basin. Stand this in hot water until the gelatine has dissolved completely.

Pick over the blackberries, and cut up the apples roughly. Stew together with the 2 x 15 ml spoons (2 tablespoons) sugar and a spoonful of water. When soft, put through a mouli or rub through a sieve. Leave to cool.

Whisk the eggs and the sugar together, preferably with an electric whisk, until thick and fluffy. Strain the gelatine into the mixture, then fold in 300 ml (½ pint) of the cooled blackberry purée. When on the point of setting, lightly whip the cream and fold it in. Pour this into a soufflé dish and leave to set. Freeze. Freeze the remainder of the purée separately.

To serve Thaw the mousse and the purée overnight in the refrigerator. Just before serving, pour the purée over the top of the mousse. Whip the cream and pipe a lattice pattern over the top with a small star pipe. Alternatively, omit the purée altogether and just decorate the mousse with whipped cream.

Landais or Bavarois Praliné

Praline Cream

15 g (½ oz, 1 sachet) gelatine
5 x 15 ml spoons (5 tablespoons) cold water
450 ml (¾ pint) milk
4 egg yolks
100 g (4 oz) castor sugar
1 x 5 ml spoon (1 teaspoon) vanilla sugar
3 x 15 ml spoons (3 tablespoons) kirsch, brandy or rum
100 g (4 oz) praline (see recipe for delice au chocolát)
200 ml (7 fl oz) double cream

For decoration

150 ml (¼ pint) double cream

Soak the gelatine in the water in a small basin. Stand in a pan of hot water until the gelatine has dissolved. Heat the milk. Mix the egg yolks and sugars together in a bowl and pour the hot milk on to them. Stir well and return to the pan. Cook gently, stirring all the time until the custard thickens. Remove from the heat and stir in the dissolved gelatine. Strain into a bowl and leave to cool, stirring occasionally.

When the custard is on the point of setting, stir in the kirsch, brandy or rum and the praline. Whip the cream lightly and fold it in. Pour into a soufflé dish and leave to set in the refrigerator. Freeze.

To serve Thaw overnight in the refrigerator and decorate with the cream, stiffly whipped.

Note For a lighter mousse, fold in 2-3 stiffly beaten egg whites after the cream and before putting the pudding into the serving bowl. (Do not try to freeze this version.)

Babas au Rhum

Rum Babas

The dough used here is exactly the same as savarin dough, except that

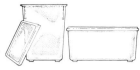

savarin is cooked in a ring mould and does not include currants. It is soaked in syrup and brushed with apricot glaze in the same way that rum babas are.

225 g (8 oz) flour
pinch salt
25 g (1 oz) sugar
15 g (½ oz) yeast
1 x 15 ml spoon (1 tablespoon)
 warm water
3 eggs
75 g (3 oz) melted butter
50 g (2 oz) currants

For the syrup
350 g (12 oz) sugar
600 ml (1 pint) water

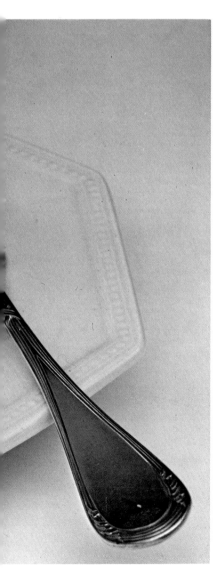

peel of 1 lemon
vanilla pod
rum to taste

For the apricot glaze
450 g (1 lb) apricot jam
4-5 x 15 ml spoons
 (4-5 tablespoons) water

Sift the flour, salt and sugar into a warm bowl. Dissolve the yeast in the water. Make a well in the centre of the flour and pour in the yeast. Beat the eggs lightly and add to the bowl. Then beat the ingredients together with your hand, gradually incorporating the flour to form a smooth mixture. When the mixture is quite smooth, add the melted, cooled butter and beat together well. Add the currants. Cover the bowl and leave in a warm place for 1 hour, until the dough has doubled in size. Knock down and put into 10-12 well-buttered castle pudding tins, filling them two-thirds full. Put in a warm place to let the dough 'prove', (by which time it will have risen to the top of the tins). Bake for 10-15 minutes at 210°C, 425°F/Gas 7. Turn out of the tins and cool. Open-freeze until hard, then put together in a polythene bag, label and return to the freezer.

To serve Thaw overnight and warm through. To make the syrup, put the sugar and water in a pan with the peel from the lemon and the vanilla pod. Bring to the boil and simmer for 5 minutes. Pour boiling syrup over the warm babas and sprinkle each one with rum. Handle very carefully as they tend to break up when properly soaked. To make the apricot glaze, put the jam and water in a pan, bring to the boil, then sieve and re-boil until the mixture is well reduced. Brush the babas liberally with the hot glaze. Serve the babas warm or at room temperature.

Babas au Rhum and the Savarin shown here both use the same basic dough. The Savarin does not include currants and is cooked in a ring mould rather than the smaller, individual baba tins.

Gâteau Basque
Covered Almond and Jam Flan
225 g (8 oz) flour
100 g (4 oz) softened butter
75 g (3 oz) sugar
50 g (2 oz) ground almonds
3 egg yolks or 2 small eggs
grated rind of 1 lemon
450 g (1 lb) apricot or other jam
egg white
castor sugar

Put the flour on a board and make a well in the centre. Put the softened butter, sugar, almonds, eggs and lemon rind into this. Work all the ingredients together with your fingertips into a smooth paste. Knead this lightly and put it in a cool place to relax for 30 minutes.

Cut off one-third of the pastry and roll out the remainder quite thickly. Use it to line a 20-cm (8-in) flan ring. Prick the base and fill to three-quarters full with jam. Roll out the remaining pastry and cover the flan, trimming round the edges and pressing the pastry together firmly. Brush the top with egg white, and use the back of a knife to decorate the tart with curved lines from the centre to the edge. Dust with castor sugar and leave for 10 minutes. Bake for about 30 minutes at 200°C, 400°F/Gas 6, reducing the heat after 10-15 minutes if the top is browning too quickly. Leave to cool on a rack, then freeze.

To serve Thaw overnight and warm slightly before serving.

Pastry
A 225-g (8-oz) quantity of shortcrust pastry, using 225 g (8 oz) flour, is sufficient to line and cover a 20-cm (8-in) flan or pie dish, or line 2 x 15-cm (6-in) flan dishes. As a smaller quantity than this is hard to make, use any leftover trimmings to make tartlet cases, which will freeze well.

Gâteau Flamand

Cherry and Kirsch Flan
You could use rich shortcrust pastry
(see Greek honey pie) instead of
pâte sucrée for this gâteau if you
prefer.

For the pâte sucrée
150 g (5 oz) flour
75 g (3 oz) butter
50 g (2 oz) sugar
2 egg yolks

For the filling
75 g (3 oz) crystallized cherries
2 x 15 ml spoons (2 tablespoons)
* kirsch or rum*
100 g (4 oz) butter
100 g (4 oz) sugar
2 eggs
100 g (4 oz) ground almonds
25 g (1 oz) flour
25 g (1 oz) flaked almonds

To finish
4-6 x 15 ml spoons (4-6
* tablespoons) glacé icing*

To prepare the pâte sucrée, put the
flour on a board and make a well in
the centre. Put the rest of the pastry
ingredients into this and work together with the fingers of one hand,
gradually drawing in the flour. Mix
to a firm paste, then put on one side
to relax for 20-30 minutes.

To prepare the filling, cut the
cherries in half and macerate them
in the kirsch or rum. Cream the
butter and sugar together, beat in
the eggs, then stir in the almonds and
the flour, with the kirsch drained
from the cherries.

Roll out the pastry and line a deep
20-cm (8-in) flan ring. Prick the
base and leave it for 10 minutes.
Arrange most of the cherries in the
bottom, reserving a few for decoration, then pour in the filling. Sprinkle the flaked almonds over the top.
Bake for 40-45 minutes at 190°C,
375°F/Gas 5 and cool on a rack.
Freeze.

To serve Thaw overnight. Just
before serving brush the top with
thin glacé icing and decorate with
the remaining cherries.

Greek Honey Pie

Rich shortcrust pastry
150 g (5 oz) flour
75 g (3 oz) softened butter
1 egg yolk
1 x 5 ml spoon (1 teaspoon) sugar
lemon juice

For the filling
225 g (8 oz) cream or cottage
* cheese*
25 g (1 oz) castor sugar
4 x 15 ml spoons (4 tablespoons)
* clear honey*
2 eggs
pinch cinnamon

To prepare the pastry, put the flour
on a board and make a well in the
centre. Put all the other pastry
ingredients into this and work them
together to a smooth paste with your
fingertips. Leave on one side to
relax for 20-30 minutes, then roll
out and line a 20-cm (8-in) flan ring.
Leave for 10 minutes while you
prepare the filling.

Mash the cheese with a fork and
beat in the sugar. Warm the honey
very slightly and beat the eggs. Beat
these into the cheese with the cinnamon. Pour into the flan case and
bake for 30 minutes at 200°C,
400°F/Gas 6. Sprinkle with a little
more cinnamon or cinnamon sugar.
Cool and freeze.

To serve Thaw the flan overnight
and heat through slightly. Serve
warm.

Tarte Beauceronne

Cream Cheese and Raisin Flan
pâte sucrée made with 150 g (5 oz)
* flour (see gâteau flamand) or*

Rich shortcrust pastry
225 g (8 oz) flour
150 g (5 oz) butter
1 x 5 ml spoon (1 teaspoon) sugar
1 egg yolk
lemon juice
iced water
pinch of salt

For the filling
50 g (2 oz) butter
2 x 15 ml spoons (2 tablespoons)
* sugar*
225 g (8 oz) curd or cream cheese

50 g (2 oz) raisins
2 x 15 ml spoons (2 tablespoons)
* double cream*
3 eggs
2 x 15 ml spoons (2 tablespoons)
* flour*

Make the pâte sucrée or the rich
shortcrust pastry in the usual way
(see *gâteau flamand* or Greek honey
pie respectively). Leave in a cool
place to relax, then roll out and line
a 20-cm (8-in) flan ring.

To prepare the filling, cream the
butter and sugar together in a warm
bowl. Sieve the cheese and stir in
with the raisins and cream. Separate
the eggs and beat in the yolks and
then the flour into the cheese mixture. Whisk the egg whites stiffly
and fold into the mixture. Pour this
into the flan ring and bake for 35-40
minutes at 190°-200°C, 375°-400°F/
Gas 5-6. Remove from the oven and
leave to cool in the ring. Open-
freeze until hard, then wrap, label
and put back in freezer.

To serve Thaw overnight and serve
cold with whipped cream.

Tarte aux Cerises Danoise

Danish Cherry Flan
rich shortcrust pastry made with
* 225 g (8 oz) flour*
225 g (8 oz) stoned black cherries
* or 1 x 400-g (14-oz) can cherries*
100 g (4 oz) ground almonds
100 g (4 oz) icing sugar
2 eggs

Make the pastry in the usual way.
Roll out and line a 20-cm (8-in) flan
ring. Prick the base and fill with the
cherries (well drained if using canned
ones). Mix the ground almonds and
sugar together and beat in the eggs,
one at a time. Pour this mixture over
the cherries and bake for 25-30
minutes at 200°C, 400°F/Gas 6. Cool
on a rack and freeze when cold.

To serve Thaw overnight and
serve cold, with whipped cream if
desired.

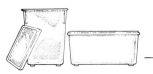

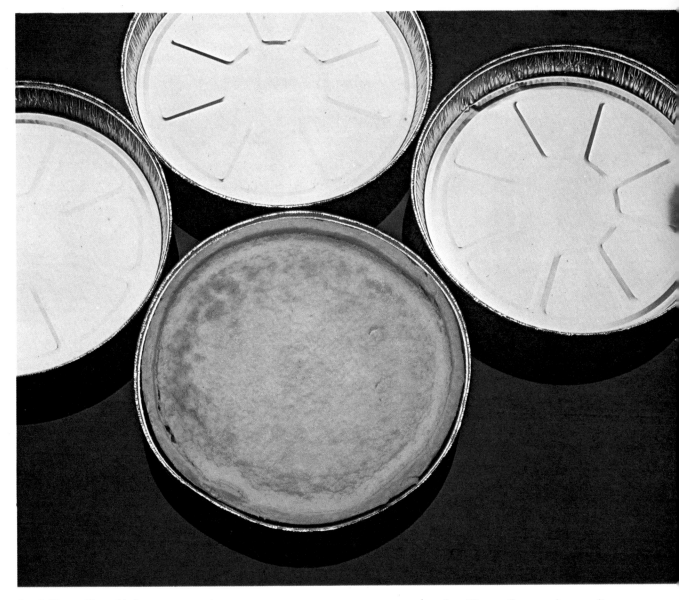

Greek Honey Pie—this is an unusual flan of rich shortcrust pastry filled with a mixture of cream cheese, honey and spice

Tarte Canelle

Blackcurrant Cinnamon Flan
*225 g (8 oz) blackcurrants
sugar
1 x 15 ml spoon (1 tablespoon)
water*

For the pastry
*175 g (6 oz) flour
75 g (3 oz) softened butter
75 g (3 oz) sugar*

*2 egg yolks
2 x 5 ml spoons (2 teaspoons)
cinnamon*

Pick the blackcurrants off the stalks and put in a pan with lots of sugar and the water. Cook gently, then increase the heat and cook quickly to a thick purée. Cool this on a plate. (This freezes well on its own as a compôte.)

To make the pastry, put the flour on a board and work in all the other ingredients in the usual way. Leave in a cool place for 30 minutes to relax. Then roll out and use to line a 15-cm (6-in) flan ring. Trim off any excess pastry, prick the base and fill with the blackcurrant purée. Roll out the pastry trimmings, cut into strips and arrange in a lattice pattern across the filling. Brush with water and dust with castor sugar. Bake for 20-25 minutes at 200°C, 400°F/Gas 6. Remove the ring and cool on a rack. Freeze.

To serve Thaw overnight in the refrigerator or for 6-8 hours at room temperature. Warm slightly before serving.

Emergency Dishes and Ices

This small section comprises dishes which can be cooked (or served) straight from the freezer. Dishes from other sections, for example *coquilles de poisson au cidre* and *moules aux herbes* from Soups and Starters, could be treated in the same way, providing they are frozen in suitably small portions. The croquettes in this section can be taken from the freezer and deep-fried in their frozen state, or can be partially thawed first. Serve them immediately after frying.

Homemade ices vary considerably in their consistency when they come out of the freezer. They should be checked a few hours before serving. If they are very hard, put them in the refrigerator for an hour or so to soften them a little. The serving bowl should be chilled

Croquettes de Volaille

Chicken and Mushroom Croquettes
> *100 g (4 oz) button mushrooms*
> *lemon juice*
> *2 x 15 ml spoons (2 tablespoons) water*
> *65 g (2½ oz) butter*
> *50 g (2 oz) flour*
> *450 ml (¾ pint) milk*
> *3 egg yolks*
> *50-75 g (2-3 oz) cooked chicken*
> *dried breadcrumbs, flour, beaten egg for coating*
> *fat for frying*
> *parsley*
> *salt and pepper*

Wipe the mushrooms and put in a pan with a squeeze of lemon juice, the water, 15 g (½ oz) butter and pepper and salt. Cover and bring to the boil. Remove from the heat and leave to stand for 5 minutes.

Then prepare a béchamel sauce, by melting the remaining butter in a pan, adding the flour and cooking for 2-3 minutes, stirring all the time. Add the milk and bring to the boil, still stirring. Cook for a further 2-3 minutes. Remove the pan from the heat, season the sauce well and beat in the egg yolks. Chop the chicken

and the cooked mushrooms and add to the sauce. Adjust the seasoning and pour the mixture into a shallow greased tin. Level the surface with a palette knife and leave to go cold, preferably overnight in the refrigerator.

When completely cold, plunge the tin into hot water and turn the mixture on to a floured pastry board. Cut into even-sized pieces and coat these first in flour, then in beaten eggs and finally in dried breadcrumbs. If you beat the egg with a little salt and 1 x 15 ml spoon (1 tablespoon) oil, it will stick to the croquettes better. Neaten the croquettes with a palette knife and leave for at least 30 minutes before frying. Alternatively, freeze them at this stage, before frying.

Heat a pan of oil so that it is almost smoking (about 185°C, 365°F). Lay the croquettes in a frying basket and plunge into the fat. Cook for 1-2

Croquettes Bruxelloises—a perfect stand-by meal for the unexpected guest

minutes. Remove and drain on kitchen paper. Do not fry for too long or the filling will boil and burst the outer crust. Let the croquettes cool, and when quite cold, open-freeze until hard. Put into a polythene bag, seal, label and return to the freezer.

To serve Either take the croquettes from the freezer and fry them straight away in hot fat, or let them thaw a little first. Fry some parsley at the same time, and serve this with them.

Croquettes Bruxelloises

Cheese Croquettes
> *50 g (2 oz) butter*
> *50 g (2 oz) flour*
> *450 ml (¾ pint) milk*
> *50-75 g (2-3 oz) cheese*
> *3 egg yolks*
> *flour, beaten egg and dried crumbs for coating*
> *deep fat for frying*
> *parsley*
> *salt and pepper*

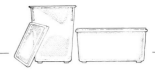

First, make a béchamel sauce by melting the butter, stirring in the flour and cooking for 2-3 minutes. Add the milk gradually and bring the sauce to the boil, still stirring. Cook for a further few minutes. Remove from the heat and season well. Grate the cheese and beat it in, followed by the egg yolks. Adjust the seasoning. Pour the mixture into a shallow, greased tin, level the surface with a buttered palette knife, and leave, preferably overnight, to go completely cold. Finish, freeze and serve exactly as for *croquettes de volaille*.

Curried Fish Croquettes

225-350 g (8-12 oz) haddock or
* coley fillet*
1 shallot or small onion
150 ml ($\frac{1}{4}$ pint) milk
salt, pepper and nutmeg
For the sauce
25 g (1 oz) butter
approx. 1 x 5 ml spoon (1
* teaspoon) curry powder*
25 g (1 oz) flour
2 egg yolks
salt and pepper
For the coating
1 egg
1 x 15 ml spoon (1 tablespoon) oil
flour
dried crumbs

Skin the fish and put in a buttered fireproof dish. Chop the shallot or onion and scatter it over the fish. Season well and pour the milk on top. Cover with buttered paper and cook for about 15 minutes at 180°C, 350°F/Gas 4. Cool the fish, drain and reserve the liquor, and flake the flesh, discarding the bones.

To make the sauce, melt the butter and add the curry powder. Cook for 1-2 minutes, then stir in the flour and cook for 1-2 minutes more, stirring all the time. Add 300 ml ($\frac{1}{2}$ pint) of the reserved cooking liquor, stirring all the time. Bring to the boil and cook for 1-2 minutes. Remove from the heat and beat in the egg yolks. Season well, stir in the fish and turn the mixture

into a well buttered shallow tin. Leave to go completely cold, preferably overnight in the refrigerator. Finish, freeze and serve exactly as for *croquettes de volaille*.

Sardine Puffs

225 g (8 oz) puff pastry (see Basic
* Recipes) or use pastry trimmings*
1 can sardines
lemon juice
1 egg
salt, pepper and paprika

Make the puff pastry and leave it on one side. Drain the sardines and mash them, discarding the bones, with a little lemon juice and seasoning.

Roll out the pastry thinly and cut into 2 rectangular strips 7.5 x 30 cm (3 x 12 in). Put the sardine mixture on one half of each strip and brush the edge with beaten egg. Fold over as for a sausage roll, pressing the edges together well to seal them. Cut into 5-7.5-cm (2-3-in) lengths. Place on a baking sheet and freeze. Pack into freezing containers when hard and put back in freezer.

To serve Take the puffs from the freezer and place on baking sheets. Brush with egg and cook for 10-15 minutes at 210°C, 425°F/Gas 7 until they are brown and crisp.

Note The puffs can also be deep-fried, in which case cut the pastry into circles, place a small amount of filling on half of them, brush the edges with beaten egg and cover each one with another pastry circle. Leave for 15 minutes and fry as for croquettes for 4-5 minutes.

Gâteau Ganache

Chocolate and Hazelnut Gâteau
Raspberries or strawberries, mixed with whipped cream or a praline-flavoured cream can be used as alternative fillings.

4 egg whites
250 g (9 oz) castor sugar
125 g (4$\frac{1}{2}$ oz) ground hazelnuts,
* browned*
For the filling and sauce
150 g (6 oz) plain chocolate
150 ml ($\frac{1}{4}$ pint) water
50 g (2 oz) sugar
300 ml ($\frac{1}{2}$ pint) double cream
icing sugar

Butter 2 x 20-cm (8-in) sandwich tins and dust them with flour. Line the bases with discs of non-stick paper.

Whisk the egg whites until they are very stiff and fold in the sugar, then the ground hazelnuts. Divide this mixture between the 2 tins and bake for 30-40 minutes at 190°C, 375°F/Gas 5. Turn out and allow to cool on a rack. Freeze.

To serve Allow 1 hour for the meringue to thaw, but take it from the freezer some time before you want to serve it (see below).

To prepare the filling break up the chocolate and put it in a pan with the water. Let it melt slowly, then stir well and add the sugar. Simmer for 10-15 minutes and cool. Whip the cream lightly and fold in 2-3 x 15 ml spoons (2-3 tablespoons) of the chocolate mixture. Spread the cream on one half of the cake and cover with the other half. Leave in the refrigerator for at least 4 hours, so the cake softens a little. Dust with icing sugar and serve the rest of the chocolate sauce separately.

Parfait au Café

Coffee Parfait

Parfaits are traditionally made in a parfait mould, which is narrow and conical in shape. However, any suitable mould or plastic container can be used.

100 g (4 oz) castor sugar
5 egg yolks
strong instant coffee
300 ml (½ pint) double cream

Put the sugar in a pan with 2-3 x 15 ml spoons (2-3 tablespoons) water and boil until a thread forms in cold water (125°C/240°F). Pour the boiling syrup on to the egg yolks and beat until the mixture is cold, thick and fluffy (this is best done in an electric mixer). Flavour with strong instant coffee. Whip the cream lightly and fold into the egg mixture. Pour into a mould, cover and freeze.

To serve Unmould by dipping the mould in cold water and turning the parfait on to a plate. Serve with tuiles or other dessert biscuits.

Note This type of ice can be frozen satisfactorily in the ice-making compartment of a refrigerator. It does not need to be stirred while it freezes.

Parfait Praliné

For a chocolate-flavoured ice add 100 g (4 oz) melted plain chocolate instead of the praline.

50-75 g (2-3 oz) praline made
with 50 g (2 oz) each sugar
and unblanched almonds
100 g (4 oz) castor sugar
2-3 x 15 ml spoons
(2-3 tablespoons) water
5 egg yolks
300 ml (½ pint) double cream

Make the praline (see *landais* or *bavarois praliné*—Sweets and Puddings).

To prepare the ice, put the castor sugar in a pan with the water and boil until a thread forms in cold water. This occurs at 125°C, 240°F. Pour the boiling syrup on to the egg yolks and beat until the mixture is cold, thick and fluffy, using an electric mixer. Flavour with the praline. Whip the cream lightly and fold into the egg and praline mixture, then pour into a parfait mould and freeze.

To serve As for *parfait au café.*

Glace aux Fraises

Strawberry Ice Cream

450 g (1 lb) strawberries
100 g (4 oz) icing sugar
juice of half a lemon
double cream

Rub the strawberries through a nylon sieve and measure the resulting purée. Stir in the icing sugar and lemon juice. Take an equal quantity of double cream, whisk lightly and fold into the strawberry purée. Freeze for at least 2 hours, stirring frequently. Transfer to a plastic container and store in freezer.

Glace aux Abricots

Apricot Ice Cream

450-700 g (1-1½ lb) apricots
75 g (3 oz) sugar
1 x 15 ml spoon (1 tablespoon)
lemon juice
1 x 15 ml spoon (1 tablespoon)
Cointreau or apricot brandy
200 ml (7 fl oz) double cream

Wash the apricots, sprinkle with

sugar and bake in a covered casserole at 130°C, 250°F/Gas ½-1 until soft. Put through a sieve or mouli, allow to cool and add the lemon juice and liqueur. Whip the cream lightly and fold into the purée. Put into the freezing tray of a refrigerator and stir every 20-30 minutes until the mixture is nearly firm. Pack into an ice-cream mould and put in the freezer.

Glace aux Framboises

Raspberry Ice Cream

150 g (5 oz) sugar
5 x 15 ml spoons (5 tablespoons)
water
4 egg yolks
450 g (1 lb) raspberries
water or lemon juice (see recipe)
450 ml (¾ pint) double cream

Put the sugar in a pan with the water and bring to the boil. Bring to 125°C/240°F, then pour the boiling syrup on to the egg yolks and beat, preferably with an electric mixer, until the mixture is thick, white and fluffy. Leave to cool.

Put the raspberries through the fine blade of a mouli or nylon sieve. If necessary, make the resulting purée up to 450 ml (¾ pint) with water or lemon juice.

Whip the cream lightly. Mix the purée into the egg mixture, then fold in the cream. Pour this into a shallow tray and freeze, stirring every 30 minutes or so until the mixture begins to harden. Put into a mould and freeze.

Note Raspberries are sometimes too acid to add to cream without the addition of the egg mousse. This method of making fruit ices is used with most acid fruit purées, to avoid curdling the cream.

Orange Water Ice

7 large oranges
1 lemon
175 g (6 oz) sugar
300 ml (½ pint) water
1-2 egg whites
Cointreau or Grand Marnier

Orange Water Ice—a cool and refreshing way to end a meal and particularly welcome after rich or highly spiced dishes

Pare the outer skin from 1 orange and the lemon, using a potato peeler. Put in a pan with the sugar and water and bring slowly to the boil. Boil gently for 6-7 minutes. Cool.

Cut the tops of the remaining oranges and carefully scoop out the pulp. (The handle of a metal spoon makes a good scoop.) The oranges must be clean inside but the skin *must not* be broken.

Crush the pulp in a liquidizer or put through a vegetable mill and strain into a measure. Add the juice from the lemon and the extra orange and, if necessary, make it up to 300 ml ($\frac{1}{2}$ pint) with water. Strain the cold syrup into the orange juice and mix well. Put in a freezing tray and freeze, stirring the mixture every 15 minutes until it is mushy.

Whisk the egg whites stiffly and fold in. Mix well and freeze again until the mixture is stiff (there is no need to stir it now). Put a few drops of liqueur into the orange shells and place in the refrigerator. Fill with the ice-cream when it is firm, replace the lids and keep in the freezer until required.

Note This ice can be frozen in a normal plastic container, but it looks more attractive served in the orange skins.

Gooseberry Cream Ice

> 450 g (1 lb) gooseberries
> 2-3 x 15 ml spoons
>   (2-3 tablespoons) sugar
> 2-3 x 15 ml spoons
>   (2-3 tablespoons) water
> 150 g (5 oz) sugar
> 4 egg yolks
> 300 ml ($\frac{1}{2}$ pint) double cream
> green food colouring

Wash the gooseberries and put them in a pan with the first quantity of sugar and the water. Cover and stew gently until tender. Put through a vegetable mill, then cool.

Put the remaining sugar in a pan with just enough water to dissolve it. Bring to the boil and boil to 125°C/ 240°F. Pour on to the egg yolks and beat until the mixture is thick, white and fluffy, preferably using an electric mixer. Leave to cool.

Whip the cream lightly. Fold in the purée into the egg mixture and colour it a delicate green. Fold in the cream. Place in the freezer and freeze until mushy. Pack into a container and freeze until hard.

Gooseberry Water Ice

If possible, add elderflowers to the gooseberries as you cook them.

> 300 ml ($\frac{1}{2}$ pint) gooseberry purée
> 225 g (8 oz) sugar
> 300 ml ($\frac{1}{2}$ pint) water
> 1 lemon
> green food colouring

Prepare the gooseberry purée in the same way as for gooseberry cream ice. Put the sugar and water together in a pan. Pare the rind of the lemon and add to the sugar and water. Boil together for 7-8 minutes, then cool. Squeeze the lemon and add the juice to the syrup, removing the lemon rind. Add the gooseberry purée to the syrup and colour it a very delicate green. Chill the mixture, then freeze until slushy, stirring frequently. Pack into a container and place in the freezer until required.

Basic Recipes

As well as completely prepared dishes, it is very useful to keep a selection of stocks, sauces and stuffings in the freezer to use with dishes as required. Make these in fairly large quantities and then store them in smaller, convenient-sized cartons. A stock of these can enable you to make a comparatively complicated dish quickly and easily.

Other recipes on the following pages include different types of pastries and also sponge fingers, which are used in several of the puddings.

Duxelle

This is a form of mushroom stuffing which is used in many dishes. It is a good way in which to keep flat mushrooms. Wipe them, but do not peel or wash them unless they are very dirty.

1 large onion
225 g (8 oz) mushrooms
25-50 g (1-2 oz) butter
salt and pepper

Peel and finely chop the onion and wipe and finely chop the mushrooms. Melt the butter and fry the onion until golden. Add the mushrooms and cook briskly, stirring very occasionally, until the mixture is quite dry. Season well and leave to cool. Freeze in 100 g (4 oz) containers. Thaw for 4-6 hours in a warm room or overnight in the refrigerator before using.

Note Parsley or tomato purée can be added to duxelle. Freeze the dish plain and add the other ingredients when it is thawed and ready for use.

Breadcrumbs

Breadcrumbs are not easy to make from sliced bread. It is better to buy an uncut tin loaf, let it go stale for a day or two, then crumb the whole loaf. A large loaf produces about 350 g (12 oz) crumbs, which will freeze well and thaw very quickly. Freeze them in a large bag (a small amount can be broken off as required) or several small bags, as preferred. Dry the crusts in the oven and use for dried crumbs to coat food for deep frying.

Basic Herb Stuffing

3 large onions
50 g (2 oz) butter
350 g (12 oz) fresh breadcrumbs
50 g (2 oz) suet
2 lemons or 1 lemon and 1 orange
1 egg
chopped herbs, parsley, majoram and sage
salt and pepper

Peel and finely chop the onions and fry them in the butter until soft. Cool and add the rest of the ingredients, seasoning well. Divide into 4 and freeze in small containers. Do not freeze this stuffing for longer than 6 weeks, and make sure it is completely thawed before use.

Alternative flavourings

chopped, soaked apricots
chopped celery
chopped apple
chopped, soaked prunes

Omit the herbs and add any of the above ingredients to the *thawed* stuffing.

White Stock

veal or beef bones
1 large onion
1 large carrot
1 stick celery
1 leek
salt and pepper

Put the bones in a saucepan and cover with cold water. Bring to the boil and skim thoroughly. Peel the onion and carrot, wash the celery and leek (leaving them all whole) and add to the pan. Season well and simmer gently for 3 hours. Strain and cool, then skim the stock and freeze it.

A pressure cooker considerably cuts down the cooking time and makes excellent stock. If you can find a pig's trotter or some chickens' feet to add to the stock, it is more likely to set well.

Make chicken stock in the same way as above, using the chicken carcass and giblets (except the liver) instead of veal or beaf bones.

Make brown stock using beef or lamb bones, but brown these and the onions and carrots in the oven first. Then transfer them to a pan with the other vegetables and seasoning. Deglaze the roasting pan with water and add this to the saucepan, then proceed in the same way as for white stock.

Chestnuts

There is no quick way to skin chestnuts—it is always a slow business. The easiest way to do it, however, is to make a nick in the top of each one, then plunge a few at a time into boiling water.

Allow them to boil for 2-3 minutes, then remove with a slotted spoon and peel off the inner and outer skin. Apart from discolouring slightly, chestnuts freeze well for six weeks or so, which helps in getting ahead with advance Christmas preparations.

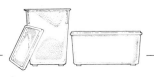

Fish Stock or Fumet

This is very useful for fish soups and for making sauces for fish dishes.

>900 g (2 lb) fish skin and bones
> from white fish
>1 onion
>parsley
>salt and pepper

Wash the fish skin and bones and put in a pan. Just cover with water. Peel and thinly slice the onion and add to the pan with the parsley, salt and pepper. Bring to the boil and simmer for 20 minutes. Strain, cool and freeze.

Note Do not simmer fish stock for longer than 20-30 minutes as it becomes bitter.

Sauce Provençale

This sauce is superb for re-heating prawns or mussels and is delicious with spaghetti and other pasta. Add garlic to taste. Traditionally, this sauce is strongly flavoured.

>1 large onion
>2 x 15 ml spoons (2 tablespoons)
> oil
>100 g (4 oz) mushrooms
>2-3 cloves garlic
>1 x 15 ml spoon (1 tablespoon)
> flour
>1 wineglass white wine
>300-450 ml (½-¾ pint) stock
>1 x 15 ml spoon (1 tablespoon)
> tomato purée
>bouquet garni
>salt and pepper

Peel and finely chop the onion. Fry in the oil until it is golden. Wipe and chop the mushrooms and crush the garlic with a little salt. Add half the mushrooms and all the garlic to the onions and fry briskly for 2-3 minutes. Stir in the flour and cook for a few minutes before adding the wine, stock, tomato purée, bouquet garni, salt and pepper. Simmer for 20 minutes, then strain and add the rest of the mushrooms. Simmer for a further 2-3 minutes. Cool and freeze.

Stocks and sauces, used with discretion, can transform the most humble dish into a dinner party treat. A selection of basic sauces and stocks can be ready to use in the freezer

Sauce Tomate

This is a very good way of freezing surplus tomatoes, which do not freeze satisfactorily whole.

>450 g (1 lb) tomatoes
>1 onion
>1-2 bacon rinds
>25 g (1 oz) butter or dripping
>25 g (1 oz) flour
>150 ml (¼ pint) stock
>1 x 5 ml spoon (1 teaspoon) tomato
> purée
>1 x 5 ml spoon (1 teaspoon) sugar
>½ clove garlic
>bouquet garni

Roughly chop the tomatoes, peel and chop the onion and dice the bacon rind. Fry the onion and bacon rind in the butter until soft, then stir in the flour and cook for 2-3 minutes, stirring all the time. Add the stock, chopped tomatoes, tomato purée, sugar, garlic (crushed with a little salt) and the bouquet garni. Season well, bring to the boil and simmer gently for 20 minutes. Pass through a sieve or a vegetable mill and use as required.

Sponge Fingers

Sponge fingers are very useful for serving with fruit fools or to put round charlottes. Although it is easy to use bought ones, homemade ones have a better flavour and are not too difficult to make. However, they do need a certain dexterity, so make them when you have lots of time and freeze them. If you are going to use them fresh (without freezing) make them at least 24 hours before you need them, or they will be too soft. They keep well in a tin for 3-4 days.

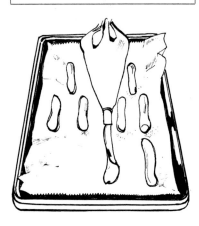

Sponge Fingers

3 eggs
90 g (3½ oz) castor sugar
75 g (3 oz) flour
vanilla sugar

Separate the eggs and cream the yolks with the sugar until the mixture is thick and fluffy. Sift the flour and vanilla sugar together and pour it on top of the yolk mixture.

Do *not* mix it in. Whisk the egg whites stiffly and then fold into the yolk mixture with the flour, *taking great care not to overfold*. Put the mixture into a forcing bag with a 1 cm (½ in) plain pipe. Pipe fingers on to baking sheets covered with greaseproof paper. Dust with icing sugar and bake for 10-15 minutes at 150°-160°C, 300°-350°F/Gas 2-4. Carefully remove from the paper with a knife and cool on a rack. When quite cold, pack gently into boxes and freeze.

Pâte Feuilletée

Puff Pastry
225 g (8 oz) plain flour
225 g (8 oz) butter
approx. 150 ml (¼ pint) water
pinch salt

Sift the flour on to a pastry board or marble slab. Make a well in the centre, add a pinch of salt and 75-100 ml (3-4 fl oz) ice cold water. Draw the flour into the centre, little by little, with your fingers until you have a sauce-like consistency. Now rub the flour lightly between your fingers until it is flaky and crumbly. Add the rest of the water gradually, kneading the dough lightly until soft and smooth. Wrap in a clean cloth and leave in a cool place for 20 minutes, or overnight if more convenient.

Put the dough on a floured surface and roll it out to the size of a tea-plate. Tap the butter lightly with the rolling pin until it is the same consistency as the dough. Place on dough. Fold the edges of the dough over the butter. Make sure the edges meet and that no butter is showing. Tap the edges gently with the rolling pin to seal them and to elongate the dough slightly.

Keeping the edges straight and the ends as square as possible, roll out the dough in a long strip (but do not roll quite to the ends). Fold the strip into three (one end to the middle, the other end overlapping). Give the pastry a half turn so the fold is on the left side. Tap it with

the rolling pin to seal it, then repeat the process. Fold again in the same way. Leave the pastry to relax in a cool place for 20 minutes, then repeat the rolling and folding process twice more. Leave to relax for a further 20 minutes, then give the pastry two more rollings and foldings. (Each roll and fold is known as a 'turn', and six turns complete the pastry.) Leave to relax for another 20 minutes: the pastry is then ready to use.

Pastry

Most types of pastry freeze well. Puff pastry, either bought or homemade, freezes very well in a raw state, but is best eaten on the day it is cooked. Thaw the frozen pastry overnight in the refrigerator before using.

Choux pastry will also freeze well cooked and is particularly easy to make. It is mainly associated with eclairs and profiteroles, but also makes an excellent container for savoury fillings, such as those made for vol-au-vents. If it is to be served hot, the choux can be cooked in advance and frozen. Re-heat by filling with hot filling and baking for about 5-10 minutes only.

Rich shortcrust pastry, as used for pissaladière (Soups and Starters), freezes well both cooked and raw. When freezing it raw, shape it into the flan case or ring first, otherwise it takes a very long time to thaw.

Eat your way round the calendar

Like the weather, dishes have seasons. Some famous recipes would be wholly inappropriate at the wrong time of the year. The dishes that follow are divided into seasonal suitability. There are enticing recipes for spring, summer, autumn and winter—for the sunshine months and the bleak, stormy months. Quantities given are sufficient for eight people unless otherwise stated.

**Smoked Mackerel
Mousse**

**Carré d'Agneau
Lorraine
Pigeons à la Normande**

**Macaroons
Montmorency**

*Smoked Mackerel Mousse—so good
it looks more like a super dessert
than a delicious and subtly
flavoured first course*

This delicious menu includes a
choice of main courses, as pigeons
are not always easy to obtain.

The lamb dish is a very tasty
alternative. Serve it with haricot
beans cooked in stock, drained well,
and with a good knob of parsley
butter stirred in.

Smoked mackerel is now widely
available. Its strong taste makes it
ideal for mousses and pâtés. This
mousse recipe freezes well, so it can
be made in advance. Allow 24
hours' thawing time in the refrigerator and decorate only an
hour or so before serving.

There is a recipe for macaroons,
which forms the basis of the pudding, in the Basic Recipes section.
If you prefer, you could use commercially made ones.

Smoked Mackerel Mousse

*2 smoked mackerel, weighing
700 g (1½ lb) altogether
250 g (8 oz) cream cheese
1 x 5 ml spoon (1 teaspoon)
creamed horseradish
2 x 15 ml spoons (2 tablespoons)
mayonnaise
5 x 15 ml spoons (5 tablespoons)
double cream*

For the sauce

*1 small onion
300 ml (½ pint) milk
1 bay leaf
25 g (1 oz) butter
25 g (1 oz) flour
15 g (½ oz, 1 sachet) gelatine
4 x 15 ml spoons (4 tablespoons)
white wine, or water and lemon
juice
salt and pepper*

For decoration

*cucumber, black olives and/or
shelled prawns*

To prepare the sauce, peel and slice
the onion finely and put it in a pan
with the milk, bay leaf, salt and
pepper. Bring to the boil gently,
then put on one side for 10 minutes
to infuse. Melt the butter in a pan
and add the flour. Cook gently for
1-2 minutes, stirring all the time.
Gradually strain in the flavoured
milk, stirring continuously to keep
the sauce smooth. Bring to the boil,
stirring continuously and cook for
2-3 minutes. Meanwhile, put the
gelatine and wine in a small bowl
and stand in hot water until the
gelatine has dissolved. Strain into
the sauce, beat well, cover and leave
on one side to cool.

Remove all the skin and bones
from the mackerel, pound the flesh
and put in a liquidizer. Add the
cream cheese and the cold sauce and
liquidize together. Add seasoning,
to taste, and the creamed horseradish. Turn into a bowl and fold in
the mayonnaise. Lightly whip the
cream and when the mousse is on
the point of setting, fold in the
cream.

Turn the mixture into a 15-cm

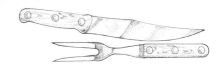

(6-in) soufflé dish and put in the refrigerator to set. Decorate and serve with cucumber and olives.

Carré d'Agneau Lorraine

Best End Neck of Lamb à la Lorraine
2 best end necks of lamb,
  each with 8 bones
5 rashers streaky bacon
4 shallots or small onions
6 carrots
4 leeks
3 x 15 ml spoons (3 tablespoons)
  olive oil
garlic
6 tomatoes
300–450 ml (½–¾ pint) stock
bouquet garni
breadcrumbs
chopped parsley
salt and pepper
beurre manié (optional)

Remove chine bones from the joints and trim the cutlets, or ask the butcher to do this for you. Remove rind from bacon and chop. Peel and chop the shallots or onions and carrots. Wash the leeks thoroughly and slice them. Heat the oil in a large flameproof casserole. Fry the meat until golden on all sides. Remove, then fry the chopped bacon and onion until golden. Add the carrots and leeks and brown lightly. Replace the joints on top of the vegetables. Crush the garlic with a little salt. Skin the tomatoes, remove the pips and chop the flesh. Add the garlic and tomatoes to the pan. Season, pour in the stock and add the bouquet garni. Cover with the lid and cook at 180°C, 350°F/ Gas 4 for about 1 hour. Ten minutes before dishing up, remove the lid and sprinkle the joints with bread-crumbs and chopped parsley. Allow to brown.

To serve, put the joints on a warm serving dish. Skim off any fat from the sauce and boil the sauce briskly for 1–2 minutes. If you like, thicken with beurre manié made with 12 g (½ oz) each of butter and flour. Pour the sauce around the meat.

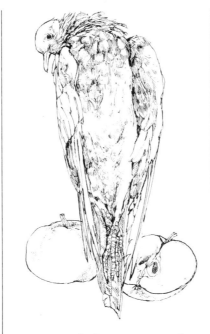

Pigeons à la Normande

Pigeons in Cider with Apples
6–8 pigeons
75 g (3 oz) butter or dripping
4 large onions
6 cooking apples
1 x 15 ml spoon
  (1 tablespoon) flour
600 ml (1 pint) stock
300 ml (½ pint) dry cider
bouquet garni
butter for frying
8 rashers streaky bacon
chopped parsley
salt and pepper

Melt the butter or dripping in a large flameproof casserole and brown the pigeons well on all sides. Remove from the pan. Peel and slice the onions and add to the pan. Peel, core and cut 3 of the apples into slices and add to the pan. Let the onions and apples brown well, then stir in the flour and cook for 2–3 minutes. Add the stock, cider, bouquet garni and seasoning.

Split the pigeons in half and remove the backbone with scissors. Return the birds to the pan, cover with a lid, then simmer very gently for 1–2 hours, depending on the age of the pigeons. (The older they are the longer they will take to cook.)

Add more stock to the pan during cooking if necessary. Meanwhile peel and core the remaining apples, cut into rings and fry in a little butter until golden brown. Remove the rind from the bacon, roll up the rashers and cook in the oven or under the grill until crisp. Keep apples and bacon warm.

Serve the pigeons on a warm dish. Strain the sauce, skim and boil rapidly to reduce it slightly. Pour over the birds and garnish with apple rings and bacon. Sprinkle with chopped parsley.

Macaroons Montmorency

2 x 400-g (14-oz) cans black
  cherries
6 large macaroons (make double
  quantity if using homemade
  recipe)
2–3 lumps of sugar
2 oranges
600 ml (1 pint) double cream
2 egg whites
2 x 5 ml spoons (2 teaspoons)
  arrowroot
kirsch

Drain the cherries and remove the stones. Boil the cherry syrup and reduce until it thickens. Leave to cool, then pour a little into a glass dish. Break up the macaroons and add half to the syrup in the dish. Cover with the cherries and add the rest of the macaroons. Rub the sugar lumps on the orange rind so they absorb the zest. Crush the lumps finely. About 3 hours before serving, whip the cream until just thick, then fold in the orange sugar. Whisk the egg whites stiffly and fold into the cream. Pile on top of the macaroons and chill in the refrigerator.

Squeeze the juice from the oranges and add to the rest of the syrup. Bring to the boil, then thicken with arrowroot, first mixed to a smooth paste with a little water. Cool this sauce and flavour with kirsch to taste. Serve separately from the pudding.

Spring Menu No. 2

Bisque de Crevettes

Canard au Cidre

Mousse au Café
Tartlettes au
Gingembre

The delicately flavoured soup that starts this special meal is particularly well worth making if you can obtain the small shrimps, which are more economically priced than the larger variety.

Duck is also something of a luxury as there is less meat for weight on a duck or goose than on other birds. Cooked in this way, the cider and apples counteract the rich flavour of the bird, making it particularly delicious. If you have to keep it hot in its sauce for long before serving, re-skim the surface of the sauce at the last minute.

The duck needs to be prepared on the day of the dinner party, but the soup and both puddings could be largely prepared in advance. The strong, clean taste of coffee makes a good finale to this meal, as do the sharply flavoured ginger tartlets. These are basically a variation on brandy snaps. A variety of fillings can be used for them. Mandarin oranges or cherries mixed with lightly whipped cream would be delicious. The quantities given here make 24 tartlets. Unfilled, they will keep well in a tin, but handle them carefully as they are very fragile. The filling is sufficient for 10-12 tartlets. Whatever filling you choose, do not put it into the tartlets until just before you serve them as they will go soft very quickly once they are filled.

Garlic
A crown or head of garlic is composed of several segments called cloves. These vary greatly in size, which together with the fact that individual tastes also differ makes it difficult to specify the exact amount of garlic required in a recipe. Apart from a few Provençal or Mediterranean dishes, nothing should taste really strongly of garlic. It should always be a background flavour. Experience will tell you how much you need to use, but do not use more than one or two cloves unless a recipe stipulates more.

Cloves of garlic should be peeled and crushed with a little salt. This enables them to be worked into a paste, which will dissolve during cooking. Garlic presses, though widely used, only serve a really useful purpose when garlic has to be added raw to a salad or an uncooked pâté.

Do not buy more than one or two crowns of garlic at a time as it withers fairly quickly, particularly in the autumn, winter and spring months. This does not apply to fresh garlic bought in strings in French or Spanish markets, which will keep its flavour for some time if stored in a cool, airy place.

Bisque de Crevettes
Shrimp Soup
> 450 g (1 lb) unshelled shrimps
> 1 large carrot
> 2 large onions
> 2 sticks of celery
> garlic
> 25 g (1 oz) butter
> 1 x 15 ml spoon
> (1 tablespoon) oil
> 1 wineglass white wine
> 1-1.5 litres (1½-2 pints) light
> chicken or fish stock
> 3-4 tomatoes
> (or 1 x 400-g/14-oz can)
> 1 x 5 ml spoon (1 teaspoon)
> tomato purée
> 15 g (½ oz) cream of rice or
> arrowroot
> 2 x 15 ml spoons (2 tablespoons)
> brandy or sherry
> chopped parsley
> paprika, salt and pepper

Peel and finely chop the carrot and onions. Wash and finely chop the celery, and crush the garlic with a little salt. Melt the butter and oil in a heavy-based pan and fry the chopped vegetables for about 5 minutes. Add the unshelled shrimps, reserving 15-20 of the largest for garnish, and continue to cook the soup, stirring frequently, for another 5 minutes. Add the wine, stock, tomatoes (roughly chopped) and tomato purée. Season to taste with paprika, salt and pepper.

Simmer the soup for 20-30 minutes. Liquidize or put through a mouli. Strain back into a clean pan. Re-heat and adjust the seasoning.

Mix the cream of rice or arrowroot to a smooth paste with a little cold water and add slowly to the boiling soup, stirring continuously until it thickens slightly. Add the brandy or sherry. Serve garnished with the remaining shelled shrimps and chopped parsley.

Canard au Cidre
Duck in Cider
> 2 ducklings, weighing 1·5-2
> kg (3½-4 lb) each
> 100 g (4 oz) butter
> 1·5 kg (3 lb) apples
> 1 lemon
> ½ litre (1 pint) dry cider

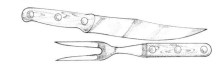

200 ml (7 fl oz) double cream
potato flour
salt and pepper

Unless you have a particularly good carver in the family, it is usually wiser to carve ducks in the kitchen and serve the joints on a serving dish. You will find it speeds the serving considerably.

Truss the ducks and season them well. Rub the breasts with 50 g (2 oz) butter and then roast at 190°C, 375°F/Gas 5 for 40-50 minutes. Turn and baste regularly. Pour 2 x 15 ml spoons (2 tablespoons) of water down the side of the ducklings 15 minutes before the end of the cooking time. Remove the birds from the oven and keep them warm.

Meanwhile, peel, core and quarter the apples. Squeeze the juice from the lemon, rub the apple flesh with it and sauté the quarters in the remaining butter. Keep them warm.

Strain the fat from the roasting pan and add the cider. Bring to the boil, stirring round the pan to deglaze. Boil rapidly to reduce the liquid by a third, then add the cream. Season well and boil for 2-3 minutes. If this liquid appears too thin, thicken with a spoonful of potato flour, first mixed to a smooth paste with a little water.

Carve the duck and arrange on a warm serving dish. Put the apple pieces around it and pour the hot sauce on top.

Mousse au Café

Coffee Mousse
15 g (½ oz, 1 sachet) gelatine
4 eggs
75 g (3 oz) castor sugar
1½ x 15 ml spoons (1½ tablespoons)
 instant coffee
500 ml (¾ pint) milk
25 g (1 oz) walnuts
300 ml (½ pint) double cream

Put the gelatine in a small basin with 5 x 15 ml spoons (5 tablespoons) cold water. Stand in a pan of hot water until the gelatine dissolves. Leave to cool.

Canard au Cidre

Separate the egg yolks from the whites and cream the yolks thoroughly with the sugar. Dissolve the coffee in 2 x 15 ml spoons (2 tablespoons) hot water. Heat the milk, add the coffee and pour over the yolks and sugar. Mix well, return to the milk pan and cook over a low heat, stirring continuously, until the custard coats the back of the spoon. Do not boil. Remove from the heat and leave to cool slightly. Then stir in the softened gelatine. Leave in a cool place, stirring from time to time, until the custard begins to set round the edge. Chop the walnuts and add to the custard. Whisk the egg whites stiffly and whisk the cream lightly. Fold in the cream and then the egg whites. Pour into a glass dish or soufflé dish and leave in the refrigerator to set. Decorate with stars of whipped cream.

Tartlettes au Gingembre

Ginger Tartlets
75 g (3 oz) plain flour
1 x 5 ml spoon (1 teaspoon)
 ground ginger
75 g (3 oz) butter

75 g (3 oz) golden syrup
75 g (3 oz) sugar
1 lemon

For the filling
300 ml (½ pint) double cream
6-7 pieces stem ginger
1 x 15 ml spoon (1 tablespoon)
 brandy
1 egg white

Sift the flour and ginger together on to a warm plate. Melt the butter, syrup and sugar together, but do not overheat. Squeeze the lemon juice and stir into the syrup mixture with the flour and ginger (re-sifted). Mix thoroughly. Place small spoonfuls on a buttered baking sheet, allowing room between each as they will spread in the cooking. Bake at 150°C, 300°F/Gas 2 for 7-10 minutes. Remove carefully and cool over the base of inverted jam jars, which should be lightly oiled for the first batch of tartlets. Put on a wire rack when they are cool and crisp.

To make the filling, whip the cream until stiff. Chop most of the ginger and stir into the cream with the brandy. Whisk the egg white stiffly and fold into the cream. Then fill each tartlet with some of this mixture and top each one with a small slice of ginger.

Spring Menu No. 3

Grapefruit Special
Potage Bonne Femme

Poulet aux Amandes

Oranges à la Reine

A large amount of the preparation for this meal can be done in advance. If you are serving the soup you can make it, omitting the cream, herbs and butter, and freeze it until required. In any event, take advantage of leeks being in season at this time and freeze a batch of the basic soup to make into vichyssoise later. If serving the grapefruit starter, the dressing could be made the day before and kept in the refrigerator, but assemble the fruit and vegetables just before serving for maximum freshness and crispness.

The basic chicken dish could also be frozen adding the almonds when it is re-heated. The pulp can be scooped from the oranges and frozen together with the shells. Always allow 24 hours for casseroles to thaw and 5-6 hours for cakes and cooked pastry.

Grapefruit Special

4 small grapefruit
3-4 dessert apples
6-8 sticks celery
1 x 225-g (8-oz) can whole
  kernel sweet corn
150 ml (¼ pint) double cream
lemon juice
sugar, salt and pepper

For the dressing

1 egg
2 x 15 ml spoons (2 tablespoons)
  tarragon vinegar
2 x 15 ml spoons (2 tablespoons)
  castor sugar
paprika

Make the dressing. Put the egg, vinegar and sugar in a bowl and stand this over a pan of hot water. Whisk the mixture until it begins to thicken. Remove from the pan and whisk until cool. Chill.

Cut each grapefruit in half and remove the flesh from the pith. Put flesh in a nylon strainer and stand over a bowl to drain. Remove all pith from the inside of the grapefruit and chill the halves. Cut the apples into quarters, remove the core and chop the flesh roughly. Wash and chop the celery and drain the sweet corn. Combine with the drained grapefruit flesh in a bowl.

Whip the cream lightly and add some of the reserved grapefruit juice and a little lemon juice. Stir in the dressing to taste and season well. Just before serving, stir the fruit and vegetables into the cream mixture and pile into the grapefruit halves. Sprinkle with a little paprika.

Potage Bonne Femme

3 large leeks
750 g (1½ lb) potatoes
50-75 g (2-3 oz) butter
2 litres (3 pints) water or chicken
  stock
salt and pepper
4 x 15 ml spoons (4 tablespoons)
  double cream
chopped parsley, chives or chervil
extra butter

Wash the leeks thoroughly and slice finely. Peel the potatoes and dice into small cubes. Melt the butter in a large pan and cook the leeks gently until soft and shining. Add the potatoes and cook for a further 2-3 minutes. Add the stock, season well and bring to the boil. Simmer gently for 25-30 minutes. Put soup through the coarse and then the fine plate of a vegetable mill. Alternatively, liquidize and strain or put

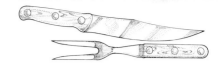

through a mouli. Re-heat and adjust seasoning. Just before serving, add cream, chopped herbs and a nut of butter to each individual dish.

Poulet aux Amandes
Chicken with Almonds
2 chickens, weighing 1·5 kg
  (3½ lb) each
50-75 g (2-3 oz) butter
1 x 15 ml spoon (1 tablespoon)
  oil
4 large onions
6 large tomatoes
cinnamon
saffron
1 litre (1¾ pints) chicken stock
75 g (3 oz) blanched almonds
100 g (4 oz) sultanas
325 g (12 oz) patna rice
chopped parsley
salt and pepper

Joint the chickens. Heat 50 g (2 oz) of the butter and oil in a large pan and fry the chicken joints until they are golden brown. Remove from the pan. Peel and chop the onions. Skin the tomatoes, remove the pips and chop the flesh. Add the onions and tomatoes to the pan and cook until the onions are soft, stirring frequently to prevent the ingredients sticking. Season with salt, pepper and a pinch of cinnamon and saffron. Add the stock to the pan. Replace the chicken, bring to the boil and simmer gently for 30 minutes.

Meanwhile, heat the remainder of the butter and toss the almonds in it until they are crisp and golden. Add to the chicken with the sultanas and cook for a further 10 minutes.

Cook the rice in boiling salted water for 14 minutes. Drain, then rinse, first under cold, then under hot water. Put in a dish with a nut of butter and leave to dry off in a warm oven.

When ready to serve, pile the chicken joints in the centre of the serving dish and arrange the rice around them. Re-boil the sauce, adjust the seasoning if necessary, and pour over the chicken. Sprinkle with chopped parsley.

Note If the sauce is a little thin, thicken with 1 x 5 ml spoon (1 teaspoon) arrowroot, mixed to a paste with water. Add this to the sauce and let it boil for a minute or two, until it thickens.

Oranges à la Reine
Orange Creams
  8 oranges
  additional orange juice (optional)
  icing sugar
  20 g (¾ oz, 7½ sheets, 1½ sachets)
    gelatine
  300 ml (½ pint) double cream
  red colouring
  pistachio nuts or crystallized violets

Grapefruit Special and Oranges à la Reine—both dishes give great scope for presentation

Cut the tops off the oranges and scoop out the pulp. Pass through a vegetable mill and make up the liquid to 600 ml (1 pint) with water or additional orange juice. Sweeten to taste with icing sugar. Put the gelatine in a small basin with 6 x 15 ml spoons (6 tablespoons) cold water and stand in a pan of hot water until the gelatine has dissolved. Add to the orange juice and strain. Stir the orange mixture until almost set in a basin standing on ice. Half fill the orange shells and put in the refrigerator to set.

Whip the cream stiffly and fold into the remaining jelly. Colour pink with a few drops of red colouring. Put the mixture in a piping bag fitted with a star pipe and pipe into the tops of the orange shells. Just before serving, decorate with pistachio nuts or crystallized violets.

Jointing a chicken
Remove the trussing string, and with the bird on its side, lift each leg away from the body and cut through the skin Pull the thigh joint out of its socket then remove the entire leg by cutting through the tendons. Put the bird on its back, pulling out the wings to balance it. Remove the wings with a good slice of breast meat allowing the knife to 'fall' on—and cut through— the wing joint. The top section of the carcass can be cut away with scissors and the breast cut in two. Divide each leg into two by cutting through the joint, leaving the piece of the lower leg on the drumstick until cooked to prevent shrinkage.

Avocado Mousse

Mouton Farcie
aux Epinards

Orange Curd Cream
Raspberry Shortcake

The slight richness of this main course is well offset by the delicately flavoured avocado mousse starter and the tangy orange pudding or the fresh raspberry shortcake. Take advantage throughout the summer of the soft fruits in season and use them wherever possible.

The avocado mousse can be made economically by using slightly brused avocados, which are often sold quite cheaply. It can be made the day before, but should not be unmoulded until the last possible minute as it will discolour very quickly.

The lamb is stuffed with an unusual mixture of lambs liver, pork and spinach and is served with a red wine sauce. Ask your butcher to bone the meat when you buy it or order it; it is quite difficult to do yourself unless you know the procedure.

Assemble the raspberry shortcake at the last possible moment. Even fresh fruit will make the cake go soggy if left for long.

Avocado Mousse

2–3 ripe avocado pears,
depending on size
15 g ($\frac{1}{2}$ oz, 1 sachet) gelatine
300 ml ($\frac{1}{2}$ pint) stock
1 lemon
150 ml ($\frac{1}{4}$ pint) cream
$\frac{1}{2}$ onion
50 g (2 oz) shelled prawns
4 x 15 ml spoons (4 tablespoons)
mayonnaise (see Basic Recipe)
Worcestershire sauce
salt and pepper
For the garnish
1 green pepper
watercress
olives

Avocado Mousse made with prawns, onion, cream and mayonnaise

Soak the gelatine in 5 x 15 ml spoons (5 tablespoons) cold water. Add 3 x 15 ml spoons (3 tablespoons) boiling stock to dissolve it, then add to the rest of the stock. Squeeze the juice from the lemon and add this. Lightly whip the cream. Peel and grate the onion and chop the prawns. Mash the avocado pears thoroughly, then fold in the grated onion, chopped prawns, mayonnaise, cream and stock (when on the point of setting). Season to taste with salt, pepper and Worcestershire sauce. Pour the mixture into a lightly oiled 1-1.5-litre (2-2$\frac{1}{2}$-pint) ring mould and leave to set in the refrigerator for at least 4 hours or, better still, overnight.

Just before serving the mousse, blanch the green pepper and chop it. Dip the mould into hot water, dry and turn out on to a flat serving dish. Decorate with chopped pepper, watercress and olives (or any other crisp salad).

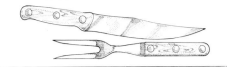

Mouton Farcie aux Epinards

Spinach-stuffed shoulder of lamb
1 boned shoulder of lamb weighing
  approx. 2 kg (4½ lb)
100 g (4 oz) lambs liver
225 g (8 oz) pork fillet
2 shallots
450 g (1 lb) fresh spinach or 1 large
  packet frozen leaf spinach
1 clove garlic
1 egg
butter or dripping
salt and pepper
For the sauce
300 ml (½ pint) stock
150 ml (¼ pint) red wine
1 x 5 ml spoon (1 teaspoon)
  tomato purée
2 x 5 ml spoon (2 teaspoons) potato
  flour
salt and pepper
Chop the lambs liver and fry lightly in butter. Mince the liver with the

pork fillet. Peel and finely chop the shallots and fry until soft. Wash the spinach well and blanch for 2-3 minutes in boiling water. Rinse under cold water and drain well, squeezing out any excess water, then chop it roughly. Add the spinach to the minced meat with the fried shallots, garlic crushed with a little salt, beaten egg and some salt and pepper. Mix thoroughly, stuff the mixture into the boned shoulder and sew up. Roll up the meat and tie at frequent intervals. Put in a roasting tin, rub the outside with butter or dripping, sprinkle with salt and pepper and cook for 1½-2 hours at 190°C, 375°F/Gas 5.

When the lamb is cooked, remove from the tin, discard the strings and put on a warm serving dish. Drain the excess fat from the roasting tin and add the stock and wine. Stir around as the liquid comes to the boil, then add the tomato purée and some seasoning. Slake the potato flour with a little cold water and add it gradually to the boiling sauce, until the required consistency is reached.

Slice the meat and serve with a little sauce poured over it. Serve the remainder of the sauce separately.

Orange Curd Cream

4 oranges
450 g (1 lb) cream or curd cheese
100 g (4 oz) castor sugar
300 ml (½ pint) double cream
Grate the rind from the oranges on to the cheese. Remove all the skin and pith and put the flesh in a liquidizer with the sugar. Liquidize, then add the cheese and liquidize again. Whip the cream lightly and add to the liquidizer. Liquidize for a second. Pile the mixture into individual glasses and chill until ready to serve; this dish should be eaten the same day.

Decorate with a little extra grated or pared orange rind or orange segments.

Raspberry Shortcake

Raspberries that have been frozen without sugar can be used for this recipe, although fresh ones are better. Wet fruit tends to soak the biscuit base, making it soggy very quickly.
100 g (4 oz) flour
75 g (3 oz) butter
35 g (1½ oz) icing sugar
1 egg yolk
450 g (1 lb) raspberries
4 x 15 ml spoons (4 tablespoons)
  redcurrant or raspberry jelly
150 ml (¼ pint) double cream
Sieve the flour on to a board and make a well in the centre. Add the softened butter, sugar and egg yolk. Use the tips of your fingers to work all the ingredients together into a crumbly texture and then knead it to form a smooth dough. Leave in a cool place for at least 30 minutes, before rolling out into a 20 cm (8 in) circle, about 0·5 cm (¼ in) thick. Place on a baking sheet, prick well and cook for 15-20 minutes at 180°C, 350°F/Gas 4. Slide on to a rack and cool.

Shortly before serving, arrange the raspberries on the base. Heat the jelly to a smooth glaze with a little water and brush over the raspberries. Whip the cream and pipe it round the edge of the cake.

**Melon Salad
Cream of Broad Bean
Soup**

Poulet Froid Sultane

**Délice de Fraises au
Fromage
Galette de Noisettes
aux Pêches**

This melon salad makes a fresh tasting starter for a summer evening's dinner party. Fresh herbs, which are almost always available at this time of year, will put this dish into the luxury class. However, if you feel that in view of the cold main course a hot starter would be preferable, use the fresh broad beans that are in season to make a delicious soup. Quantities of this can be frozen (without the cream and herbs) for a welcome addition to an autumn or winter meal.

Serve a selection of fresh salads (rice, lettuce and watercress, onion and tomato) with the cold chicken, which has a mild curry flavour.

Both puddings take advantage of fruits that are in season. The strawberry pudding takes only moments to prepare and should not be made more than a few hours in advance, leaving just enough time to chill it slightly before serving. The peach pudding involves a little more preparation, but the pastry circles will store for two or three days in an airtight tin. They need very careful handling as they are fragile.

Melon Salad

*1 large ripe honeydew melon
225 g (8 oz) grapes
1 large cucumber
450 g (1 lb) tomatoes*

*1 x 15 ml spoon (1 tablespoon)
chopped parsley
1 x 15 ml spoon (1 tablespoon)
chopped mint, chives and chervil*
For the dressing
*2 x 15 ml spoons (2 tablespoons)
wine vinegar
1 x 5 ml spoon (1 teaspoon) sugar
1 x 5 ml spoon (1 teaspoon)
French mustard
6 x 15 ml spoons (6 tablespoons)
oil
salt and pepper*

Cut the melon in half and discard the seeds. Scoop out the flesh using a teaspoon or small ball cutter. Skin and de-seed the grapes. Peel the cucumber, remove the seeds, dice, sprinkle with salt and leave for 20 minutes. Skin and pip the tomatoes and cut into segments.

Drain and dry the cucumber and mix in a bowl with the melon, tomatoes and grapes. Mix all the dressing ingredients together and pour over the ingredients in the bowl. Cover and chill for 2-3 hours. Just before serving, stir in the herbs. Serve in soup cups or bowls.

Cream of Broad Bean Soup

*700 g (1½ lb) shelled broad beans
sprig of savory or thyme
1 small onion
50 g (2 oz) butter
35 g (1½ oz) flour
2 litres (3 pints) stock
8 x 15 ml spoons (8 tablespoons)
double cream
chopped parsley or chervil
salt and pepper*

Cook the beans in boiling salted water (just enough to cover) with the savory or thyme. Drain and reserve the liquid. Refresh beans under the cold tap and drain well again.

Meanwhile, peel and chop the onion finely. Fry in melted butter until soft. Stir in the flour and cook for another 2-3 minutes. Add the stock and bring to the boil. Season to taste and simmer for 10 minutes. Reserve a few beans for garnish

and add the rest to the soup. Simmer for a few minutes, then pass through a vegetable mill.

Just before serving, remove the outer skins from the reserved beans and add, with some of the cooking liquor, to the soup. Mix the cream and parsley or chervil together in a bowl. Bring the soup back to the boil and pour a little on to the cream mixture. Stir well, tip back into the pan and re-heat gently. Adjust seasoning and serve.

Poulet Froid Sultane

Sultan's Cold Chicken
*2 chickens, weighing 1·5 kg
(3½ lb) each
1 x 15 ml spoon (1 tablespoon) oil
15 g (½ oz) butter
2 large onions
1 x 15 ml spoon (1 tablespoon) curry
powder
1 x 15 ml spoon (1 tablespoon)
flour
300 ml (½ pint) white wine
300-500 ml (½-¾ pint) stock
(jellied if possible)
1 x 5 ml spoon (1 teaspoon)
tomato purée
3 peppers (red and green)
300 ml (½ pint) double cream
salt, pepper and paprika*

Joint the chickens (see Spring Menu No. 3). Heat the oil and butter in a

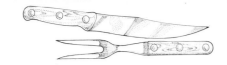

large pan and fry the joints until golden brown. Remove from the pan. Peel and finely chop the onions and fry for 2-3 minutes. Stir in the curry powder and cook for another 1-2 minutes. Add the flour, cook for a few more minutes, then add the wine, stock and tomato purée. Bring to the boil and season well. Replace the chicken joints and simmer gently for 30-40 minutes, until the chicken is tender. Allow to cool.

Meanwhile, de-seed the peppers and chop them coarsely. Blanch in boiling salted water for 1-2 minutes, then refresh under the cold tap. Drain. Remove the chicken when almost cold and arrange on a dish. Skim the sauce. Lightly whip the cream and fold in with the peppers when the sauce is about to set. Spoon over the chicken and chill.

Note: If the stock was not jellied, add 1 x 5 ml spoon (1 teaspoon) dissolved gelatine to the sauce while warm.

Délice de Fraises au Fromage

Strawberry Cream Cheese Delight
  1 kg (2 lb) strawberries
  325 g (12 oz) cream cheese
    (Petit Suisse or similar)
  2 x 15 ml spoons (2 tablespoons)
    milk
  300 ml (½ pint) cream
  75 g (3 oz) castor sugar
Sieve two-thirds of the strawberries, reserving the best ones for decoration. Beat the cheese with the milk until smooth. Half-whip the cream and beat into the cheese mixture until stiff. Add the sugar gradually continuing to beat the mixture. Finally, stir in the strawberry purée. Pile into a glass bowl or individual dishes and decorate.

Galette de Noisettes aux Pêches

Hazelnut Cake with Peaches
When fresh peaches are not available use canned white ones. The pastry in this recipe needs very careful handling and can be difficult to lift on to a baking sheet. To overcome this, roll it out on the sheet. When cooked, leave the pastry to cool for 5 minutes before transferring to a wire rack.
  75 g (3 oz) hazel nuts
  100 g (4 oz) flour
  75 g (3 oz) castor sugar
  75 g (3 oz) butter
  4 fresh peaches
  300 ml (½ pint) double cream
  icing sugar
Roast the nuts in the oven until they are brown. Rub them in a cloth to remove the outer skins, then grate them in a nut mill. Sieve the flour on to a board and make a well in the centre. Into this put 50 g (2 oz) sugar, the softened butter and the nuts. Mix the butter and sugar together, gradually working in the nuts and flour until you have a smooth dough. Leave in a cool place for 20 minutes, then roll out and cut into three circles of about 20 cm (8 in) diameter (use a saucepan lid as a guide). Put on buttered baking sheets, prick well and bake for 15-20 minutes at 180°C, 350°F/ Gas 4. Cool on a rack.

Scald, skin and slice the peaches. Put in a basin and sprinkle with the remaining sugar. Leave for 20-30 minutes. Whip the cream and, as it begins to thicken, gradually add the juice that will have gathered in the peach bowl. Whisk until thick, then fold in the sliced peaches.

Just before serving, sandwich the layers of pastry with the peach mixture and dredge icing sugar over the top. Pipe additional whipped cream round the edge.

Galette de Noisettes aux Pêches

Tomates Guacamole

Truite Saumonée au Vin Rosé

Velvet Cream
Pineapple Water Ice

Salmon trout are never cheap, but they are at their best and least expensive in the summer. This delicious recipe does full justice to this special fish. Salmon could also be prepared in this way.

The other dishes in this menu to some extent offset the expense of the salmon trout. Both avocados and tomatoes are at their cheapest at this time of the year and pineapples should be available at reasonable prices.

The tomato shells for the starter can be prepared in advance, but it is best not to make the avocado filling too early, as it will quickly discolour. The hollandaise sauce required in the main dish could be made the day before if time is going to be a problem on the day. You will find a recipe for it on the page of Basic Recipes.

Both puddings could be made the day before and the pineapple ice cream could be made even earlier if this is more convenient. If it is not made too long in advance, serve it in the pineapple shells— this looks extremely attractive. The velvet cream is a nutty version of a chocolate mousse and is delicious. If preparation time permits it is a good idea to serve both puddings. Some people might find the chocolate pudding a little rich and the water ice will make a cool, refreshing alternative.

Tomates Guacamole

8-10 large ripe tomatoes
½ green pepper or 2-3 sticks celery
2 large ripe avocado pears
1 lemon
garlic
chilli powder
chopped parsley
salt and pepper

If the tomatoes are firm, skin them. Cut off the tops, scoop out the seeds, sprinkle the insides with salt and leave upside down to drain. Deseed the pepper and chop finely. Blanch the flesh in boiling salted water for 2-3 minutes, then refresh under the cold tap and drain. If using celery, chop it finely. Remove the stones from the avocados, scoop out the flesh and mash it using a silver fork or a wooden spoon. Squeeze the lemon and add the juice, together with the garlic, crushed with a little salt, chilli powder and chopped peppers. Season well and mix together thoroughly. Pile into the tomato shells and sprinkle with chopped parsley. Top with the lids.

Truite Saumonée au Vin Rosé

Salmon Trout with Rosé Wine
1 salmon trout weighing 2 kg
  (4½ lb)
1 onion
½ bottle rosé wine
1 wineglass water
salt and pepper
For the garnish
2 large cucumbers
1 bunch spring onions
butter
chopped parsley
For the sauce
15 g (½ oz) butter
15 g (½ oz) flour
4 x 15 ml spoons (4 tablespoons)
  double cream
6-8 x 15 ml spoons (6-8
  tablespoons) hollandaise sauce
  (see Basic Recipes)

Clean and trim the trout. Peel and chop the onion finely. Butter a fireproof dish and sprinkle the onion in it. Put the fish on top, season well and pour on the wine and water. Cover with a buttered paper and foil and cook for 1-1½ hours at 180°C, 350°F/Gas 4.

To prepare the garnish, peel the cucumber and cut into 7.5 cm (3 in) pieces. Quarter these and remove the seeds. Trim the spring onions and blanch with the cucumber in boiling salted water for 2-3 minutes. Refresh under the cold tap and drain well.

When the fish is cooked, remove from the cooking dish and put on a serving plate. Keep warm. Strain the cooking liquor into a clean pan and boil rapidly until it is reduced by about half. Melt the butter in a pan, add the flour and cook for 1-2 minutes, stirring all the time. Gradually stir in the fish liquor. Bring to the boil. Season well and add the cream. Remove from the heat and beat in the hollandaise sauce. Do *not* re-boil it at this stage.

Toss the garnish vegetables in melted butter and add chopped parsley. Remove the skin from the trout and spoon a little of the sauce over it. Arrange the vegetables around it and serve the rest of the sauce separately.

Velvet Cream

225 g (8 oz) cream cheese
25 g (1 oz) castor sugar
3 large eggs

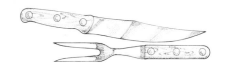

100 g (4 oz) plain chocolate
35 g (1½ oz) walnuts
3 x 15 ml spoons (3 tablespoons)
  brandy or sherry
300-450 ml (½-¾ pint) double
  cream
extra chocolate to decorate

Beat the cheese until it is soft, add the sugar and beat again. Separate the eggs and add the yolks to the cheese mixture. Beat until smooth. Put the chocolate in a bowl and cover with boiling water. Leave to stand for 3-4 minutes, pour off the water and add the softened chocolate to the cheese mixture. Mix well. Chop the nuts finely, reserving a few for decoration, and add to the mixture with the brandy or sherry.

Whip the cream lightly and fold into the cheese and chocolate mixture. Whisk the egg whites stiffly and fold them in. Turn into a glass bowl or individual glasses and chill for at least 3-4 hours (or overnight). Just before serving, decorate with the remaining walnuts and some grated chocolate.

Pineapple Water Ice

1 large or 2 small pineapples
175 g (6 oz) granulated sugar
600 ml (1 pint) water
1 lemon
1 egg white

Dissolve the sugar in the water. Thinly pare off the lemon rind and add to the pan. Boil for 6-8 minutes. Squeeze the lemon juice and add to

Pineapple Water Ice

the pan. Strain the syrup and leave to cool.

Split the pineapple(s) in half lengthwise and scoop out the flesh. Remove the central core and either mash or liquidize the flesh into a purée and measure the quantity. There should be about 600 ml (1 pint). Mix the pineapple pulp with an equal quantity of syrup and freeze this until it is slushy. Whisk the egg white stiffly and fold it into the pineapple mixture. Pack into a freezer container and freeze until required.

If serving the same day, chill the pineapple halves and serve filled with scoops of ice cream.

and make up one-and-a-half times the amount of stuffing. Calabrese or french beans and creamed potatoes make a good accompaniment.

Both puddings are quick to prepare. The meringues for Eton Mess can be bought, but they are very easy to make (see Basic Recipes). The rest of this pudding should be made a few hours in advance and kept in the refrigerator, but do not fold the meringues into the cream purée until moments before serving, otherwise they will go soggy and lose their crunchiness. The fruit purée and custard for the fool can be made the day before, but should not be combined with the cream until a few hours before serving. Sponge fingers make a good accompaniment to all fruit fools.

Egg and Anchovy Mousse

7 eggs
1 x 5 ml spoon (1 teaspoon)
anchovy essence
1 x 5 ml spoon (1 teaspoon)
Worcestershire sauce
1 x 5 ml spoon (1 teaspoon)
mushroom ketchup
1 x 15 ml spoon (1 tablespoon)
Parmesan cheese
300 ml ($\frac{1}{2}$ pint) aspic jelly or
jellied stock
300 ml ($\frac{1}{2}$ pint) double cream
salt and pepper

For the garnish
cucumber slices and/or mock caviar

Cook the eggs for 12 minutes in boiling water. Plunge them into cold water and leave them to cool. Separate the yolks from the whites and rub the yolks through a sieve into a large bowl. Reserve a little for decoration and mix the remainder with the anchovy essence, the Worcestershire sauce, the mushroom ketchup and the cheese. Mix together thoroughly and season well.

Melt the jelly or stock, then stir over ice until it is on the point of setting. Stir it into the yolk mixture. Whip the cream lightly and fold in.

Egg and Anchovy Mousse

Ballotine de Caneton aux Abricots

Eton Mess Gooseberry or Blackcurrant Fool

The light but tasty mousse starter to this meal clears the palate in readiness for the richness of the apricot-

Egg and Anchovy Mousse—although this is a light first course, the anchovies give a distinctive flavour

stuffed duck. It can be made the day before the party and kept covered in the refrigerator. Decorate it shortly before serving.

The duck recipe takes a little time to prepare as the duck has to be boned, but it is well worth it. Take extra care when boning duck. There is hardly any flesh at all along the breastbone and it is very easy to cut through the skin. The duck could be boned and stuffed the day before if it makes preparation time easier on the day of the party. If catering for very hungry people with keen appetites, allow two smaller ducks

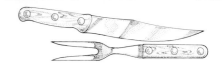

Chop the egg whites finely and fold in, reserving a little for decoration. Pile the mixture into a glass bowl and leave to set in a cool place.

When ready to serve, decorate with the reserved egg yolk and white, slices of cucumber and/or mock caviar.

Note If ordinary stock is used in this recipe, add 1 x 5 ml spoon (1 teaspoon) gelatine dissolved in 2 x 15 ml spoon (2 tablespoons) water. The mousses could be made in individual ramekins if preferred.

Ballotine de Caneton aux Abricots

Stuffed Duck with Apricots
> 1 duckling, weighing 1·75 kg
>   (4 lb)
> butter
> 1 onion
> 300 ml (½ pint) stock
> 1 wineglass Madeira

For the stuffing
> 1 onion
> 25 g (1 oz) butter
> 225 g (8 oz) lean pork
> 1 apple
> 2 sticks celery
> 50 g (2 oz) walnuts
> 50 g (2 oz) fresh breadcrumbs
> 4-5 apricots (canned, fresh or
>   dried, soaked overnight)
> 1 egg
> salt and pepper

For the sauce
> 1 x 425 g (15 oz) can apricots or
>   225 g (8 oz) fresh apricots
> 150 ml (¼ pint) stock
> 6 x 15 ml spoons (6 tablespoons)
>   Madeira
> scant 1 x 5 ml spoon (1 teaspoon)
>   ground ginger
> pinch cinnamon
> potato flour
> salt and pepper

First prepare the stuffing. Peel and chop the onion finely and fry it gently in the melted butter until soft. Leave to cool. Mince the pork. Chop the apple, celery and walnuts. Put in a bowl with the breadcrumbs. Chop the apricots and add to the bowl with some seasoning. Beat

the egg, add to the bowl and mix everything together thoroughly.

Bone the duck (see Autumn Menu No. 2) removing the leg and wing bones. Put the stuffing on the inside of the bird and roll it up. Sew loosely down the back using a trussing needle. Tie at intervals.

Rub the outside of the bird with softened butter and put it in a roasting tin. Peel and roughly chop the onion and put this with the bird. Add seasoning and pour over the stock. Roast for 1-1¼ hours at 190°C, 375°F/Gas 5.

Meanwhile, prepare the sauce. If using fresh apricots, stew them. Then liquidize all the ingredients (except the potato flour) until smooth. Pour into a saucepan and bring to the boil. Adjust seasoning, and thicken with a little potato flour mixed to a smooth paste with water.

When the duck is cooked, remove it from the roasting tin and keep it warm. Pour off the excess fat and pour the Madeira into the tin. Stir around to deglaze the pan, then strain this into the sauce. Remove the string and slice the duck. Serve the sauce separately.

Cold Mousse

When folding cream and/or stiffly beaten egg whites into cold mousses, it is essential that the mousse base is on the point of setting, with the consistency of unbeaten egg white. In hot weather, it may be necessary to stir it over ice to reach this stage. If the cream and egg white is folded into the mixture too soon, the mousse will separate out to jelly at the bottom and froth on the top.

Eton Mess

This is one of M. Escoffier's recipes —he must have had some Old Etonians among his clients. In fact

kirsch and meringues have been later additions to this old favourite.
> 450 g (1 lb) strawberries
> 3 x 15 ml spoons (3 tablespoons)
>   kirsch
> 1 x 15 ml spoon (1 tablespoon)
>   castor sugar
> 300-450 ml (½-¾ pint) double
>   cream
> 6 meringues

Reserve a few of the strawberries for decoration and crush the rest roughly. Sprinkle with kirsch and sugar. Whip the cream fairly stiffly and fold in the fruit. Break up the meringues and fold them in too. Chill, but serve within 1-2 hours, decorated with the reserved whole strawberries.

Gooseberry or Blackcurrant Fool

> 1 kg (2 lb) gooseberries or
>   blackcurrants
> 3 x 15 ml spoons (3 tablespoons)
>   water
> 100 g (4 oz) sugar
> 2 egg yolks
> 50 g (2 oz) sugar
> 150 ml (¼ pint) milk
> 300 ml (½ pint) double cream

Wash the fruit and put it in a heavy-based pan. Add the water and cook very gently until the juice begins to flow. Add the sugar and continue cooking until the fruit is soft. Rub it through a sieve or vegetable mill and leave to cool.

To prepare the custard, cream the egg yolks and sugar together in a basin. Bring the milk to boiling point and pour it on to the egg mixture. Return it to the pan and cook it gently (do *not* boil) until it thickens. Cool.

When the fruit purée and the custard are both cold, mix them together. Lightly whip the cream and fold into the mixture. Serve in a large glass bowl or in individual glasses; with sponge fingers.

Note You can thicken the purée with a little arrowroot if it is too thin. This is more likely to apply to blackcurrants than gooseberries.

**Prawn Cocktail
Tomates aux Crevettes
Gervais**

**Loin of Lamb
Bretonne**

Dacquoise

This menu has two starters to choose from, both featuring prawns or shrimps. If large firm tomatoes are still available, the *tomates aux crevettes* is a little more unusual and is very easy to make. Prawn cocktail is always a great favourite, and a homemade one is infinitely better than those which are generally served in restaurants.

The lamb dish is very tasty and has a substantial garnish of haricot beans. You could serve potatoes as well for those with hearty appetites but otherwise it is hardly necessary.

The sharp taste of apricots makes a good finish to the meal and the Dacquoise is a very exotic and impressive pudding, as well as being delicious. The almond meringue circles will store well for several days in a plastic container.

Prawn Cocktail

Frozen prawns or shrimps may be used for this recipe, but they must be thoroughly thawed and drained before being added to the sauce.

*450 g (1 lb) shelled prawns or
 shrimps*
300–450 ml ($\frac{1}{2}$–$\frac{3}{4}$ pint) mayonnaise
300 ml ($\frac{1}{2}$ pint) double cream
Tabasco sauce
paprika
tomato purée
tomato ketchup
lemon juice
salt and pepper
1 large lettuce

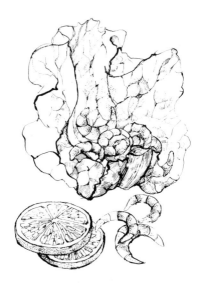

Make up the mayonnaise in the usual way (see Basic Recipes). Whisk the cream lightly and fold into the mayonnaise. Flavour to taste with the Tabasco sauce, paprika, tomato purée, tomato ketchup, lemon juice, brandy, salt and pepper. Combine with the prawns or shrimps.

Wash and shred the lettuce and divide it between individual glasses. Pile the shrimp mixture on top and chill. Just before serving, sprinkle the top of each with a little more paprika.

Tomates aux Crevettes Gervais

Stuffed Tomatoes Gervais
If you are unable to buy Gervais cheese use demi-sel or Philadelphia instead.

8 large tomatoes
*225 g (8 oz) shelled prawns or
 shrimps*
75 g (3 oz) Gervais cheese
*2 x 15 ml spoons (2 tablespoons)
 mayonnaise*
*2 x 15 ml spoons (2 tablespoons)
 cream*
chopped parsley and chives
salt and pepper
For the garnish
lettuce or watercress
Skin the tomatoes and cut a slice off the top of each one. Carefully scoop

out the seeds, then sprinkle the insides with salt and leave upside down to drain for 10-15 minutes.

Chop the prawns or shrimps roughly. Sieve the cheese and beat in the mayonnaise (see Basic Recipes), cream and chopped herbs. Season to taste and stir in the prawns. Spoon the mixture into the tomatoes and replace the lids. Chill.

Arrange on a serving dish garnished with lettuce or watercress and sprinkled with a few extra herbs.

Loin of Lamb Bretonne

2 x 1–1·5 kg (2–3 lb) loins of lamb
dripping
450 g (1 lb) haricot beans
pinch bicarbonate soda
1 carrot
1 onion
garlic
bouquet garni
flour
browned crumbs
175 g (6 oz) piece lean bacon
*4 x 15 ml spoons (4 tablespoons)
 double cream*
125 g (4 oz) butter
chopped parsley
50 g (2 oz) soft white breadcrumbs
For the sauce
1 wineglass sherry or red wine
300–450 ml ($\frac{1}{2}$–$\frac{3}{4}$ pint) stock
*2 x 5 ml spoons (2 teaspoons)
 tomato purée*
*1 x 15 ml spoon (1 tablespoon)
 redcurrant jelly*
*1 x 5 ml spoon (1 teaspoon)
 potato flour*
salt and pepper
For the stuffing
2 large onions
50 g (2 oz) butter
*10 x 15 ml spoons (10 tablespoons)
 fresh breadcrumbs*
*2 x 15 ml spoons (2 tablespoons)
 mixed chopped fresh herbs
 (e.g. parsley, thyme, sage)*
1 orange
1 egg
Ask the butcher to chine and bone the loins of lamb. Soak the beans overnight in cold water, then drain. Place in a large pan, cover with cold

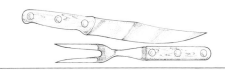

water and add the bicarbonate of soda. Bring to the boil and simmer for 5 minutes. Drain and wash the beans, then replace in the pan and cover with fresh water. Chop the carrot, onion and garlic and add to the pan with the bouquet garni and seasoning. Bring to the boil again, then simmer until the beans are tender (2½–3 hours).

Make the stuffing. Peel and finely chop the onions and fry gently in the butter until soft. Mix with the breadcrumbs, chopped herbs and some seasoning. Grate the rind from the orange, squeeze the juice and add. Bind the mixture together with a little beaten egg, reserving the remainder. Spread the stuffing over the inside of the meat, then roll up and tie at intervals. Dust the joint with flour, brush with the remainder of the egg and roll in the browned crumbs. Heat a little of the dripping in a pan and brown the meat all over. Roast at 190°C, 375°F/Gas 5 for 1¼ hours.

When the beans are cooked, strain off the excess liquid. Taste for seasoning and add more if necessary. Cut the bacon into small strips and fry until crisp. Stir into the beans with the cream, half the butter and the chopped parsley. Cover with the soft breadcrumbs, dot with the remainder of the butter and brown in the oven for 15–20 minutes.

When the joint is cooked, remove from the roasting pan and keep warm on a serving dish. Strain the fat from the pan and pour in the sherry or wine. Bring to the boil, stirring well to deglaze the pan, Add the stock, tomato purée and redcurrant jelly. Season well and bring to the boil. Strain into a smaller pan and skim the surface.

Mix the potato flour with a little water to a smooth paste and use to thicken the sauce. Remove the string from the joint and carve. Serve the beans and sauce separately.

Loin of Lamb Bretonne—served with haricot beans and sauce

Dacquoise

75 g (3 oz) unblanched almonds
225 g (8 oz) castor sugar
4 egg whites
pinch cream of tartar

For the filling and decoration

125 g (5 oz) dried apricots
1 lemon
100 g (4 oz) sugar
150 ml (¼ pint) water
450 ml (¾ pint) double cream
25 g (1 oz) plain chocolate

Blanch the almonds, remove the skins and dry the kernels well. Put through a nut mill.

Sieve the sugar on to a piece of paper. Whisk the egg whites until stiff, then beat in a large spoonful of sugar and the cream of tartar. Fold in the rest of the sugar with the the almonds. Divide the mixture into 2 and spread in 20 cm (8 in) circles on non-stick paper placed on baking trays. Bake for 1½ hours at 140°C, 275°F/Gas 1, turning down the heat if the meringue browns too much. Cool slightly, then peel off the paper and cool completely, leaving to stand on a wire rack.

Soak the apricots overnight in just enough water to cover. Cook gently in the soaking liquor with a strip of lemon rind. When tender, rub through a sieve or a mouli. Leave to cool. Squeeze the juice from the lemon and put in a small pan with the sugar and water. Bring to the boil and boil for 3–4 minutes. Leave to cool.

Whip the cream stiffly and put a third into a forcing bag with a star tube. Add about a third of the apricot purée to the remainder of the cream and sweeten to taste. Just before serving, sandwich the two meringue circles together with the apricot cream, then decorate the top circle with piped cream and grated chocolate. Add the sugar syrup to the rest of the apricot purée and serve this sauce separately.

Potage Niçoise

Faisan Périgord

Suprême au Moka
Poires Chantilly

The soup and puddings in this menu can all be prepared a day in advance. The soup is fresh but spicy which makes it a good fore-runner to counteract the greater richness of the main course.

The pheasant dish involves quite a lot of preparation as the birds have to be boned. This is quite a fiddly job with such small birds but it is worth taking the time and trouble. If time is short on the day of the party, the pheasants could be boned and stuffed the day before and the sauce demi-glacé could also be made (see Basic Recipes).

The coffee pudding is quite rich and a little will go a long way. It is a good idea to serve the *poires Chantilly*. Some people will prefer the fresh orangey taste as a finish to this superb meal.

Potage Niçoise

Soup Niçoise
The cheese croûtons make this soup a substantial starter. If preferred, omit them and sprinkle each bowl with a little chopped parsley instead.

2 large onions
1 green pepper
450 g (1 lb) tomatoes or 1 x 400 g
(14 oz) can tomatoes
50 g (2 oz) butter
35 g (1½ oz) flour
2 litres (3 pints) stock
bouquet garni plus a sprig of
tarragon
salt and pepper
For the cheese croûtons
20 g (¾ oz) butter
20 g (¾ oz) flour
300 ml (½ pint) milk
75 g (3 oz) cheese
French bread

Peel and finely chop the onions. De-seed the pepper, chop the flesh finely and blanch in boiling salted water for 2-3 minutes. Refresh under cold water and drain. Skin the tomatoes, remove the seeds and chop the flesh.

Melt the butter in a large pan and fry the onion gently until it is soft (not brown). Add the flour and cook for 2-3 minutes, stirring well. Add the peppers, tomatoes, stock, bouquet garni, and garlic crushed with a little salt. Season well, bring to the boil and simmer gently for 30 minutes. Remove the bouquet garni and adjust seasoning as necessary.

Make the croûtons. Melt the butter, stir in the flour and cook for a minute or two. Gradually add the milk, stirring all the time to keep the sauce smooth. Bring to the boil and cook for 2-3 minutes. Grate the cheese and add 25 g (1 oz) to the sauce. Season the sauce and spread on slices of French bread. Sprinkle these with the remainder of the grated cheese and brown under the grill. Cut into small dice and float on the top of each soup bowl, if required.

Faisan Périgord

Pheasant Périgord
2 plump pheasants
butter
1 wineglass sherry
1 wineglass stock

For the stuffing
100 g (4 oz) lambs' or calves' liver
150 g (6 oz) lean veal or pork
fillet
2 shallots
25 g (1 oz) butter
1 x 100 g (4 oz) can pâté de foie
4 x 15 ml spoons (4 tablespoons)
fresh breadcrumbs
2 x 5 ml spoons (2 teaspoons)
chopped fresh herbs
(include parsley)
2 x 5 ml spoons (2 teaspoons) brandy
1 egg
salt and pepper
For the sauce
300-450 ml (½-¾ pint) sauce
demi-glacé (see Basic Recipes)
1 truffle or 50 g (2 oz) mushrooms
1 wineglass sherry

Prepare the stuffing. Mince the liver and veal or pork. Finely chop the shallots and fry in melted butter until soft. Mix with the liver, veal or pork, pâté, breadcrumbs, herbs and brandy, pounding everything together thoroughly. Season well and add sufficient beaten egg to bind.

Bone the pheasants leaving the wings and drumsticks in place. Spread the stuffing on the inside of the birds, then sew them up using a trussing needle and string. Reshape and truss the pheasants, then cover with butter and place in a roasting tin. Add the sherry and stock, then roast for 1-1½ hours at 200°C, 400°F/Gas 6, reducing the heat to 190°C, 375°F/Gas 5 if the birds brown too quickly. Baste from time to time.

Prepare the sauce demi-glacé (see Basic Recipes). Then slice the mushrooms or truffle and fry in a little melted butter. When the pheasants are cooked, remove from the roasting dish and keep warm. Add the remaining glass of sherry to the dish, bring to the boil, stirring well to deglaze the pan. Strain this into the sauce demi-glacé, season well and add mushrooms or truffle. Re-heat carefully.

Remove all string from the pheasant, carve in slices and serve with the sauce on top.

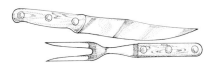

*Poires Chantilly—a dash of
Cointreau or Grand Marnier
adds a touch of distinction*

Boning Poultry

Lay the bird, plucked and
drawn, on its breast. Cut the
skin down the back from the
neck to the parson's nose.
Holding the knife like a pen,
cut away the flesh keeping
close to the bones. Cut
through the wing and thigh
joints, carefully removing the
meat from the breast bone.
Finish one side and repeat on
the other, then cut along the
top of the breast bone
ensuring not to break the skin.
Remove the carcass. Remove
the thigh bones from the
inside. The bird can now be
stuffed if required before
trussing with fine string.
Alternatively, the drum sticks
and wing bones can be boned
out, splitting the skin on the
inner side of the pockets
formed. Spread out flat, stuff,
and roll up like a large
sausage.

Suprême au Moka

Coffee Supreme
  225 g (8 oz) unsalted butter
  100 g (4 oz) castor sugar
  4 egg yolks
  500 ml (1 pint) strong coffee
  2 packets boudoir biscuits
  25 g (1 oz) flaked almonds

Soften the butter by putting it in a
bowl over hot water. Beat until
creamy, then beat in the sugar. Add
the egg yolks one at a time, beating
well in between. Add 2 x 15 ml
spoons (2 tablespoons) coffee and
beat until the mixture is really
smooth.

Put the rest of the coffee in a soup
plate and dip a third of the boudoir
biscuits into it. Arrange them side
by side in the bottom of a shallow
dish. (Make sure that the coffee is
cold, and avoid soaking the biscuits
so long that they break up.) Cover
the biscuits with a thin layer of
coffee cream. Dip the next third of
biscuits into the coffee and put
them on top of the coffee cream.
Cover with another layer of coffee
cream and top this with the remainder of the biscuits dipped in
coffee. Cover the top and sides of
the biscuits with the rest of the
coffee cream. Chill for 2-3 hours
or overnight.

Brown the almond flakes. Just
before serving, sprinkle them over
the top of the pudding.

Poires Chantilly

Chantilly Pears
  300 ml ($\frac{1}{2}$ pint) water
  100 g (4 oz) sugar
  6 large pears
  $\frac{1}{2}$ lemon
  3 egg yolks
  75 g (3 oz) castor sugar
  3 x 5 ml spoons (3 teaspoons)
    arrowroot
  2 oranges
  450 ml ($\frac{3}{4}$ pint) milk
  150 ml ($\frac{1}{4}$ pint) double cream
  2 x 15 ml spoons (2 tablespoons)
    Cointreau or Grand Marnier
For decoration
  angelica, cherries or candied
    orange peel

Put the water and sugar in a pan and
bring to the boil. Peel and core the
pears and rub with the cut side of
the half lemon. Poach in the syrup
until tender. Allow to cool slightly,
then drain on a rack until completely
cold.

Put the egg yolks, castor sugar
and arrowroot in a bowl and add
grated rind from one of the oranges.
Mix together well. Bring the milk
to the boil and pour on to the egg
mixture. Return to the pan and
heat the mixture to just boiling
point, stirring all the time. Turn
into a bowl to cool.

Pare the rind from the remaining
orange using a potato peeler and
cut into fine julienne strips. Put in a
small pan, cover with cold water
and bring to the boil. Boil for 2
minutes, then drain and rinse under
cold water. Drain again and add to
the custard.

Whip the cream lightly and fold
half of it into the custard when it
is quite cold. Pour the custard into
a glass dish and arrange the pears,
cut side uppermost, on top. Sprinkle
with the liqueur and decorate with
the rest of the cream and the
angelica, cherries or candied orange
peel.

115

Terrine Normande aux Noix
Choux Normands

Poulet au Gingembre

Crème Asphodèle

Either of these starters makes a good, substantial beginning to this meal. The terrine could be made well in advance as it will keep for ten to twelve days uncut in the refrigerator. The choux buns and the filling could be made the day before the party, then combined and re-heated, as suggested in the recipe, just before serving.

The spicy chicken dish is a good way of injecting some flavour into frozen birds, which are often rather tasteless. It needs nothing more to accompany it than boiled rice and a crisp green salad.

The lemony tang of the *crème Asphodèle* freshens the palate after the ginger taste of the chicken and it can be made a day in advance to save time on the day.

Terrine Normande aux Noix

Normandy Nut Terrine

450 g (1 lb) pigs' liver
350 g (12 oz) trimmed belly of pork
garlic
125 g (4 oz) hazelnuts
50 g (2 oz) lard
4 x 15 ml spoons (4 tablespoons) white wine
4 x 15 ml spoons (4 tablespoons) Calvados or whisky
450 g (1 lb) fat green bacon rashers
salt and pepper

Mince the pigs' liver and the trimmed belly of pork. Crush the garlic with a little salt. Toast the hazelnuts lightly, rub off their skins and chop roughly. Melt the lard and add to the liver, pork, garlic and chopped hazelnuts, with the wine and Calvados or whisky. Season well and mix everything together thoroughly.

De-rind the bacon and flatten the rashers with the back of a knife. Line a terrine with them, then press the mixture into this. Cover and cook in a bain-marie for 1½ hours at 180°C, 350°F/Gas 4. When cooked, press with a 1 kg (2 lb) weight until the terrine has been allowed to cool.

> **Casseroles**
> A large oval enamelled cast-iron casserole dish is invaluable for many dishes, including the chicken recipe here. Always heat slowly.

Choux Normands

90 g (3½ oz) flour
75 g (3 oz) butter
175 ml (6 fl oz) water
3 eggs
salt and pepper
For the filling
1·5 kg (3 lb) mussels
100 g (4 oz) button mushrooms
lemon juice
butter
100 g (4 oz) shelled prawns
For the sauce
25 g (1 oz) butter
25 g (1 oz) flour
450 ml (¾ pint) mixed mushroom and mussel liquor
2 egg yolks
3 x 15 ml spoons (3 tablespoons) cream

Sift the flour on to a piece of paper. Cut the butter in small pieces and put into a pan with the water. Bring to the boil. Remove from the heat and tip the flour into the pan.

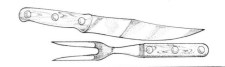

Beat well until the mixture has formed into a smooth paste. Break the eggs into a bowl and beat. Add gradually to the paste, beating well. Reserve a spoonful of egg to brush the choux. Put the mixture into a large forcing bag with a 1-cm (½-in) plain pipe and pipe small mounds the size of a walnut on to greased baking sheets. Brush with the reserved egg and bake for 10 minutes at 200°C, 400°F/Gas 6. Turn down the heat to 190°C, 375°F/Gas 5 and cook for a further 15-30 minutes. Remove the tops from the choux and cool on a wire rack.

To prepare the filling, scrape the mussels well and wash 3 times in cold water. Discard any that open. Put in a large clean pan and cover with a lid. Cook for 3-4 minutes over a high heat, shaking the pan occasionally. Strain into a colander and reserve the liquor. Remove the mussels from the shells and put in a bowl. Wash the mushrooms and put in a pan with about 4 x 15 ml spoons (4 tablespoons) water, a good squeeze of lemon juice, a knob of butter and salt and pepper. Cover, bring to the boil and cook for 1 minute. Allow to cool slightly in the pan. Strain, adding the liquor to the mussel liquor (keep this for the sauce) slice the mushrooms and add both these and the prawns to the mussels.

To make the sauce, melt the butter and stir in the flour. Cook, stirring continuously, for 2-3 minutes. Add the mushrooms and mussel liquor, stirring all the time to keep the sauce smooth. Simmer gently for 4-5 minutes. Mix the egg yolks with the cream in a bowl and pour on a little of the boiling sauce. Stir well and return to the pan. Cook for a minute or so without boiling and adjust the seasoning as necessary.

Stir the mushrooms, prawns and mussels into the sauce and heat through again. Fill the choux buns with the mixture, then heat for 10-

Ingredients for Choux Normands

15 minutes at 180°C, 350°F/Gas 4. **Note** If the choux buns and the filling have been made in advance, re-heat the filling and spoon it into the cold buns. Heat them for 10-15 minutes at 190°C, 375°F/Gas 5.

Poulet au Gingembre

Chicken with Ginger
2 x 1·6 kg (3½ lb) chickens
4 x 15 ml spoons (4 tablespoons)
  redcurrant jelly
15 g (½ oz) butter
1 x 15 ml spoon (1 tablespoon) oil
2 x 15 ml spoons (2 tablespoons)
  flour
2 lemons
300 ml (½ pint) stock
potato flour (optional)
chopped parsley
salt and pepper
For the marinade
3 large onions
3 cloves garlic
1 x 5 ml spoon (1 teaspoon) salt
2 x 5 ml spoons (2 teaspoons)
  sugar
1 x 5 ml spoon (1 teaspoon)
  ground coriander
2 x 5 ml spoons (2 teaspoons)
  ground ginger
pinch ground cloves
pinch chilli powder
2 x 15 ml spoons (2 tablespoons)
  oil
2 x 15 ml spoons (2 tablespoons)
  wine vinegar
300 ml (½ pint) white wine

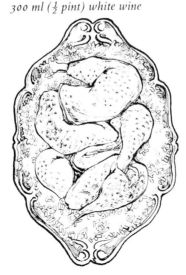

Joint the chicken. Prepare the marinade. Peel and slice the onions and crush the garlic with the salt. Place in a liquidizer with the rest of the marinade ingredients and liquidize to a paste. Pour this over the chicken joints and leave for at least 2-3 hours.

Heat the butter and oil in a flameproof casserole. Wipe the chicken joints and sauté them until they are golden. Stir in the flour and cook for 2-3 minutes. Grate the rind, extract the juice of the lemon and add these with the marinade, stock and redcurrant jelly to the chicken. Season. Cover and cook at 180°C, 350°F/Gas 4 for about 1 hour.

Arrange the joints on a dish. Adjust the seasoning and thicken the sauce with a little potato flour, mixed to a paste with water, if necessary. Pour this over the chicken and serve sprinkled with chopped parsley.

Crème Asphodèle

Double the quantity of this recipe is needed for 8 people, but it is easier to make the recipe twice with these quantities than to attempt to make it all at once with double the ingredients.
3 eggs
3 lemons
15 g (½ oz) gelatine
5 x 15 ml spoons (5 tablespoons)
  hot water
165 g (5½ oz) castor sugar
Separate the eggs and beat the yolks with the sugar, using an electric whisk, until light and fluffy. Grate the rind of 2 lemons and squeeze the juice from all 3. Dissolve the gelatine in the hot water. Add the lemon rind and juice to the eggs and sugar and strain in the gelatine. Stir well and leave in a cool place until it is beginning to set. At this point, whisk the egg whites stiffly and fold them into the mixture. Pour into a glass bowl and chill until set.

Decorate with a little grated lemon rind or a few flaked nuts.

Salade aux Poires

**Boeuf en Daube
Provençale**

**Charlotte aux
Noisettes
Chartreuse de Pommes**

This is a good menu for a busy weekend party. The *boeuf en daube* can be made well in advance and frozen (allow 24 hours for it to thaw). A fresh green vegetable and mashed potatoes are the ideal accompaniments.

If you find fresh tomatoes are very expensive, two large cans can be used successfully instead: drain them well and use the juice in the cooking. Chop the tomatoes and add as instructed for fresh ones in the recipe.

The *charlotte aux noisettes* can be made the day before, but do not turn it out and decorate it until shortly before serving. The pear starter should also be assembled at the last possible minute, although the filling and the sauce could be prepared in advance. Canned pears can be used instead of fresh ones, but the flavour will not be as good. Chopped walnuts make a tasty and attractive garnish but do not combine well with canned pears. Serve thinly sliced brown bread and butter with this salad.

The light apple pudding is best made in the morning and left in the refrigerator to set and chill before serving.

Salade aux Poires

Pear Salad
> 4 ripe pears
> 1 lemon
> 50 g (2 oz) Roquefort or

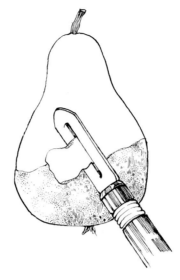

> Gorgonzola cheese
> 25 g (1 oz) butter
> single cream or milk
> 75-100 g (3-4 oz) cream cheese
> paprika
> salt and pepper
> lettuce leaves

Peel the pears, cut in half and remove the cores. Squeeze the lemon and rub the pears with the juice to prevent discolouring.

Cream the Roquefort or Gorgonzola with the butter and a little cream to give a firm consistency. Season to taste. Fill the central cavity of the pears with this mixture. Beat the cream cheese with milk or cream to a pouring consistency and add a squeeze of lemon juice. Season well.

Put the pears on lettuce leaves on individual dishes and coat them with with the cheese mixture. Sprinkle with paprika.

Boeuf en Daube Provençale

Provençal Beef Stew
> 1.75 kg (4 lb) top side or chuck
>   steak
> 1 large onion
> 1 carrot
> 1 stick celery
> sprig each parsley and thyme
> 1 bay leaf

> 1 x 15 ml spoon (1 tablespoon)
>   olive oil
> 1 bottle red wine
> dripping
> 225-g (8-oz) piece bacon
> 2 x 15 ml spoons (2 tablespoons)
>   flour
> extra wine or stock
> 1 pig's trotter
> garlic
> 1 x 5 ml spoon (1 teaspoon)
>   tomato purée
> salt and pepper
> potato flour (optional)
> 1 kg (2 lb) tomatoes
> 12 green olives

Trim any fat or gristle from the meat and cut into 5-cm (2-in) squares. Put in a large bowl. Peel and finely slice the onion and carrot and finely slice the celery. Add these to the meat with the herbs tied together in a bunch and the olive oil. Pour the wine on top and leave to marinate for at least 24 hours.

The next day, remove the meat and dry it well. Strain the marinade and reserve it. Heat the dripping in a heavy pan and, when it is smoking, brown the meat on all sides. Remove the meat and brown the vegetables strained from the marinade. Cut the bacon into cubes and brown. Dust in the flour and cook for 2-3 minutes, stirring once or twice. Add the wine from the marinade and replace the meat in the pan. Add some extra wine or stock to cover the meat and vegetables if necessary. Blanch the pig's trotter by putting it in cold water, bringing it to the boil and boiling for 2 minutes. Wash well and add to the meat and vegetables. Add the garlic, crushed with a little salt, with the tomato purée and the herbs from the marinade. Season well, cover and cook for at least 3 hours.

When cooked, remove the pieces of meat and keep them warm in a casserole dish. Remove any flesh from the pig's trotter and add to the meat. Strain the sauce and skim it thoroughly, then thicken with a little potato flour. Skin and de-seed the tomatoes, chop the flesh and add

Charlotte aux Noisettes

to the casserole with the olives. Pour the sauce on top and simmer for another 20 minutes.

Praline

This is most useful for flavouring cream or butter cream as a filling for cakes, or for use as a decoration or flavouring for puddings and ices. It may be made with hazelnuts or unblanched almonds but must always be cooked slowly so that the nuts are golden right through.

50 g (2 oz) hazelnuts or unblanched almonds
50 g (2 oz) castor sugar

Put the nuts and sugar together in a heavy pan and cook gently until the sugar caramelizes. Stir once, then continue cooking until the sugar is a rich brown. Pour on to an oiled baking sheet and leave to go cold. Grind in a coffee grinder or in a cheese or nut mill and reduce to a fine powder in a liquidizer.

Charlotte aux Noisettes

Hazelnut Charlotte

15 g (½ oz, 1 sachet) gelatine
5 x 15 ml spoons (5 tablespoons) cold water
450 ml (¾ pint) milk
4 egg yolks
75 g (3 oz) castor sugar
2 x 15 ml spoons (2 tablespoons) honey
75 g (3 oz) hazelnut praline (see box)
450 ml (¾ pint) double cream
1 packet langue de chat biscuits (or similar)
whole toasted hazelnuts

Soak the gelatine in the cold water and dissolve in a small basin placed in a pan of hot water. Heat the milk to boiling point. Beat the egg yolks, sugar and honey together and pour on to the milk. Return to the pan and cook, stirring all the time, until the custard thickens (do not let it boil). Strain into a bowl, cool slightly and add the gelatine.

When the mixture is on the point of setting, stir in the praline. Lightly whip the cream and fold two-thirds into the custard. Pour this into a lightly oiled 1–1·5-litre (2–2½-pint) charlotte tin. Leave in the refrigerator for at least 4 hours or preferably overnight.

When ready to serve, unmould the charlotte on to a round dish. Cover with the remaining whipped cream in a thin layer, reserving some for decoration. Arrange the *langue de chat* biscuits, overlapping, round the outside of the charlotte. If necessary, whip the cream a little more until it is stiff enough to hold its shape, then pipe this on to the top of the pudding. Decorate with hazelnuts.

Chartreuse de Pommes

Apples Chartreuse

1 large cooking apple
300 ml (½ pint) water
225 g (8 oz) castor sugar
1 lemon
15 g (½ oz, 1 sachet) gelatine
1·5 kg (3 lb) crisp apples (Charles Ross, Cox, Russet)
100 g (4 oz) mixed crystallized fruit (cherries, angelica, pineapple and apricot)

For the sauce
4 x 15 ml spoons (4 tablespoons) smooth apricot jam or sweetened apricot purée
2 x 15 ml spoons (2 tablespoons) rum
lemon juice and water

Wipe the cooking apple and slice thinly into a pan containing the water. Cover and cook gently to a pulp. Tip this into a strainer over a bowl, and leave to drip until all the juice is through. Pour 300 ml (½ pint) juice into a clean pan and add the sugar. Pare the rind from the lemon and squeeze the juice. Add to the pan. Bring to the boil and simmer for 5 minutes. Meanwhile soak the gelatine in a little cold water. Take the pan from the heat, remove the lemon rind from the syrup.

Peel and core the remaining apples and slice in 3-mm (⅛-in) slices, directly into the apple syrup. Cover the pan and cook very gently for 10–12 minutes. Remove the lid and continue cooking until the syrup has nearly evaporated. Stir in the gelatine. Chop the crystallized fruits and stir in gently, taking care not to break up the apples. Cool, then tip the apples into a glass bowl and leave in a cool place to set. Chill in the refrigerator.

Make the sauce by combining the apricot jam or purée and rum. Add sufficient water and lemon juice to give a runny consistency. Serve this separately from the pudding with a bowl of whipped cream.

the lemon and grate or finely chop the onion. Stir both into the avocado pulp. Add the Worcestershire sauce and Tabasco to taste and season. Chill, covered with clingwrap.

Soupe au Poisson
Fish Soup
- 100 g (4 oz) unshelled prawns
- 1 large leek
- 1 large onion
- 1 carrot
- 2 x 15 ml spoons (2 tablespoons) olive oil
- 2 cloves garlic
- 1 x 400 g (14 oz) can tomatoes
- 150 ml (¼ pint) white wine
- 1·25 litres (2 pints) fish stock
- chervil and saffron
- 12-18 mussels
- 225 g (8 oz) haddock fillet
- 1 x 15 ml spoon (1 tablespoon) potato flour
- chopped parsley
- aioli (see Basic Recipes)

For the stock
- 700-900 g (1½-2 lb) sole or plaice skin and bones
- 1 onion
- parsley
- 2 litres (3 pints) water
- salt and pepper

To prepare the fish stock, wash the fish bones and skin and put in a large pan. Slice the onion thinly and add with the parsley, water and seasoning. Bring to the boil and simmer for 15-20 minutes. Strain.

Shell the prawns and reserve the shells. Wash the leek thoroughly and peel the onion and carrot. Chop the vegetables finely and fry gently in the oil in a large pan until they are soft. Add the prawn shells. Crush the garlic with a little salt, add to the pan and cook for a further 4-5 minutes. Add the tomatoes and wine and simmer gently for 20 minutes. Add the prepared fish stock, the chervil and a pinch of saffron. Season well. Bring to the boil and cook for 10 minutes. Pass the soup through a mouli or liquidizer and strain into a clean pan.

Scrub the mussels and put them

Avocado Appetizer
Soupe au Poisson

Côtes de Porc Savoy

Crème Ambassadrice
Orange Caramel Trifle

This is another menu in which much of the preparation can be done in advance. The fish soup can be re-heated, but the fish, mussels and prawns should not be added until the last minute. Incidentally, served with chunks of fresh bread, it makes a lovely supper dish on its own.

The avocado appetizer is a great standby as it takes next to no time to prepare. It loses nothing if you use slightly bruised pears. Make it as late as possible and keep covered with cling-wrap in the refrigerator.

The main course here is also very quick to prepare, and is very tasty because the flavours of pork and

Soupe au Poisson with prawns, mussels, haddock and white wine

apple complement each other beautifully. This recipe allows for really thorough cooking which will help to ensure the chops are as tender as they can be.

Crème ambassadrice is a delicious pudding. It is a rich custard mixed with crystallized fruits, which are easiest to obtain in winter. The orange caramel trifle is a lovely winter version of this ever-popular pudding and makes a good alternative to the *crème ambassadrice*.

Avocado Appetizer
- 3 avocado pears
- 1 large lemon
- 225 g (8 oz) cream cheese
- ½ onion
- Worcestershire sauce
- Tabasco sauce
- paprika
- salt and pepper

For decoration
- lettuce

Cut the avocado pears in half and remove the stones. Scrape the pulp into a bowl. Squeeze the juice from

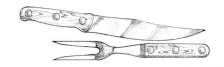

in a clean pan. Cover with a lid and cook them over a high heat for 4-5 minutes until their shells open. Remove the mussels from their shells and mix with the prawns. Skin the haddock fillet and cut into small cubes. Add to the prawns and mussels.

Strain the mussel liquor into the soup. Season the soup and bring to the boil. Mix the potato flour with a little cold water to a smooth paste and add it gradually to the boiling soup until it reaches the desired consistency. Five minutes before serving, add the prawns, mussels and haddock. Simmer gently.

Serve the soup piping hot, sprinkled with chopped parsley, with a bowl of aioli as accompaniment (see Basic Recipes).

Côtes de Porc Savoy

Savoy Pork Chops
    8 pork chops
    50 g (2 oz) butter
    2 x 5 ml spoons (2 teaspoons)
    *   flour*
    300 ml (½ pint) cider
    5 x 15 ml spoons (5 tablespoons)
    *   sherry or Madeira*
    2 lemons
    100 g (4 oz) sultanas
    2 large apples
    stock
    salt and pepper

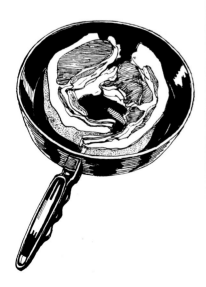

Brown the chops on both sides in the butter and put them in a fireproof dish. Sprinkle the flour into the pan and cook gently, stirring all the time, until it begins to brown. Stir in the cider and sherry or Madeira. Grate the rind from the lemons and squeeze the juice. Add to the pan with the sultanas. Peel, core and dice the apples and add to the pan. Season to taste and then pour over the chops. Cook at 180°C, 350°F/ Gas 4 for 45-60 minutes, adding a little stock if the dish seems too dry.

Crème Ambassadrice

    175 g (6 oz) crystallized fruit
    *   (cherries, angelica, pineapple*
    *   and apricots, not mixed peel)*
    2 x 15 ml spoons (2 tablespoons)
    *   rum or kirsch*
    6 eggs
    75 g (3 oz) castor sugar
    concentrated vanilla sugar
    50 g (2 oz) flour
    600 ml (1 pint) milk
    300 ml (½ pint) double cream
    2 x 15 ml spoons (2 tablespoons)
    *   apricot jam*
    6 macaroons

Chop the crystallized fruit and put in a bowl with the rum or kirsch. Leave to stand, stirring occasionally.

Separate 4 of the eggs and put the yolks in a bowl with the 2 whole eggs, the castor sugar and vanilla sugar. Mix well, add the flour and mix again. Heat the milk to boiling point and pour it on to the egg mixture, stirring well. Return to the pan and bring it up to boiling point, stirring all the time. Cook gently for a few minutes, then pour into a clean bowl, cover with foil and put on one side to cool.

When the custard is cold, whisk the cream and fold three-quarters of it into the custard. Whisk the egg whites stiffly and fold them in too. Put half of this mixture into a glass serving dish. Mix the crystallized fruits with the apricot jam and spread on top of the egg mixture. Sprinkle with crushed macaroons. Cover with the remainder of the egg mixture, smoothing over the surface. Chill in the refrigerator.

Decorate the top with whipped cream, piped from a forcing bag.

Orange Caramel Trifle

    4 eggs
    75 g (3 oz) sugar
    600 ml (1 pint) milk
    6 lumps sugar
    4 oranges
    1 packet trifle sponges
    Grand Marnier
    300 ml (½ pint) double cream
For the caramel
    100 g (4 oz) sugar
    2 x 15 ml spoons (2 tablespoons)
    *   water*

Break the eggs into a bowl and mix with the sugar. Bring the milk to boiling point and pour it on to the eggs. Mix well and strain back into the pan. Cook gently without boiling, stirring all the time, until the custard begins to thicken. Pour into a bowl and leave on one side to cool.

Prepare the caramel. Put the sugar and water in a pan, bring to the boil and cook until it is a rich brown colour. Plunge the base of the pan into a bowl of cold water and immediately pour the caramel on to an oiled plate or tin to cool and set.

Rub the sugar lumps over the oranges until they have absorbed the zest. Peel the oranges and remove all the pith. Holding them one at a time over a bowl to catch any juice, cut out the segments with a sharp knife leaving all skin behind.

Split the sponge cakes and put a layer in a glass bowl. Sprinkle with orange juice and Grand Marnier. Cover with a layer of orange segments and a layer of custard. Repeat this layering once more, ending with a layer of custard. Leave in the refrigerator to chill.

Whip the cream lightly and cover the surface of the custard with it. Break up the caramel with a rolling pin and sprinkle this and the crushed sugar lumps over the top.

Winter Menu No. 2

Prawns in Whisky

Paupiettes de Boeuf Marinées

Walnut and Maple Pie

The main course and pudding in this menu can be prepared in advance. The prawns in whisky are an exotic starter and need little preparation. The starter should be served as soon as it is cooked rather than re-heated. Remember it is an appetizer, not a main course, so serve only a little rice with it. It looks most attractive presented on individual dishes as opposed to one big serving dish. The walnut and maple pie could be made the day before.

A green vegetable and mashed or mousseline potatoes are all that is needed to go with the beef olives. Take note of the box: the cut of the meat is all important.

Prawns in Whisky

450 g (1 lb) shelled prawns
50 g (2 oz) butter
2 x 15 ml spoons (2 tablespoons) olive oil
2 small onions or 2 large shallots
2 cloves garlic
6 x 15 ml spoons (6 tablespoons) whisky
1 wineglass white wine
1 small can tomatoes
1 x 5 ml spoon (1 teaspoon) tomato purée
1 x 5 ml spoon (1 teaspoon) potato flour or arrowroot
5 x 15 ml spoons (5 tablespoons) double cream
cayenne
salt and pepper

Melt the butter and oil in a pan. Peel and finely chop the onions or shallots and fry them gently until transparent. Crush the garlic with a little salt and add to the pan with the prawns. Cook for a few minutes Add half the whisky, setting light to it to flame it. Pour on the wine and the rest of the whisky. Squeeze the seeds from the tomatoes and chop roughly. Add to the pan with the juice from the can and the tomato purée. Season well and simmer for 5-10 minutes. Mix the potato flour or arrowroot with a little water and use to thicken the sauce slightly. Stir in the cream.

Note Serve this dish very hot with plain boiled rice, either in individual shell dishes or in one large fireproof dish.

Paupiettes de Boeuf Marinées

Marinated Beef Olives
8 slices topside beef, weighing 1.5 kg (3 lb) in all
50 g (2 oz) butter
1 x 15 ml spoon (1 tablespoon) oil
1 x 15 ml spoon (1 tablespoon) flour
450 ml (¾ pint) stock
75 ml (3 fl oz) red wine or sherry

For the marinade
1 x 15 ml spoon (1 tablespoon) oil
4 x 15 ml spoon (4 tablespoons) red wine

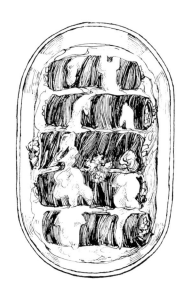

Prawns in Whisky—an exotic way to begin a meal and easily prepared

1 x 5 ml spoon (1 teaspoon) vinegar
salt and pepper

For the stuffing
1 onion
25 g (1 oz) butter
225 g (8 oz) smoked gammon
6-8 anchovy fillets
1 x 15 ml spoon (1 tablespoon) tomato purée
2 x 15 ml spoons (2 tablespoons) chopped parsley

Mix all the ingredients for the marinade together and pour over the beef slices. Leave to stand for at least 1 hour.

To prepare the stuffing, peel and chop the onion finely and fry in the butter until soft. Mince the gammon and chop the anchovy fillets. Mix these together thoroughly with the fried onion, the tomato purée, chopped parsley and seasoning. Add a few breadcrumbs if desired.

Remove the beef slices from the marinade and pat them dry. Spread with the stuffing, roll them up and tie securely at intervals.

Heat the butter and oil together in a heavy pan and brown the olives well on all sides. Remove from the pan and put in a fireproof dish. Add the flour to the pan and stir until it

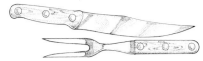

line a 20-cm (8-in) flan case or ring. Chill for 10 minutes.

To prepare the filling, melt the butter in a pan and mix in the sugar and maple syrup. Add a pinch of salt. Cool this mixture and add the eggs, one at a time, beating well. Chop the walnuts coarsely and spread over the pastry base. Pour the syrup mixture on top and bake for 30-40 minutes at 190°C, 375°F/ Gas 5, until the filling is firm. If the pastry begins to brown too quickly, but the filling is still not firm, reduce the heat slightly. Let the pie cool on a rack and decorate with piped whipped cream and extra walnuts shortly before serving.

browns. Add the stock, wine and marinade mixture. Season well and bring to the boil. Strain over the olives, then cook for 1-1½ hours at 180°C, 350°F/Gas 4.

When cooked, remove the string and put the olives on a warm serving dish. Skim the sauce and pour it over the olives.

Paupiettes
These are thin slices of meat, usually cut from the topside of beef. They should be about 12.5 x 7.5 cm (5 x 3 in) in size, cut along the length of the grain of the meat— that is, sliced down the side of the joint. There should be no division of muscle in the slice. It is not easy to cut slices like this and, in fact, butchers usually cut slices across the top of a piece of topside. A French butcher cuts meat carcasses quite differently and it is easy to obtain such a cut from a continental butcher.

The slices should be flattened with a damp knife before stuffing and rolling. An escalope is the same cut, using veal or pork.

Walnut and Maple Pie
If you cannot obtain maple syrup easily use a mixture of 50 ml (2 fl oz) black treacle and 175 ml (6 fl oz) golden syrup for this pie.

For the pastry
225 g (8 oz) plain flour
150 g (5 oz) butter
1 egg yolk
squeeze lemon juice
salt
2-3 x 15 ml spoons
  (2-3 tablespoons) water

For the filling
75 g (3 oz) butter
150 g (6 oz) castor sugar
225 ml (8 fl oz) maple syrup
pinch of salt
4 eggs
100 g (4 oz) walnuts

For decoration
walnut halves
double cream

To make the rich shortcrust pastry, sieve the flour on to a board and make a well in the centre. Into this put the softened butter, the egg yolk, a squeeze of lemon juice and a pinch of salt. Using the fingers of one hand, work the butter and egg yolk together, gradually drawing in the flour until everything is combined and the mixture is flaky. Add the water and knead to a firm dough. Leave in a cool place for 30 minutes, then roll out and use to

Pastry
All pastry, including ordinary shortcrust is less likely to shrink during cooking if it is allowed to stand for 10-15 minutes before baking.

Winter Menu No. 3

Devilled Tuna Pâté
Coquilles de Moules
à la Rochelaise

Jambon à la
Bayonnaise

Boodles Fool
Délice aux Marrons

Two fishy starters to choose from, the tuna pâté being the most economical and the quickest to make. The *coquille de moules* is a little more special, but requires considerably more preparation. However, it can be made the day before as it re-heats well, or the mussels can be cooked in advance and frozen in the liquor until required. Bottled and canned mussels are not really suitable for this recipe: bottled mussels are usually steeped in vinegar and canned ones in brine, which gives them a poor texture.

Gammon makes a good main course in winter and this recipe is both delicious and substantial. It has the advantage of needing nothing more than a green vegetable or salad to go with it.

The chestnut pudding is very rich and calorie-loaded, but so good that it is worth breaking any diet. The quantity given in this recipe is really for six, but bear in mind that a little goes a long way. It is wise to serve an extra pudding when serving one that contains chestnuts, which may not be to everyone's taste. The Boodles fool is a classic pudding from the famous London club. There are many versions but this is one of the best.

Devilled Tuna Pâté

2 x 200-g (7-oz) cans tuna
225 g (8 oz) cream cheese
2 x 15 ml spoons (2 tablespoons)
  double cream
curry paste
Tabasco sauce
squeeze lemon juice
salt and pepper

Mash the tuna (in its oil) with the cheese to a smooth, well mixed paste. Beat in the cream gradually, together with the curry paste, Tabasco sauce, a good squeeze of lemon juice and salt and pepper to taste. Mix thoroughly (this can be done in a liquidizer). Chill and serve with hot brown rolls or toast.

Coquilles de Moules à la Rochelaise

Mussels with White Wine and Mushrooms
2 kg (5 lb) mussels
flour or oatmeal
4 shallots
2 sticks celery
225 g (8 oz) button mushrooms
chives
50 g (2 oz) butter
1½ wineglasses white wine
75-100 g (4-5 oz) fresh white
  breadcrumbs
chopped parsley
nutmeg
salt and pepper

Soak the mussels in cold water with a handful of flour or oatmeal for 1-2 hours. Scrape them well and wash in at least 3 changes of cold water.

Chop the shallots finely. Wash the celery, wipe the mushrooms, and chop both finely. Chop the chives. Fry the shallots in butter in a large pan until they are soft. Add the celery, mushrooms and chives (reserving some). Add the white wine and the mussels and season well. Cover and cook over a high heat for 4-5 minutes, shaking the pan from time to time. The mussels are cooked when the shells are open. Do not overcook them.

Remove the mussels from the pan and reduce the liquor by half by boiling briskly. Add enough fresh breadcrumbs to bind the sauce. Stir in a large spoonful of chopped parsley and chives. Put a little sauce in the bottom of coquille shells or ramekins. Remove the mussels from their shells and divide between the dishes. Cover with the rest of the sauce and brown for 5-10 minutes at 210°C, 425°F/Gas 7.

Cooking Rice

Risottos and pilaffs easily become rather soggy and puddingy when they are re-heated or kept hot.

If you want to cook rice in advance, tip it into a large, shallow, fireproof dish as soon as it is cooked. Cover it with buttered paper and foil and keep it warm (or re-heat it) in a low oven at about 150°C, 300°F/Gas 2.

If serving a meat and sauce recipe with rice, never put the rice round the edge of the serving plate and the meat and sauce in the middle in advance. The rice will absorb the sauce in no time at all, leaving the meat dry.

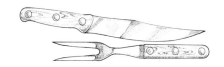

Jambon à la Bayonnaise

Braised Gammon and Rice

1·5-1·75 kg (3½-4 lb) middle-cut
gammon
1 wineglass Madeira, sweet
sherry or port
300 ml (½ pint) sauce demi-glacé
(see Basic Recipes)

For the pilaff

325 g (12 oz) Patna or Italian
rice
1 large onion
1 litre (1½ pints) stock
100 g (4 oz) butter
3 tomatoes
225 g (8 oz) chipolata sausages
.100 g (4 oz) button mushrooms
salt and pepper

Soak the gammon in cold water for
2-3 hours. Put in a large pan, cover
with cold water and bring slowly
to the boil. Season, cover and
simmer for 1 hour. Remove the
gammon, strip off the rind and any
excess fat. Put in a casserole dish
(just large enough to hold it) and
pour the Madeira, sherry or port,
over it. Cover and cook at 180°C,
350°F/Gas 4 for a further hour.

Meanwhile, prepare the sauce
demi-glacé (see Basic Recipes) and
the rice pilaff. Peel and chop the
onion finely. Fry the onion in 25 g
(1 oz) butter until soft. Add the
rice. Fry for 3-4 minutes, stirring
occasionally. Then add the stock
and bring to the boil. Skin the
tomatoes, discard the pips and add
the flesh to the pan. Fry the sausages,
cut into chunks and cut the mushrooms into quarters. Add to the
rice and simmer until the rice is
tender and has absorbed the stock
(about 25 minutes altogether). Melt
the remaining butter and pour it
over the rice.

Remove the gammon from the
casserole and stir the juices into the
sauce demi-glacé. Bring to the
boil, skim the surface and adjust
the seasoning if necessary. Arrange
the rice round the edge of a warm
serving dish. Slice the gammon
and put it in the centre. Spoon a
little sauce over and serve the rest
separately.

Boodles Fool

4 oranges
2 lemons
2 x 15 ml spoons (2 tablespoons)
castor sugar
500 ml (1 pint) double cream
6 sponge cakes or 24 sponge fingers

Grate the rind from 2 oranges and
1 lemon. Squeeze the juice from all
the fruit and measure. It should
not exceed 300 ml (½ pint) as the
cream will not absorb more than
this without curdling. Sweeten the
juice to taste with the sugar, then
add to the cream, whipping in
gradually, until the mixture is semi-
stiff. Break up the sponge cakes or
fingers and put in a glass bowl.
Pour the cream over and leave in a
cool place for at least 4 hours or
overnight. Serve very cold.

Délice aux Marrons

Chestnut Delight

100 g (4 oz) plain chocolate
12 g (½ oz) unsweetened chocolate
75 g (3 oz) castor sugar
6 x 15 ml spoons (6 tablespoons)
water
1 x 450-g (1-lb) can unsweetened
chestnut purée
2 eggs
175 g (6 oz) unsalted butter
1-2 x 15 ml spoons
(1-2 tablespoons) brandy or rum

For decoration

150 ml (¼ pint) double cream
chocolate flake or vermicelli

Oil lightly a 1-litre (1¾-pint) charlotte mould and put a circle of oiled
paper in the base.

Break up the chocolate and put it
in a pan with the sugar and water.
Heat gently until it has turned into
a thick cream. Let it cool. Beat it
into the chestnut purée. Separate
the eggs, and beat the yolks into the
chocolate mixture. Beat in the
softened butter and add brandy or
rum to taste.

Whisk the egg whites stiffly and
fold them into the chestnut mixture.
Pour into a mould and leave in the
refrigerator for at least 4 hours, or
overnight.

When ready to serve: whip the
cream stiffly and put in a forcing
bag with a star pipe. Turn the mould
out on to a serving plate and
decorate with piped cream and the
chocolate flake or vermicelli.

*Jambon à la Bayonnaise—a
delicious way of serving thick slices
of gammon on a bed of pilaff*

Pâté de Foie de Volailles

Dinde Magique

Ginger Ice
Tangerine Sabayon

This is a lovely menu for the Christmas season. The turkey requires a little more trouble than the traditional roast feast but it is an unusual variation and the superb flavour makes it well worth trying. A large capon could be treated in the same way. To make the pastry for the cranberry tartlets, use the recipe for rich shortcrust given in the Walnut and Maple Pie in Winter Menu No. 2.

The chicken liver pâté is a rich one, but very simple to make. If it is covered with clarified butter, it will keep for at least two weeks in a refrigerator.

Vary the amount of ginger in the ginger ice cream according to whether a really strong gingery flavour or something a little more subtle is wanted. Remember to check the consistency before serving; ice cream is usually too hard if taken direct from the freezer and will benefit from 30 minutes or so in the refrigerator before serving to allow it to soften.

The tangerine pudding provides a delicious way of using these traditional Christmas fruits. Complete the final preparation no more than an hour or so before serving, as the juice from the fruit makes the sabayon separate.

Pâté de Foie de Volailles
Chicken Liver Pâté
1 kg (2 lb) chicken livers
2 shallots or 1 small onion
450 g (1 lb) butter
2 x 15 ml spoons (2 tablespoons) brandy
3 x 15 ml spoons (3 tablespoons) sherry
garlic salt
pepper

Remove sinews and any yellow matter from the chicken livers and chop the livers roughly. Peel and chop the shallots or onion finely.

Melt 50 g (2 oz) butter in a heavy pan and fry the shallots gently without browning. When soft, add the chicken livers a few at a time. Cook for 10-15 minutes, very gently so they do not brown too much. Stir from time to time.

Then either liquidize the mixture or pour into a mortar and pound until smooth. Add the remainder of the butter gradually until it is absorbed. Unless using a liquidizer, also rub the mixture through a sieve.

Put the liver mixture in a clean bowl and add the brandy, sherry, garlic salt and pepper to taste. Put in a covered dish and leave in the refrigerator for at least 24 hours before serving.

Dinde Magique
Magic Turkey
4.5-5.5 kg (10-12 lb) turkey
3 x 15 ml spoons (3 tablespoons) Calvados
2 kg (4 lb) apples
2 x 15 ml spoons (2 tablespoons) double cream
100 g (4 oz) cream cheese
100 g (4 oz) butter
rich shortcrust pastry made with 225 g (8 oz) flour (see maple and walnut pie)
cranberry jelly or jam
300 ml (½ pint) stock
cream or arrowroot
salt and pepper

Draw and truss the turkey (or ask your butcher to do so). Using a syringe and hypodermic needle, inject Calvados into each side of the breast and leave overnight (the flavour will be excellent).

Peel and core about 6 of the apples and chop finely. Mix with the cream and the cream cheese and spread in the bottom of a roasting pan. Put the turkey on top, spread it with butter and roast for 1¾ hours at 200°C, 400°F/Gas 6, basting frequently.

Meanwhile, roll out the pastry and line into tartlet moulds or boats. Prick the pastry and bake (at the same temperature as the turkey) for 10-15 minutes. Remove from the tins and fill with cranberry jam or jelly.

Peel and core the remaining apples, leaving them whole. Put a knob of butter in each. When the turkey has cooked for 1¾ hours, put the apples round it in the tin and cook together for another 45 minutes.

Put the turkey on a warm serving dish and surround with the apples and tartlets. Keep warm while you pour the excess fat off the roasting tin and add the stock. Bring to the boil, stirring well. Season, add a few spoonfuls of cream or a little arrowroot mixed to a smooth paste with cold water. Serve this sauce separately.

Ginger Ice
300 ml (½ pint) milk
4 egg yolks
2 x 15 ml spoons (2 tablespoons) castor sugar
4-5 x 15 ml spoons (4-5 tablespoons) ginger syrup
75-100 g (3-4 oz) preserved ginger
300 ml (½ pint) double cream
2-3 x 15 ml spoons (2-3 tablespoons) rum (optional)

Put the milk in a pan and bring to the boil. Beat the egg yolks and sugar together and pour on the boiling milk. Return to the pan and cook, stirring all the time, until the mixture begins to thicken (do not boil). Pour the custard into a clean bowl and add the ginger syrup. Let it cool, then chill in the refrigerator.

Chop the ginger and whip the

Ginger Ice—as strong and gingery as you care to make it

cream lightly. Fold both into the custard with the rum, if using it. Pour the mixture into a shallow tin and freeze. Stir 2-3 times while freezing to break up the crystals. Put in a plastic container and leave in the freezer until required.

Tangerine Sabayon

4 *tangerines*
8 *lumps sugar*
$\frac{1}{2}$ *lemon*
50 g (2 oz) *granulated sugar*
4 x 15 ml spoons (4 tablespoons) *water*
4 *egg yolks*
4 *ripe pears*
4 *bananas*
4 *oranges*
Cointreau or Grand Marnier (optional)
300 ml ($\frac{1}{2}$ pint) *double cream*

To prepare the tangerine syrup (or sabayon), rub the tangerines with the lump sugar until they have absorbed the zest. Squeeze the juice from the tangerines and the half lemon and strain. Add 3 x 15 ml spoons (3 tablespoons) of this to the lump sugar and stir until the lumps have dissolved. Put the granulated sugar in a pan with the water and boil it to the thread stage (this is reached at 120°C, 238°F).

Pour this on to the egg yolks and whisk until the mixture is cold, thick and fluffy. Whisk in half the tangerine syrup and chill.

Peel and core the pears and slice them into a glass bowl. Peel and slice the bananas and put on top of the pears. Remove peel and pith from the oranges and cut out the segments so they are free from skin. Add to the other fruit in the bowl and moisten it all with the rest of the tangerine juice and, if liked, a little Cointreau or Grand Marnier to taste.

Whip the cream stiffly and fold in the sabayon. Pour over the fruit and chill for 1-2 hours before serving.

127

Basic Recipes

There are cross-references to these recipes, essential elements of more elaborate dishes, throughout the preceding dinner-party menus. You will find them all invaluable both in day-to-day cookery and in dishes for entertaining.

Mayonnaise

2 egg yolks
1 x 15 ml spoon (1 tablespoon)
  wine vinegar or lemon juice
300 ml (½ pint) oil
salt, pepper and mustard (optional)

Put egg yolks in a bowl, add a pinch of salt and pepper (and the mustard if using it) and mix together well. Stir in a few drops of vinegar or lemon juice. Add the oil, drop by drop, stirring all the time. (Use a wire sauce whisk or a wooden spoon.) As the mayonnaise begins to thicken, you can add the oil a little more quickly, but be careful. The final consistency when you have stirred in all the oil should be that of whipped cream. Add a little water or more vinegar or lemon juice if the mayonnaise becomes too thick.

One egg yolk will absorb up to 300 ml (½ pint) oil at the maximum. If the mayonnaise curdles during preparation, put 1 x 5 ml (1 teaspoon) cold water in a clean basin and pour the curdled mixture on very slowly, whisking continuously.

Aioli

This is a garlic-flavoured mayonnaise.

8 cloves garlic
2 egg yolks
300 ml (½ pint) mixture of
  olive and salad oil
squeeze lemon juice
salt and pepper

Peel the garlic cloves and crush them to a paste with a little salt. Stir in the egg yolks and mix well. Add the oil drop by drop, whisking all the time until the mayonnaise begins to thicken. At this point you can add the oil a little more quickly,

still whisking all the time. Season well and add the lemon juice.

Hollandaise Sauce

This sauce should not be kept hot. Re-heat it when you want to use it, whisking it all the time.

175 g (6 oz) butter
3 egg yolks
3 x 15 ml spoons (3 tablespoons)
  white wine
lemon juice
salt and pepper

Melt the butter over a gentle heat until it is just liquid. Do not over-heat so that it begins to froth. Put the egg yolks and wine in a small pan (preferably stainless steel) and whisk together, over the heat, until they are the consistency of smooth scrambled egg. Remove from the heat and gradually pour in the butter, whisking all the time. Season and add lemon juice to taste.

Sauce Demi-glacé

1 large carrot
1 large onion
1 rasher bacon or bacon rinds
35 g (1½ oz) dripping or oil
25 g (1 oz) flour
1·25 litres (2 pints) stock
1 stick celery
mushroom stalks and peelings
parsley stalks
1-2 tomatoes or 1 x 5 ml spoon
  (1 teaspoon) tomato purée
2 x 15 ml spoons (2 tablespoons)
  sherry or other wine

Peel and chop the carrot and the onion. Dice the bacon. Melt the dripping or oil in a heavy pan and add the carrot, onion and bacon. Cook until brown, stirring to prevent sticking. Add the flour and cook, stirring continuously, until it browns. Add stock, finely chop the celery and add to the pan with the mushrooms and parsley stalks. Chop the tomatoes and add these, or the purée.

Bring to the boil, season lightly, then simmer gently for about 45 minutes. Strain into a clean pan,

add a little cold stock and skim the surface. Add the sherry or wine and cook for a further 10 minutes.

Meringues

2 egg whites
100 g (4 oz) castor sugar

Line baking sheets with non-stick paper. Whisk egg whites stiffly in a dry bowl, then whisk in 1 x 15 ml spoon (1 tablespoon) of the sugar. Fold in the rest. Put the mixture in a forcing bag with a 1-cm (½-in) plain nozzle and pipe small circles on to the baking sheets. Alternatively, spoon the mixture on to the trays using 2 teaspoons. Bake in a cool oven (130°3, 250°F/Gas ½) for 1½-2 hours, reducing the heat after 30-40 minutes. The meringues are cooked when they are quite dry, but should still be white. Cool on a wire rack and, when cold, store in an airtight container.

Macaroons

Homemade macaroons are more delicately flavoured than bought ones and are therefore more suitable for use as a recipe ingredient. You can also make them to the exact size you require.

100 g (4 oz) castor sugar
1 x 5 ml spoon (1 teaspoon)
  cornflour
50 g (2 oz) ground almonds
1 small egg white—a maximum of
  25 ml (1 fl oz)
rice paper
split almonds

Sift the sugar with the cornflour and ground almonds. Beat the egg white just enough to break it up and add it gradually to the sugar mixture to make a firm paste. Divide into 12 even-sized pieces and, with dampened hands, roll into balls. Place these on rice paper on a baking tray, flatten them and put a split almond in the middle of each. Brush with egg white and bake for 10-12 minutes at 180°C, 350°F/Gas 4. Cool on a rack. Pack into suitable containers and freeze until required.

Conversion Tables

All weights and measures in this book are given in the metric system, followed by the imperial in brackets. Conversions correspond, but are not necessarily exact to the last milligram or part of an ounce. However, they are correctly adjusted within one system, which makes it essential to follow *either* the metric *or* the imperial in any one recipe.

Oven Temperatures

These are given in Centigrade, Fahrenheit and Gas Regulo.

°C	°F	Gas
130 (very cool)	250	$\frac{1}{4}$
140 (very cool)	275	1
150 (cool/slow)	300	2
160 (warm/very moderate)	325	3
180 (moderate)	350	4
190 (moderately hot)	375	5
200 (moderately hot)	400	6
210 (hot)	425	7
230 (very hot)	450	8
240 (very hot)	475	9

Weights

Metric	Imperial
25 g	1 oz
50 g	2 oz
75 g	3 oz
100-125 g	4 oz
150 g	5 oz
175 g	6 oz
200 g	7 oz
225 g	8 oz
250 g	9 oz
275 g	10 oz
300 g	11 oz
325-350 g	12 oz
375 g	13 oz
400 g	14 oz
425 g	15 oz
450 g	1 lb
900 g	2 lb
1 kg	2 lb 3 oz (approx.)
1·2 kg	$2\frac{1}{2}$ lb
1·4 kg	3 lb
1·6 kg	$3\frac{1}{2}$ lb
1·8 kg	4 lb
2 kg	$4\frac{1}{2}$ lb

Liquid Measures

Metric	Imperial
25 ml	1 fl oz
50 ml	2 fl oz
75 ml	3 fl oz
100-125 ml	4 fl oz
150 ml	$\frac{1}{4}$ pint
175 ml	6 fl oz
200 ml	7 fl oz
225 ml	8 fl oz
250 ml	9 fl oz
275-300 ml	$\frac{1}{2}$ pint
575-600 ml	1 pint
1 litre	$1\frac{3}{4}$ pint

Spoon Measures

All spoon measures given in this book indicate level spoonfuls.

Metric	Imperial
5 ml	1 teaspoon
10 ml	1 dessertspoon
15 ml	1 tablespoon

Glossary

à la   in the manner of.

aspic   a clear meat jelly, used mainly for glazing savoury dishes.

au gratin   cooked with a layer of breadcrumbs (and sometimes cheese) on top and browned under the grill.

to bake blind   to cook, or part-cook, a pastry flan case before adding the filling.

to baste   to spoon fat over a roasting joint or bird as it is cooking.

béchamel sauce   a basic white sauce made by adding milk (containing a bay leaf and onion) to a roux of butter and flour.

beurre maitre d'hôtel   butter mixed with chopped parsley and lemon as a garnish.

beurre manié   butter and flour worked together to a paste. One of the liaisons for thickening soups and stews.

to blanch   to immerse fruit or vegetables in boiling water for a short time. Blanching helps remove skins as well as slowing enzyme action, while preserving natural colour, flavour and nutritional value.

to blend   to combine ingredients together with a spoon, beater or liquidizer.

to bone   to remove the bone from a joint of meat or poultry, or to remove the carcass from a whole bird.

bonne femme   cooked in the country, or simple, manner. Also a classic garnish for sole, made with hollandaise sauce and mushrooms.

bouquet garni   a bunch of herbs, usually parsley, thyme and a bay leaf, for flavouring soups and stews.

to brown (meat)   to fry meat quickly in very hot fat to seal in the juices. This gives a rich brown colour to stews and casseroles.

to caramelize   to heat sugar, moistened with a little water, until it turns brown.

cayenne   very hot powdered spice made from seeds and dried pods of various capsicums (peppers), used to give a hot peppery flavour.

charlotte mould   a plain round mould or tin used to make a charlotte dessert.

clarified butter   butter melted, skimmed of froth and strained.

cocotte   a small, fireproof, earthenware dish. Usually an individual dish used for baking eggs.

compôte   fruit poached gently in syrup usually served cold.

condé   fruit with rice, moulded.

consommé   a strong, very clear meat soup, or stock, sometimes jellified.

crêpe   pancake.

croûte   a slice of bread or brioche, fried or baked, or a pastry covering for a joint of meat.

croûton   a small cube of bread, fried, baked or toasted and served as a garnish.

cuisine minceur   literally 'thin cooking'. A new school of cooking from France that concentrates on fresh herbs for flavouring and avoids such ingredients as butter, oil, flour.

to curdle   to form a separated mixture, which results when two fats do not combine.

dariole mould   an individual castle-shaped mould for savoury jellies or puddings.

to de-glaze   to add wine or stock to a meat pan to mix the cooking juices into a sauce.

to devil   to use very hot sauces and spices for meat, poultry or fish before being grilled.

to dice   to chop into small cubes.

dressing   oil and vinegar mixed with a variety of seasonings and used with salads. Also used to describe the preparation of poultry for the table.

dripping   the fat from a roast bird or joint.

to fold in   to combine one ingredient with another, very gently, using a metal spoon.

forcing bag   a funnel-shaped bag, with various nozzles, used for piping cream or potatoes, to garnish a dish.

fromage blanc   a fresh cheese made from skimmed milk that contains no fat solids. Used extensively in *cuisine minceur* as a liaison or thickening agent.

fruit fool   dessert made from stewed and/or puréed fruit, mixed with sugar and whipped cream or custard.

galantine   a meat loaf, glazed with aspic jelly and served cold.

to garnish   to decorate a savoury dish with parsley, chopped chives.

gelatine   a setting agent of animal origin, used for jellies, mousses, cold soufflés.

glacé   iced, frozen or glazed.

to glaze to brush with milk, syrup, beaten egg or jelly.

(à la) grecque cooking in the Greek style, characterized by oil and vinegar or lemon juice.

griddle another name for a girdle—a flat, heavy, metal plate used for cooking.

to hull to remove stalks and leaves from berry fruit.

julienne strips vegetables, such as carrots, cut into very fine strips for garnish.

liaison a thickening agent of cream, eggs, flour or flour and butter.

marinade an acid liquid such as lemon juice and oil, wine or vinegar, generally with herbs added, in which meat, poultry and fish are steeped to make tender and give flavour.

to marinate to leave in a marinade.

meringue a confection of egg white and sugar, baked in a cool oven until crisp.

meunière a method of cooking fish, by lightly flouring, seasoning and frying in butter. Lemon juice is squeezed over the cooked fish.

moule à manqué a cake tin which has a wider circumference at the base.

mousse a light set mixture, savoury or sweet, which can be hot but is more usually served cold.

niçoise containing tomatoes, garlic and olives; originating from Nice.

paprika red mild-flavoured, powdered spice made from sweet red peppers.

parmentier containing potatoes.

pastry an amalgam of fat, flour and water which is shaped and cooked to form a crisp case for other ingredients or, in certain yeasted cakes, is combined with these before cooking.

pâté a savoury mixture of game, meat, bacon and liver, either baked in an earthenware dish and served cold or contained in an enclosed pastry case and served hot or cold.

pâte sucrée a sweet pastry.

to pipe to force (cream, meringue, mashed potato, icing) through a tube to decorate various dishes.

to poach to cook in gently simmering water.

praline almonds covered with caramelized sugar.

to prove to leave dough, after it has been well kneaded, to rise before baking.

provençal usually with tomatoes and olives, but always with garlic; in the regional style of Provence.

purée solid foods made into a smooth consistency by putting through a sieve, foodmill or liquidizer.

ramekins individual fireproof dishes.

to reduce to concentrate a liquid by boiling.

to reserve to set on one side for later use.

roux flour and butter cooked together, used as a base for sauces.

to sauté to fry rapidly in shallow, hot fat, shaking the pan so the food does not stick and burn.

seasoned flour flour to which salt and pepper have been added. Used generally to coat fish, meat or poultry before sealing in hot fat.

to skim to remove scum or skin from the top of a liquid (or cream from milk).

to slake to mix dry ingredients, such as flour, cornflour or arrowroot, to a smooth paste or cream with a little water.

sorbet a fruit water ice.

soufflé a delicate, smooth-textured concoction, which may be sweet or savoury, served hot or cold, raised by beaten egg whites.

soufflé dish an ovenproof, straight-sided, round china dish for cooking and serving soufflés.

to steep to marinate or soak.

terrine an earthenware dish; also a coarse pâté cooked in a terrine.

vol-au-vent large puff-pastry cases of about 15 cm (6 in) in diameter for sweet or savoury fillings.

to whip to incorporate air into various substances, such as eggs and cream, by beating.

zest the absolute outer skin of citrus fruits in which the oils of the fruit are contained.

Index

Aioli 128
Almond and raspberry flan 26
Apple and cabbage soup 66
Apricot cheesecake 15
Aspic jelly 3
Avocado, appetizer 120
  mousse 104
  and spinach soup 40

Babas au rhum 86
Bacon pâté 41
Baked cheesecake 57
Ballotine, de caneton aux abricots 111
  of chicken and apricots 77
Barbecues 48
Barbecue sauces 54
Barbecuing on skewers 52
Bar-B-Q basting sauce 54
Basic herb stuffing 94
Bavarois praliné 86
Birthday cakes 58
Biscuit au chocolat praliné 20
Bisque de crevettes 100
Bitkis 79
Boeuf, à la bourguignonne 8
  en daube provençale 118
  stroganoff 43
Bonnet russe 85
Boodles fool 125
Bramble mousse 85
Brandy snaps 60
Breadcrumbs 94
Bread rolls 52
Bridge roll toppings 60
Brownies 57
Buffet food 64
Butter cream 62

Cakes 61
  birthday 58
Canard au cidre 100
Carbonnade, d'agneau nimoise 17
  de boeuf flamande 78
Carré d'agneau lorraine 99
Carrot and coriander soup 16
Casseroles 116
Celery and almond soup 66
Charlotte, Louise 82
  Malakoff 82
  aux marrons 19
  aux noisettes 119
Chartreuse de pommes 119
Cheeseburgers 49
Cheese sablés 31
Chestnuts 94
Chicken 51, 74

and avocado salad 44
and ham mousse 42
and leek pie 24
and noodle salad 44
Children's parties 58
Chilled mushroom soup 40
Chocolate, brandy cake 83
  and chestnut meringue 9
  crispies 60
  log 61
Choux, normands 116
  pralinés aux chocolat 46
Cold mousse 111
Cold salmon mayonnaise 13
Cooking rice 124
Corned beefburgers 50
Coq au vin 74
Coquilles, de moules à la rochelaise 124
  de poisson au cidre 72
Côtes de porc, niçoise 80
  savoy 121
Crabe, diablé 72
  à la facon des pêcheurs 42
Cream 105
  of broad bean soup 106
Crème, Agnès Sorel 67
  ambassadrice 121
  asphodèle 117
  camélia 67
  doria 68
Crêpes, aux épinards 69
  landaises 24
  ripieni 68
Croque monsieur 57
Croquettes, bruxelloises 90
  de volaille 90
Cumberland rum nicky 38
Curried fish croquettes 91

Dacquoise 113
Danish liver pâté 71
Délice, au chocolat 84
  de fraises au fromage 107
  aux marrons 125
Devilled, poultry kebabs 53
  tuna pâté 124
Dinde magique 126
Drinks 45, 64
Drop scones 60
Duxelle 94

Eclairs 62
Egg, and anchovy mousse 110
  mousse 26
Elizabethan casseroled pork 80
English game pie 18

L'estouffat gascon 79
Eton mess 111

Faisan, aux marrons 78
  périgord 114
Family kebabs 53
Filet de boeuf niçoise 4
Fish 51
  stock or fumet 95
Flapjacks 61
Frankfurter bun 49
Fresh haddock mousse 71
Fruit, punch 64
  sauce 56
Fruits au vin rouge 20

Galantine de volaille 77
Galette de noisettes aux pêches 107
Gammon 51
Gâteau, Alix 84
  basque 87
  bigarreau 46
  chocolat suisse 84
  Diane 14
  flamand 88
  Fôret Noire 4
  ganache 91
  jalousie 27
  de noix des mesnards 14
Gazpacho 40
Genoese sponge 61
Glace, aux abricots 92
  aux fraises 92
  aux framboises 92
Glacé icing 62
Gooseberry, or blackcurrant fool 111
  cream ice 93
  water ice 93
Gougère 18
Goulash d'agneau 80
Grapefruit special 102
Gratin de pommes de terre Crécy 29
Greek honey pie 88
Guards' cup 39

Haddock mousse 71
Ham 51
Hamburgers 49
Haricot beans with sausages 23
Hawaiian beans 64
Hazlenut roulade 45
Herb, bread 31
  stuffing 94
Hollandaise sauce 128

Honey spice marinade 55
Hot, anchovy or garlic bread 31
  fudge sauce 56

Ice-cream cake 64
Infusing milk 71
Insulated containers 41

Jambon, à la bayonnaise 125
  roulé aux fines herbes 43

Kidney, and liver kebabs 53
  and sausage casserole 22

Lamb 51
  chops provençal 81
Lamburgers 50
Landais or bavarois praliné 86
Langue de boeuf braisée aux raisins 81
Lemon barbecue sauce 54
Lemonade 39
Lentil and tomato soup 34
Liqueurs and spirits 84
Loin of lamb Bretonne 112
Lord John Russell's pudding 8

Macaroni and ham au gratin 22
Macaroons 128
  Montmorency 99
Macédoine niçoise 25
Magda, biscuits 60
  jelly 16
Marinades 55
Marinated smoked mackerel 12
Mayonnaise 31, 105, 128
Meat, 50, 74
Melon salad 106
Meringue cake 62
Meringues 62, 128
  chantilly 45
Mexican hamburgers 49
Milkshakes 64
Minestra 16
Moules aux herbes 73
Mousse, aux abricots 20
  au café 101
  de fromage aux raisins 3
  aux langues 42
Mousses, savoury 70
Mouton farcie aux épinards 105

Mrs Dixon's chocolate cake 38
Mulled wine 39
Mushroom soup 34

Oeufs au thon 7
Orange, caramel trifle 121
    curd cream 105
    water ice 93
Oranges, caramelisées 11
    à la reine 103
Oriental kebabs 53

Pan pizza 56
Parfait, au café 92
    praliné 92
Parties for children 58, 59
Pastry 87, 96, 123
Pâte, feuilletée 32, 96
    sucrée 32
Pâté 71
    de campagne 37
    de foie de volailles 126
Paupiettes 123
    de boeuf marinées 122
Pavlova 5
Picnic, fondue 57
    tartlets 37
Pigeons à la normande 99
Pineapple water ice 109
Pipérade 36
Pissaladière 70
Pizza napolitana 69
Poires chantilly 115
Pois à la normande 28
Pommes de terre, Alphonse 29
    macaire 29
Pork 51
    and pear loaf 38
Potage, bonne femme 102
    Crécy 68
    niçoise 114
Potato salad 29
Poulet, aux amandes 103
    au currie 76
    au gingembre 117
    froid sultane 106
    salade chantilly 25
    sauté à la basquaise 74
Praline 119
Prawn, cocktail 112
    flan 43
Prawns in whisky 122
Puchero 23
Puddings 45, 46

Railway cake 62

Ranch barbecue sauce 54
Raspberry, milkshake 64
    shortcake 105
Ratatouille niçoise 29
Rice, cooking 124
Rich shortcrust pastry 32
Roulade au chocolat 26
Roulades au jambon
    dijonnais 7
Russian smoked salmon
    roulades 2

Salade, des fruits 27
    italienne 10
    niçoise 30
    aux poires
    de riz 30
Salads for barbecues 52
Salambos au Grand
    Marnier 20
Sardine, pâté 42
    puffs 91
Sauce, barbecue 54
    demi-glacé 128
    hollandaise 128
    hot fudge 56
    provençale 95
    tomate 95
Sauces, for ice cream 56
    for marshmallows 56
Savoury, basting sauce 54
    mousses 70
Scotch eggs 36
Sicilian steak 8
Smoked mackerel, mousse 98
    pâté 16
Snaffles mousse 10
Soupe au poisson 120
Soups and starters 40
Soured cream 44
Spanish salad 30
Spirits and liqueurs 84
Sponge fingers 96
Steak 50
    tourte 17
Sticky ginger cake 38
Strawberry, milkshake 64
    tartlets 14
Stuffed sausages 36
Summer chicken 4
Suprême au moka 115
Sweet and sour basting
    sauces 54

Tangerine sabayon 127
Tangy barbecue sauce 54
Tarte, beauceronne 88
    canelle 89
    aux cerises 88

à l'oignon 64
Tarragon marinade 55
Tartelettes au gingembre 101
Teriyaki marinade 55
Terrine, of chicken and
    walnuts 7
    aux herbes 2
    de lièvre 37
    normande aux noix 116
Tomates, aux crevettes 112
    guacamole 108
    mousmées 28
Tomatoburgers 49
Tourte au saumon 73
Truite saumonée au vin rosé
    108
Tuna fish mousse 70
Turinois, le 83
Turkey and ham salad 13

Vanilla biscuits 60
Velouté indienne 34
Velvet cream 108
Venison ardennaise 78
Victoria sponge 61
Vinaigrette 31

Walnut and maple pie 123
Westmorland raisin and nut
    flan 21
White stock 94
Wine marinade 55
Winter salad 30